BECOMING
DANGEROUS

Witchy Femmes,

Queer Conjurers,

and Magical Rebels

BECOMING DANGEROUS

EDITED BY
KATIE WEST AND JASMINE ELLIOTT

FOREWORD BY
KRISTEN J. SOLLÉE,
author of *Witches, Sluts, Feminists*

WEISER BOOKS

This edition first published in 2019 by Weiser Books, an imprint of
Red Wheel/Weiser, LLC
With offices at:
65 Parker Street, Suite 7
Newburyport, MA 01950
www.redwheelweiser.com

ISBN: 978-1-57863-670-9
Library of Congress Cataloging-in-Publication Data available upon request.

Cover design by Kathryn Sky-Peck
Interior by Katie West
Typeset in Fanwood and Weiss

Printed in the United States of America
IBI
10 9 8 7 6 5 4 3 2 1

Contents

Foreword

If the broom
fits witch it
is time to
ride it
act up
resist

—the Yerbamala Collective

What does it mean to resist? When "resist" is the slogan of a multibillion-dollar political machine. When #resist is a viral meme. When "resist" is printed on shirts and hats and stickers you get for joining the right email list, and resistance has been co-opted by the very systems you're trying to resist?

In *Becoming Dangerous*, witchy femmes, queer conjurers, and magical rebels offer answers. Through twenty-one wildly different essays, the authors lay bare their prismatic perspectives on what it means to challenge the social, political, and cultural forces that seek to marginalize and erase them. Rituals of reclamation. Aesthetic spellcraft. Tapping into the earth for answers. Cracking open your ancestral powers. These are their routes to redemption, the way these writers summon the strength to resist.

Now more than ever, witches, occultists, and magicians are joining the magical resistance. Healing circles for survivors, mass hexes against fascists and abusers, and collective protection spells are proliferating. The pervasive notion that the political and the spiritual are contradictory is slowly being dispelled.

When I started teaching my college course, The Legacy of The Witch, at the New School five years ago, incorporating social justice into discussions about witchcraft seemed novel to the students taking the class. Fascinating, yes, but removed from reality, they'd say. They perceived the political realm as devoid of grace and of magic. They understood witchcraft to be all aesthetic and no action. But every year since then, as the American government has doubled down on exclusionary, punitive, and oppressive policies, my students arrive more and more primed to view the necessity of studying the two in tandem. Many even come to the table well-versed in both subjects, already part of magical communities putting on their own protests and using ritual as intimate parts of their own acts of resistance.

When studying witchcraft and social justice movements of the past and present, cyclical patterns emerge. As a fraught political climate simmers and comes to a roil, the occult is often the next mode of defense, of reproach. This holds today as much as it did in the age of second wave feminism and neopaganism, and in the time of suffragists and Spiritualism. Historically, many of the greatest acts of resistance have been informed by spiritual practice. And some of the most nourishing spiritual practices have been borne within society's stifling political strictures, like so many buds finally bursting through fallow soil.

In 1843, Isabella Baumfree received an otherworldly call to serve. She christened herself Sojourner Truth. She traversed the country to share and teach and extemporize about womanhood and inequity and the painful realities of racism and sexism that were tearing America apart. Truth, a former slave, was a devout Christian. By today's standards, she was much more. Historian Nell Irvin Painter argues that Truth's syncretic spiritual practice, a mix of West African animistic beliefs, American folk magic, and Dutch Calvinism and Methodism makes her a witch in the contemporary sense of the word. Her rituals were public, massive and mesmeric, drawing hundreds hypnotized by her impassioned oratory as she planted the seeds that would later bloom into Womanism and Intersectionality.

In 1974, a community of lesbians in Wolf Creek, Oregon birthed *Womanspirit,* the first quarterly magazine dedicated to both spirituality and feminism. In the midst of the women's liberation movement, these women were frustrated with the limitations of patriarchal religion but didn't want to eschew spirituality altogether. They took the formation of consciousness-raising groups that were central to early feminism and saw the magic inherent within such sharing circles. "Feminism tells us to trust ourselves," wrote Jean Mountaingrove, one of the founders of *Womanspirit*. "We began to trust our own feelings, we began to believe in our own orgasms. These were the first things. Now we are beginning to have spiritual experiences and, for the first time in thousands of years, we trust it."

In 2017, an anonymous group of anti-fascist witches joined together to hex the white supremacist capitalist heteropatriarchy. Under the Yerbamala Collective moniker, this amorphous cadre of activists released free, downloadable zines and spellbooks decrying racism, sexism, transphobia, Islamophobia, and, above all, complacency. "Complacency is anti-magic," one poem of theirs declares. "Witches of all genders ride now."

"The Yerbamala Collective is a purposefully porous group of witches so numerous you might as well call us the stars," a member told Janus Kopfstein in an interview published on *Medium.* "We are everywhere, behind every fascist, waiting for the fist to be our own. We started as a conversation between friends, which spread to other friends around the country. We covened together in the encrypted byways of the internet to form our first response and rally cry . . . We are claiming our righteous anger and using that too as a fuel. This fight will take so much away from us. It's important we remember who we are: divine beings with divine power."

This divinity, not granted by outside forces but cultivated and claimed internally, is palpably present in *Becoming Dangerous.* Through healing rituals of logomancy, the authors of this spellbinding anthology write their realities into existence, revealing how fallible flesh can become armor, and why fighting to live life on your own terms is sacred. Each chapter can act as a response to the contemporary question of survival and resistance. What it means to actively counter narratives and structures that seek to oppress and keep us from not only surviving but thriving under patriarchy, white supremacy, late capitalism, and the searing traumas attendant to all three.

"In truth, my rituals—the same ones I use to perform my undangerous and thoroughly human body—are weapons," writes J.A. Micheline in "Ritualising My Humanity." "In unabashedly affirming my own dignity, I am becoming dangerous."

The witchy femmes, queer conjurers, and magical rebels in this volume know there is nothing more dangerous than the self-possessed. Those who know power lies in their ability to channel and harness and subvert the tools at their disposal. Those who alchemize their pain into healing and beauty, overcoming and community. They remind us that there is no one way to resist, only that it is imperative we do.

—Kristen J. Sollée, author of *Witches, Sluts, Feminists*

Introduction

The difference between the witch and the layperson is that a witch already knows they are powerful. The layperson may only suspect. To tap into this power, a witch performs rituals with purpose, with intent, and with an enviable aesthetic. Some people say witches are irrational, absurd, or ridiculous, but in response, witches smile knowingly. They see the irony in the accusations: Rituals have been and continue to be performed in all societies throughout time to such an extent that the performance of ritual could be said to be the defining characteristic of human beings. What are we if not the culmination of our efforts to construct meaning where there is none, to pull reason from the absurd?

Currently, the world is very similar in look and feel to a dumpster on fire. It's been this way for a while, so we keep trying to come up with ways to make it better, or easier, or kinder. But as of yet, nothing has really worked. Not fighting for it, dying for it, praying for it, working for it, or wishing for it. As a result, we feel powerless. In response to this failure, many have resorted to coming up with ways to explain it, to look at the world around them and see it as normal. 'This is fine.'

This book is full of the ways in which queer conjurers, witchy femmes, magical rebels, and people like you (or maybe nothing like you) resist the onslaught of a world of irrational happenings and the normalisation of their world on fire. It offers personal explorations from the authors of how they've created their own irrational actions that give them the strength, patience, community, and hope required to survive. These arbitrary activities are their rituals, and this book tells us how and why they work for them.

What makes these arbitrary actions into rituals is the intention behind them. Witches already know this. So do religions. They know that rituals don't mean anything on their own, separate from any context; it's the intention that makes a series of arbitrary actions powerful. But unlike religious rituals—which are prescribed by someone else and must be performed in a certain way—the rituals we discover and create for ourselves, like the ones described by the authors in this book, can grow out of our own bodies, spirits, and desires. The act of deliberately choosing to apply significance to our actions and to cultivate a deeper meaning to them is powerful. We can use ritual to gain control, and not just any kind of control—a specific type of control that requires no one else's approval or permission. It is completely self-wrought and that makes it incredibly powerful.

Becoming Dangerous is a book about using ritual to resist. When so many forces outside ourselves are trying to take away our rights, freedoms, and agency, adhering to practices that centre us as fully-realised people dependent on and owing only to the earth, those we love, and the development of ourselves—instead of to elected officials or systems of oppression and those who uphold them—can't be a bad idea. There is a power disparity in our world. Those with power are not keen on sharing, and those of us without are left with discovering ways to summon it for ourselves. Discovering power that hasn't been given to us begrudgingly or allocated sparingly makes us threatening. Power makes us dangerous.

I sent a draft of this introduction to my friend Cara Ellison, the first author in this book actually, and I told her 'I just want it to answer the question, "Why did I make a book about rituals?"' And Cara replied instantly, 'Because everything else hasn't worked.' Oh, right. Yes, that. That is why I made a book about rituals.

This world is hard and unreasonable and there's those within it who would prefer you to be powerless—

But:

I see you. I know you're tired. I know the world is a hard place to navigate. And you are right to have hoped it would've been, if not easier, at least better by now. Instead you're left waiting (for equal rights, for gender to be recognised as a spectrum, for reconciliation, for self-acceptance, for the right to choose, for the patriarchy to burn, for universal healthcare, for access, for it not to be audacious to demand decency and kindness). I see you. And I'm glad you're still here. Still struggling, resisting, fighting, yearning for all the above and more. And I want you to know, like so many witches already know, that you're powerful.

Find your rituals, find your power, find your reason.

Become dangerous.

Katie West
Editor, *Becoming Dangerous*
Edinburgh, January 2018

Notes from the Editors

Having a style guide for a book makes it an easier read; inconsistent expressions of punctuation, spellings, or other grammatical rules can pull the reader out of a narrative. However, at times while editing *Becoming Dangerous*, we've made exceptions or changes to our guide in order to respect the authors, their preferences, and their practices.

Some words have various spellings used throughout the book; for example, 'magic' is also expressed as 'magick', and this has been a conscious choice by each author. Another example is the capitalisation of 'Moon'—several authors prefer this spelling as it reflects the importance of the moon in their practice. There is also a pronoun in Catherine Hernandez's essay—*their—that is how her lover refers to themselves. In regards to spellings of groups of people, we've followed the rule of 'always go with what those people are calling themselves'. The word 'indigenous' has been capitalised when speaking about Indigenous people in Canada. When referring to indigenous cultures of other regions, it has been left lowercase or to the discretion of the author. The word nonbinary has been expressed without the hyphen in most cases (subject to author's preference), and our reasoning for doing so is that hyphens are often used when something new enters the English language with the help of a prefix. Once that word has been around for a while and is accepted into normal usage, it often loses the hyphen. We felt expressing it without a hyphen shows, in language, an acceptance and embracing of nonbinary people. However, we recognize that, as Maranda Elizabeth—who feels the word non-binary/nonbinary may currently be more accepted in language but not in concept and understanding of lived experience—graciously explained to us, having to identify with words that describe what people *are not* (nonbinary, genderless) rather than what they *are* isn't ideal. We've tried to do the best we can with the language currently available to us.

Katie West and Jasmine Elliott
Editors, *Becoming Dangerous*

Content Warnings

This book has twenty-one essays covering a vast range of topics from a deep pool of personal experience: from boxing to gardening, from dealing with post-traumatic stress disorder to dealing with racism, from nail extensions to slut magic. We want all our readers to be able to enjoy the experience of reading through this book, so we're including a list of content or trigger warnings for each essay in this anthology.

Our goal at Fiction & Feeling is to elevate underrepresented voices and topics, which can mean that some readers are engaging with topics, experiences, and viewpoints for the first time and may find this strange or uncomfortable. Other readers may find certain topics more difficult to deal with than others. The content of an essay may bring up painful memories or trigger panic attacks. Many topics could potentially be the trigger for such reactions, though there are some main culprits such as abuse, self-harm, violence, blood, war, rape, and eating disorders. Including a content warning at the beginning of a piece of writing that gives a quick description of what can be expected can act as a heads-up for those who need it. Content warnings are not meant to suggest a reader stays away from a piece of writing; rather, they hopefully give a reader some time to prepare themselves for what they're about to encounter. This can be true for either subjects that might cause physical and emotional distress or themes that might be uncomfortable and challenging.

Content Warnings

Unfuckable

Cara Ellison

Scotland is unfuckable.

Scotland cannot, will not, be fucked. It has always been, and to this day is, in a total and complete lack of having been fucked, fucked up, fucked over, fucked with.

I say this in defiance of a history of its misery and domination, poverty and neglect—though it has been bought and sold and barely any of its land is owned by anyone who really lives there. For certain, Scotland has been fucked *on*: Robert Burns and Edwin Morgan wrote down, in beautiful detail, the desiring of a woman's and man's body, respectively. But the way that the accepted canon of literary men talks about land, ownership, territory—Scotland is unfuckable because it is inhospitable.

I am become the land I stand on. I cannot remember exactly when the transformation took place. But I would like to tell you about where I realised it had, and the powerful ritual it gave me.

It is the grand masculine colonial tradition to talk about women as if they were a conquerable landscape — from Sir Walter Raleigh's naming of Virginia after a virgin queen, through the way that residents of the Kingdom of Fife adoringly call the Lomond Hills the 'paps of Fife', or the 'breasts of Fife'. In the pale teal mornings I would lie back on my grandmother's cold garden lawn and compare my growing chest bumps to the horizon.

But as I look closer at the history of Scotland, that very early history before and enduring the Ancient Romans, I learn that in the beginning, women were never the tilled, the claimed, the fertile land that the Romantic poets made them. They were wild: the crags, the bursting river; the unpredictable, the dangerous; those who may at any point *take it all away*. We might one day lash the world like a cat surprised, break the skin of natural order, and have the contents below burst into mess. It was that part of the land metaphor we occupied. We were not known as the passive but the prickly. The spiky. The terrifying. The vicious.

Scotland did not behave. Scotland will not behave.

As Sharon Blackie writes in her book *If Women Rose Rooted*, Celtic women had social standing that most other contemporaries in the West did not, and Christianity came to change that for the worse. In Ireland and Britain, women could be leaders and were important in political, social, and religious roles. Boudica and Cartimandua, for example, lead their people into battle, and Celtic women have been reported to have been judges, priestesses, lawyers, astronomers, artists, and doctors, often with rights to property, sexual freedom, and recourse to damages if they were physically or sexually assaulted. A Celtic woman was feared and respected. The Romans are on record saying you do not fuck with a Celtic woman.

The whole Celtic world was based on the ordaining of place, of the natural world. What we might now call the 'femme' was indivisible from the land on which people lived. This land was not something considered to belong to anyone.

I leaf through the Ulster Cycle of Irish literary tradition, a sort of Marvel Universe of the Dark Ages, the stories Celts constructed together as they cooked and drank and wove and washed and stole each other's sheep. One figure in particular stands out to me: Scáthach, a famous warrior woman and prophet who lived with her daughter on the Isle of Skye. Scáthach taught the Irish heroes how to snatch life from one another and vault ramparts like giants, like gods. There is little centred upon her alone, but she has an easy traversal through the background of stories written down about more famous Irish heroes. She stands, smiling, to the side of gilt Celtic knot lettering, behind the posturing of hundreds of words of male-ingratiated prose.

She gets up every morning to sharpen spears, kick the shins of young Irishmen, wash blood out of undershirts. Her daughter is on the wall watching her, sewing, and spotting selkies in the ocean waves.

～

There is supposed to be failure in a woman being alone. For years it bothered me that I was not 'possessed' by another or 'attached' in some way. What are you supposed to do with yourself when the ways in which society is structured make you safe or content only if you are tied, legally or socially, to another, more esteemed gender? It is not that you cannot have it: there are many men who would marry you or would at least treat you kindly. It is that happiness and a steady attention supply are not the same thing. *Happiness and a steady attention supply are not the same thing.* They are not even related. And the only reason that I thought they were was because very many of my role models were operating under the same delusion.

That you might think they are the same thing is because of magazines, social media, romantic movies, people's fickle approval, the way people talk about weddings and marriage, 'he'll make you happy': those are mythology. The only things needed for happiness are a fixed abode, safety, food, water, care, and stories. The care and stories can come from anyone, romantic or otherwise. You do not need daily attention to survive; you merely only need to experience daily *care*. The care, if it is not forthcoming, can be sought most of the time, but it must be face to face. In person. And the greatest purveyors of it, these days, tend not to be men.

Two years ago, I stopped being subject to the woodpecker opinions of the internet, stopped reassessing my worth by the comments column, deleted my popular Twitter account, and wandered into the constant dark wilderness of my home country, far away from the cities that require that you sell yourself to keep from suffocating. There, I began to write what I wanted at length in private and work at jobs that required my physical presence. I found people nearby who cared for me and I cared for. I found people who wanted to tell stories with me. This has brought me close to my motherland in a way that I have never been: I have become firm friends with the roiling dark and grey-blue frowns of the unpredictable. In fact, I revel in downpours and thunder and fierce, ripping winds, and when they catch me by surprise, I like to linger in and try to prolong them. I try to think of all the women who knew how to thatch a roof and butcher a pig and find a spring, those who may not have had care like I can have care. Atop my neighbour Calton Hill, men have placed Enlightenment monuments that poke the sky, but when it rains, the clouds envelop and sap their power. Beneath the hill, it is said, the Pale Queen sits ready to impart to local women the gifts of how to survive.

Perhaps I have finally listened.

⌒

Perth Railway Station is a Victorian building made of red and white brick triangles and inverted U shapes. If you grew up in the United Kingdom, there's a good chance you think Perth Railway Station looks a bit like a seventies Safeway supermarket. There's nothing particularly mysterious or interesting about its iron girders if what you are seeking is a reclusive martial artist from a Dark Ages tome.

Striding out towards the car park where multi-coloured pansies sit in troughs, I remember an urban childhood spent in and out of Perth and Aberdeen on the east coast of Scotland, only sometimes broken by trips to Balloch, Bennachie, Glenshee. Sometimes I'd see my aunt in Auchtermuchty, something that in proper Scots pronunciation sounds a lot like coughing twice or a compound sneeze, a place that looks like a village from *Outlander*.

We won't be needing postcard images where we're going. Remove all thoughts of twee Jacobite sex fantasies and Highland Toffee trim and the comfort of *Trainspotting*'s nearby

Class A drugs. My mind can't get past the sadness and massacre, old stains of poverty and airborne sea foam that will be at our destination, possible guesthouse fish and chips if we are lucky. We are going to Dun Sgathaich—a ruin named 'Fortress of Shadows' in Gaelic, like it might be some sort of *Dark Souls* level—and I know from thirty-two years' experience there is nothing cute about the ankle-spraining hikes of Caledonian coastal cliffs, and treating them like a lovely little jolly into Highland cow territory is what the Isle of Skye frankly *wants* from you before it opens up rockpool jaws and consumes you whole.

My friend Cat, whose expertise in both driving and photography I have hired for the weekend, shows me her supplies in the back of the car: wellie boots, waterproof trousers, windbreakers, fleeces. Possible armour for an oncoming storm. Photographers never leave anything to chance—there's a lot of expensive equipment to abandon in a sucking bog. We look at the weather forecast: as usual, the answer comes, 'Changeable.' The Isle of Skye is more than five hours' drive away to the north-west, but not on flat, wide straights. After you leave Fort William for the islands, it is a shoulder-wrench on the steering column around steep hills, up and down narrow roads populated with spiteful sheep, the force of the usual angry cloudburst and gale force winds making it likely you will drive into a springy heather trap-ditch. If you consider Scotland an old woman's face turned west towards North America, as my Highland ancestors did, then we are driving to the edge of her bushy eyebrow to try to understand what she is thinking.

In the car, I try not to think about Scáthach. But she is all I can think about.

Scáthach the warrior woman's largest role happens in an Old Irish Gaelic tale called 'The Wooing of Emer'. In the earliest form of the tale, the Ulster hero Cu Chulainn has to prove himself to the father of his prospective bride Emer. Part of the father's approval depends on Cu Chulainn going to Scotland to train with a great martial artist, our Scáthach, who resides in a place called The Fortress of Shadows. It is such a demanding regime that it is expected that Cu Chulainn will die in training. In fact, Emer's father is counting on it.

The Fortress of Shadows has a long precipice to negotiate and a solid door at the entrance. Cu Chulainn walks across the precipice and stabs his spear right through the door of the dun, or fortress. Scáthach's daughter Uathach opens the door, presumably to find out who is damaging the door (no daughter of Scáthach fears mere violence).

Uathach is immediately dumbstruck by how agonisingly hot Cu Chulainn is. (I believe the translation in the *Revue Celtique* states, 'She did not speak to him, so much did his shape move her desire.') Uathach goes upstairs to tell her mother Scáthach about him (I like to imagine he looks like Hot Chris Pratt. Maybe Chris Pratt in *The Magnificent Seven*, or in that *Jurassic Park* movie where he seduces a pack of velociraptors).

I ruminate, from time to time, on the conversation that sup- posedly passed between the two women about Cu Chulainn. Scáthach is a very famous teacher of the fuck 'em up arts, and she runs what one might consider a sprawling martial arts train- ing ground, the kind that you might see in a Bruce Lee movie, only they're all Scottish and Irish and they really like swords and haft weapons. Scáthach's by no means a stupid woman, and she's a woman who's used to huge strapping Irish heroes turning up at her door, or at least dying on the precipice before it for her entertainment. There's no direct speech suggested for what Uathach says to her about Cu Chulainn, but it's probably something like, 'Mum, there's an Irish hero at the door and he's so hot my eyes and crotch might have gone on fire.'

Scáthach's reply is something like, 'Put him in my bed then. I've been bored all this time.'

It is this ability to be completely unimpressed with the world that made Scáthach immediately dear to me.

Generally speaking, Cu Chulainn is one of the worst house guests you could possibly imagine. When he was young, he killed his host Chulainn's guard dog and had to pretend to be a guard dog for Chulainn until a replacement dog was reared, which is how Cu Chulainn got his name. At Scáthach's house, he accidentally breaks Uathach's finger and then kills one of Scáthach's guest champions. Cu Chulainn also goes out to try to slay Aoife, a neighbouring warrior woman said to be the best in the world, against Scáthach's will, and brings her back as prisoner. I imagine Scáthach's carpets, if there are any, are ruined.

Do not have Cu Chulainn round your house. He will do something awful.

And yet Scáthach seems to care about Cu Chulainn, probably because her daughter ends up betrothed to him. (I'm not really versed in Irish marriage laws, but doesn't he want to marry Emer? Doesn't this create some problems? Should it? How many children is this guy supposed to have? Didn't he swear a vow of chastity to Emer that was immediately violated when he met Scáthach? So many questions for the editor.) But she's not even ruffled by his behaviour. When he kills a visiting champion, she's just like: that is inconvenient. What are you going to do about that? It seems that to Scáthach the whole world is just teeming with impetuous young Irish imbeciles who run rampant across the land like kittens might play all over their bored, slightly sleepy mother. It's this quality that I like about her: she's the best at what she does, because she's seen it all. Scáthach is only scared of Aoife, her neighbour, but Scáthach lives in a fortress with all the heroes of the Celtic world. What has she got to worry about, really? She knows all of the secrets of the art of killing others. That's why men come to her.

⌒

The five-hour drive to Fort William feels like being in the first season of *True Detective*, the passing landscape like some ticking timebomb and the serial killer is the weather. The sky quickly blows past grey clouds and covers us in fine mist, then solid rain, then mist again. Most of Scotland's motorways pass by fields of cows or sheep or horses, pine trees, telephone poles, telephone poles, giant mountains, heather and heather and heather, cottages, squat grey villages, and sometimes a couple petrol stations. Cat, a seasoned Highlands driver, has planned to stop at the Fort William Morrison's supermarket to get lunch and a break from looking at the road's white Morse code before she stick shifts around winding single track roads. The hard part. The difficult part. The part where you might fuck it up entirely.

We have been mostly silent. Cat and I don't know each other well, but we are happy in each other's company. Anticipation feels like a person sitting dourly, dark-browed in the back, like a murderer of hopes and dreams. Probably we are both wondering what might go wrong or trying to think about what we might see from that coast. We are definitely thinking about the weather and how it will piss it down the closer we get. We are both thinking about where we will sleep and what we will eat.

The further you get to the edge of the Roman Empire in Britain, the less comfortable everything gets. They used to build us roads, you know. Straight roads Britons still use. But the Romans were not used to the water-based army Scotland kept in the sky, and they didn't care to face the land army either.

I'm telling you this because ancient history has had a direct effect on Scotland and how it works. Inverness, Edinburgh, Glasgow, Aberdeen, we all have what anyone in the United States has in terms of, well, stuff. But sometimes there are places that even Amazon won't go. It doesn't make fiscal sense. The ancient Romans worked this out early. Probably the Romans built the wall against us because they disliked the idea of fighting men and women hardened on the absence of tiled, heated floors and steam rooms, and whose primary idea of intimacy was telling each other the most heart-wrenching stories they could think of, then duelling each other to the death over them. (If you have ever wanted to live in a society entirely made of warrior-poets, this is the logical endpoint of one.)

I always think about a game the Roman soldiers used to play when they kept watch on the ramparts of Vindolanda at Hadrian's Wall. They would throw a red ball over the wall into Scotland, and every soldier would try to throw their ball closest to it. The closest ball to the red ball would win. The ball furthest away from the red ball would lose: the owner would be lowered into Scotland to pick all the balls up. I laugh to myself, every time, at the idea of a Roman soldier, in full leather armour regalia and winter fur, running about the bushes, frantic, before the Scots arrive to pick him off. Probably this was the main entertainment of the game for the not-losers, like Ancient Roman *Takeshi's Castle*. Only if you fell, a Scot jumped out and stabbed you.

~

Cat and I sit in the cafe of Morrison's over mugs of lukewarm brown coffee with that thin layer of milk fat glinting on the top of it, looking out past the last vestiges of what one might call 'urban' life on our way. Next to us are the bright yellow arches of a McDonald's restaurant, strangely not that far from the actual Clan MacDonald outposts. Scots like to brag about what we gave the world, but sometimes it bites us in the arse.

We're going to Lord of the Isles territory. (If these terms seem familiar, George R. R. Martin has probably borrowed them.) The Gallowglass come from these islands. They were a breed of Viking that settled with the Gaels as early as the mid-thirteenth century and became so good at fucking people up that the Irish, the French, and even the English hired them as mercenaries for their own private battles. People were scared of them. They were in awe of them. They carried a Sparth Axe, a long haft weapon with an axe blade that often curved around to meet the pole it sat on, and a broadsword or claymore (Scots for 'very large sword'). If you faced them, they did not have to be very close to you to put a lot of metal through you like butter. Alongside they would bring two boys, like squires, to hold other implements of war: throwing spears for those pesky ones who run away, and a snack, for after the spear has landed in the enemy's back.

Was the character of Scáthach based on these terrifying
mercenaries? The more bleak purple mountains we encounter on the drive towards her reputed fortress, the more real she
becomes to me. The more the rain threatens to bash through the
windscreen, the more I think I know how she thinks. The closer
we get to a place named after her, the less fictional she becomes.

⤙

My day job is to write stories. To make people up. Being
the creator of a story world is difficult because one particular
question sits on the shoulders all day: are you imitating the
world or shaping it? Is this something that must correspond
to your own experience, or can you write what you imagine,
what you wish something to be, what *should* be? If you are
writing something down, are you responsible for what it does
to people? Are you responsible for the reaction when it hits
someone? How responsible?

Scotland is covered in these anxious questions. The central
rail station in Edinburgh is called 'Waverley' after Sir Walter
Scott's novels about a village of the same name. The place name
'Waverley' was made up for the book. But now it is a place. It
is a real place in lowland Scotland, and Sir Walter Scott is
responsible for imagining it, and by his influence, he made it.
By writing it down, he asked for it to come into being. People
believed 'Waverley' should exist so much that it *now exists*.
Shakespeare made up places in Verona that now exist: Juliet's
Tomb is a sarcophagus you may visit in Verona with *no one
buried in it*. Shakespeare had *never been to Verona*.

And so: if you invent a warrior woman of the Gallowglass ilk
and place her in the wilderness of Skye, in a place called The

Fortress of Shadows, will she eventually arrive? How much of this was based on a real person? Or a real idea? Was it based on a real place? Did it come into being because people *believed it* into being, or did someone build a castle, name it after her, and claim that it was once hers? I can't find any historical records to explain it, and it's unlikely there is anything much that has survived. What came first? Did she come first, or did the land? Did the stories come first, or did some role model, some leader? She was never *real*, but then, when you look out of your car window at the gathering storm, when you are winding round and round, past angry sheep with those eyes like the insides of razor blades, you think: There must have been some basis in fact. There must have been someone.

᜶

We arrive at Dun Sgathaich, the fifteenth-century castle named after Scáthach, said, by local legend, to be built on the foundations of Scáthach's fortress itself. It is battering rain. We get out of the car at the edge of Skye's coast and look over an unruly field of sheep towards a small hump on the horizon. The air in the remote parts of Scotland is sharp and fresh, always so full of petrichor and the taste of wild green leaves. Sometimes breathing it feels like drinking iced water on a hot day.

We trudge through springy, soggy peat bog and up over hills until it winds into view, a grey mouth crouching on a small mound, gnarled, snarling.

'That's it!' I say to Cat, holding my waterproof's hood over my glasses. 'That's it! We found it.' There's a weird feeling in the bottom of my stomach.

Pounded by waves over the years, it has no walls, but the foundations and what look like steps are still visible on the other side, overgrown with grass and some sort of vegetation in the middle up by where the ground floor of the hall used to be.

'Do you think we can get in?' Cat asks. I don't know. We have to get closer.

We trudge towards it as the rain spatters into our eyes. Horizontal rain blinds us as we arrive at a square hole.

'There's no drawbridge,' I say. This is a stupid statement, because of course there isn't. Instead there is a huge gaping drop onto rocks below that look like jagged teeth. A thin line of slidy stones reach across it at either side, where the drawbridge once rested when it was down.

'Can you get across?' Cat says. I test a stone underneath my green wellies. The wellies are massive and they don't have very good grip. In good weather, a careful and dainty explorer might be able to edge across one of the drawbridge supports and into the castle itself. But today I'm certain trying to do this in the rain will result in my smashed corpse in the rocky moat below.

~

I lie awake that night in a cheap hotel bed and think about the stories of Scáthach. Even if Dun Sgathaich was opportunistically named after Scáthach in order to maximise its fearsome reputation, I wonder if in some manner the actual act of *believing* that a fictional figure might have lived there gives her a better chance of slipping into existence. It's a well-known story Scottish grandmothers tell that sometimes, where the forest has a cold spot, that is a *thin place*, a place where the boundary between this world and the Other World of spirits, fairies, and pixies is worn. I wonder if thin place magic has somehow worked its stuff on the castle and the weird feeling I have around it is just excess belief turning into the real.

When I was young, I was particularly enamoured with the Terry Pratchett book *Hogfather*, a comedic fantasy book about a parallel medieval world to ours, where a man analogous to Father Christmas goes missing and Death himself has to take over the job. In the book, Pratchett describes a world in which strong belief in a particular mythical figure can pop that figure into existence: the Tooth Fairy, for example, starts to exist in a physical form simply because enough children believe in her.

I always think about this book as a powerful reminder that perhaps it doesn't even matter that the Tooth Fairy does not exist: sometimes pretending that something exists, even as a symbol, is *necessary*, so that losing a tooth might seem like a less gruesome or painful experience.

Doesn't all fiction function this way?

⌁

The next day, I run full pelt towards Dun Sgathaich for the second time. Cat has parked and left me alone. It is drier now, but the wind is up. My hair whorls around me. The springy moss rises up to meet my Doc Martens. I put Grimes up very loud in my headphones and look searchingly at the looming grey walls as they near. It is the last chance I will have to really find her. I have an hour until the rain comes and makes my task impossible.

I'll do it, I think. This time, I'll do it.

In the stories, Irish heroes have to make it through a number

of trials and over a dangerous precipice to get to the door of
The Fortress of Shadows and greet Scáthach.

I edge out onto the little ledge, no more than a couple of inches
in width, and grab onto the remaining mortar beside it to steady
myself. The grips on my Doc Martens hold me there as I look
down at the drop and my stomach flips. The wind slaps my
hair on my cheek. I try to look straight out at the view of the
coast instead: stark claws slung with striped tides of blue and
green seaweed, the rocky beach curving away, purple heather
playing on the cliffs above.

I take a deep breath, and agonising, gripping the side, I take
baby steps all the way along towards the landing. I step onto the
other side into a sandy pathway. Underfoot, I feel what were
probably once perfectly flat flagstones, and I look up a winding
staircase that leads steeply up the hill. Warriors had used these
once for real. They had climbed the steps in sopping armour
with food and fur and those little round shields.

Suddenly I run all the way up the winding steps up into the
castle feeling my whole body grin: fuck you fuck you fuck you
I MADE IT. And run straight into a sea of nettles at the top, a
massive lake of them surrounding me. Some childhood instinct
makes me hold my hands up high to avoid the stinging barbs
on the leaves and I gasp.

A laugh so loud comes out of me as I look around this final
trial, surrounded, surrounded, a whole swathe of nettles up to
the waist. But I'm wearing waterproofs as armour. Scáthach
cannot beat me this way. I wade through the giant nettle field
until I come out of the other side into the clearing where the
main hall used to be. It is grassy, some foundation walls still
visible in the ground.

The heroes of Ulster left the carpet neat after all.

Then I notice there is a small hole right in the centre of the ground with very clear water in it. I scoop some into my mouth messily: fresh. The remains of the castle well. The castle is siege-proof.

At the edge of Dun Sgathaich, the remains of the walls give way to a sheer drop into the sea below. The wind pushes at my shoulders and sucks at my elbows as I look at the waves smashing the pebbles and rocks.

It is breathtakingly beautiful from here. White-speckled tidal islands are little humps out in the Irish Sea; there is nothing but grey rippling waves and those roiling rolling layers of blue-orange cloud cover. It is like looking at an animated painting where all of the rippling brushstrokes and layers are visible.

I find a place on the castle edge to sit and do nothing but look at the grass carpet and stare out over the coast, watching the birds play by a cliff lip.

This is what it would be like to have a castle of your own, I think. To live by yourself. To be self-sufficient. To need nothing and want nothing. To be contented.

'I don't fucking need you,' I blurt out.

I hardly hear it the first time: I realise I have said it and then I frown at myself. Who am I talking to? What am I talking about? I don't know. It could be anyone, anything. But it seems so fitting I say it again: 'I don't fucking need you. I don't. Fucking. Need you! I DON'T FUCKING NEED YOU!' I lose my breath and I laugh and it feels like everything, every weight I ever had comes out of me. The stones and hills and sea are the only witnesses. I can't help myself: I whisper at the well in the centre of the castle as if it is in on the secret. 'I don't fucking need you,' I say, under my breath, quietly, like it is a spell that only works on me. 'I don't. Fucking. Need you.'

I sit there silently for an hour, my mind completely blank, devoid of wanting or needing anything at all but to sit and look. I just look at Scotland and feel like I am part of it. Scotland continues. It is fine.

Slowly, as the rain sweeps in, I walk down the steps of the castle, edge out over the precipice, and walk back to the car where Cat is packing up.

I say: 'I got inside. It had a well. It was beautiful.'

'I saw you sitting on the edge,' she said. And I wonder if she saw me laughing.

⁓

I don't know what came first: the fortress or the story. In many ways, the place is more important than the story. It is evocative of stories. When I need to be calm, I say the mantra: *I don't. Fucking. Need you.* It is part of how Scáthach functions in 'The Wooing of Emer', and it is part of me now.

When I say it, all the world's insidious systems and oppressions and dark, spirit-voiding animosity recoil from my vicinity temporarily, wash back into a yonder where they cannot hurt me. I have become like the Fortress. I am the rock by the ocean, under the lashing rain, raking sun, banshee wind, shadow, hail, and that thin, consistent spitting mist Scots call 'smirr', and I am wild, and you cannot mark something that is so profoundly marked. To Scotland, all happenings, all happenings, are mere exfoliation. And I have become like Scotland, the woman who is the landscape.

You cannot fuck with that kind of woman.

Trash-Magic: Signs & Rituals for the Unwanted

Maranda Elizabeth

'Those flowers belong to the city,' somebody shouted as I retrieved a bouquet from a green dumpster on the side of a busy street, my cane resting alongside the bin so I could use both hands. I didn't look up. Whoever it was, they didn't come closer, didn't repeat themselves.

I brought the flowers home and placed them on my nightstand beside a tarot deck and a desk lamp with a hot pink cord and a dim bulb. I knew the flowers were a sign. The two-drawer nightstand was found at a junk store in the tiny village where I lived in a haunted house as a baby. While revisiting the place, I picked up a piece of broken concrete from a path leading to another haunted house, this one abandoned, weeds creeping through the cracks.

'Leave that house alone,' somebody else yelled. Again, I didn't look, didn't respond. *I'm from here!* I wanted to yell. *I belong here, too!*

Around the corner, as I raised my phone to take a photo of my yellow-brick babyhood home, a black cat trotted out from the backyard and sat on the path leading to the concrete patio my dad, a construction worker, laid shortly before our family split. She looked like she was protecting the place. She looked like she knew me, had a message for me. She looked like she belonged.

∼

One of my visualisations for getting around the city is to imagine myself, my crooked body and odd appearance, as a black cat crossing somebody's path: good luck to some, bad luck to others.

When I'm bad luck, I'm haunting. The young disabled misfit you don't wanna become. I'm ugly and mysterious. I'm in pain when I'm not 'supposed' to be. I'm the black cat dashing out in front of your car, staring you down, trespassing on your property, daring you to shoo me away.

When I'm good luck, I'm really good. I'm a sign. Catching a glimpse of me feels meaningful. A witch in tourmaline and amethyst, my cane becoming my wand, a sight of another cripple-goth, another disabled-weirdo, in a landscape too often inaccessible to us. Sometimes we share a nod. I'm the lucky talisman you find on the ground, keep in your pocket. I'm the black cat sitting at the feet of the Queen of Wands. I'm a spell come true.

Bad luck or good, I'm magic.

∼

I make rituals for different times, different spaces. Home rituals, hospital rituals, crip rituals. Dumpster rituals, writing

rituals, body rituals. Rituals of celebration, of comfort, of gratitude. Rituals to remain present, rituals to protect myself, rituals
to feel a sense of belonging—belonging wherever I am, whether
I'm at home or elsewhere, outdoors or in, always belonging in my
body. Rituals of resistance. Of affirmation. My mantras come
from books about witchcraft, books about borderline personality
disorder. They come from fiction. I make them up.

Every surface in my home has become an altar. I painted my
door lavender, hung up a plastic skeleton from the dollar store
adorned with a filmy, dusky mauve cape, glowing eyes. A deep
violet rug in the stairwell tests the parameters of my own home,
making visible a hint of my personality, my magic, to those who
pass through in the cobwebbed shared entrance. The door is
crooked, misaligned with the frame. I burn black candles here.
The building is almost one hundred years old.

My writing desk, another altar. Found at a yard sale in my
hometown for ten dollars. Spray-painted lavender, outside by
the lilac bushes in the backyard of a house I lived in almost
ten years ago. Three drawers, metal handles. Scratches on the
surface touched up with nail polish, purple glitter. I've written
dozens of zines on this desk. Several novels on this desk, so many
diaries, letters, notes, to-do lists. Invoices, too.

There's a large chunk of amethyst on the left corner, chosen
because its shape, its odd opaque points of quartz protruding
from its otherwise deep violet sharp curves, reminded me of the
Three of Pentacles. I look at it when I'm writing and imagine
I am inside it. I imagine this corner of my home is the same
corner in the image on the tarot card, the hidden nook where my
creative work is my form of prayer, my form of spellcasting. The
place where I practise, where I cry, where I scribble, where I scry.

For medical appointments, I book WheelTrans rides. Wheel-Trans is a service provided by the city for disabled folks who can't or who can rarely access public transit. It costs the same, $3.25. There are buses, but most of my rides are in cabs contracted by the city. I've had a lot of conversations with cab drivers, learned about their lives, seen how strangers treat them. In the backseat, window down, depending on my mood, I feel sometimes pathetic, sometimes grateful, sometimes like a sad cripple being driven to the hospital again, sometimes like a rich eccentric with a personal chauffeur. I keep my backpack, adorned with enamel pins as magical talismans, on my lap. Sometimes I tweet about my ride, an attempt to demystify the process, the service, connect with other crips.

A single Tylenol 3 and Xanax are the potion I imbibe before medical appointments. One for pain, the other for anxiety. I used to cry at every single appointment. For years. I still do sometimes, but less so since I decided to make art of them. Crying in public became one of my forms of resistance.

In hospitals, my cane is still my wand, and my camera becomes a magical implement, too. When I hold my cane, my fist clutches the handle, but I keep my middle finger extended, another form of protection. Documenting my medical appointments, making art of them, is one way I've found to become more myself, to practise witchcraft in medicalised environments, to be someone beyond a body-shaped object in a white room. I'm a patient and I'm a witch. I take selfies in hospital gowns, pictures of my feet in stirrups, my *witch trial* tattoo visible on my bare feet. The exam rooms become studios, studies, circles cast. It's because of my crip-body that I've been able to collect so many photos. I warn the doctors and nurses that it'll take me longer than usual to change out of my clothes, change back into them. I'm in pain. They can hear my bones, but my camera is silent.

~

Disability is rarely mentioned alongside witchcraft. For that reason, I intentionally devote time and imagination to writing as a sick mad crip borderline witch, to re-writing spells and re-defining tarot cards from my own disabled perspective(s). I'm a cripple-witch who always has psych meds and painkillers in their pockets and on their altars.

I name who I'm writing for, a form of invocation, of acknowledgement. Cripple witches, medicated witches, crazy witches. Misfits and solitaries. Anti-capitalists and mad folks, city-witches, traumatised fuck-ups, the abandoned. I write for those of us who are poor, those of us on social assistance. Those who were/are bullied for our magic, for our survival skills.

As a high school dropout, I write against nostalgia, against romanticisation. I'm un(der)educated formally, but/and contain unfathomable, underappreciated, and undervalued knowledges. A song, a zine, a protest, an essay. These are all witchcraft.

~

Creating a home is a series of rituals, too. Amethyst Cathedral is a home I've managed to hold onto for four years so far, the longest I've stayed in one place. A bachelorex painted countless shades of purple, violet, lilac, lavender, a space where I have felt more free than any other, a space where I reached my unimaginable thirties and decided *I wanna stay alive.* Amethyst Cathedral is a home built of trash. Dozens of milkcrates stolen from alleyways, mostly black, hold hundreds of books, ceramic teapots and glass bottles with dried flowers, found pottery dishes filled with crystals, prayer candles, plastic emerald-coloured bottles of vitamins, carnelian-coloured pill bottles, little potions, Hello Kitty dolls.

The sturdiness of the thick plastic milkcrates, the way they hold their shape, hold so much weight upon them; their versatility, solidity, and cheapness; their excessive presence on bright streets and in unlit alleys alike; their trustworthiness. In a way, I want to become them, want my crippled tattooed often-unpredictable body to be inspired by the presence of these objects, these inanimate entities that seem somehow to hold so much life within them. I want my body to be as indestructible as the milkcrates that contain so much of who I am, of what I want.

Raccoons build their homes from scraps. They collect whatever they can access—salvaged wood, shoeboxes, the detritus abandoned by city-dwellers, items deemed useless. What was not good enough for somebody else, what felt unneeded, becomes essential to their survival. Their paws are different from our hands—they can dig in the dark, dig underwater, and find what they need as though their palms and their claws were eyes, too. Without looking, through a kind of psychic vision experienced through the body, they know whether or not what they've found is useful, whether or not it's edible. If they've been unable to build their own home, raccoons still manage to find somewhere to live. Rooftops, balconies, porches. They're squatters. They know they belong wherever they are.

When I moved to the city, I sublet an apartment with a raccoon family living in the back. The kitchen window looked out onto an alley with a series of garages. The raccoons lived on the rooftops of the garages. There was a mother with a crooked gait, an injury to one of her back legs, and a row of six babies crawling behind her wherever she went—the runt, the tiniest one, followed at the back of the line. When she fell behind, her mom and her siblings would stop, wait, let her catch up. Over the course of a season, I watched the mother teach each of her babies how to walk, how to climb, how to hunt. When the runt couldn't climb up the drainpipe with the rest of them, her mother peeked over the edge, called out, watched her try and try again. The runt's siblings gathered, also watching. To save their injured mother from descending down and up again, one of the runt's siblings shimmied back down the drainpipe, met their sister, and led her up, nudging her partway but also encouraging her to climb on her own. When the family was reunited, they wandered off together into the night.

⁓

What would it feel like to imagine we are destroying capitalism with each spell we cast? Destroying capitalism with each candle we light, each breath we breathe? To know it's crumbling, to know we'll survive and build new worlds.

Amethyst Cathedral is meant to feel insulated from the world. Insulated, not isolated. The word 'safe' does not always resonate with me, but I do want my home to feel as safe as possible. I've survived many unstable and untenable living situations. When I talk about my apartment, I repeat like a mantra, again and again, 'I plan on living here until the building crumbles in on me.'

The day I moved in, the middle of winter and far from the water, I found a piece of beach glass welcoming me at the door. There are maple hardwood floors the same colour as my pale

ginger cat's fur, and the largest window I've ever been in pos-
session of (so to speak), three narrow rows of glass reaching from
almost floor to ceiling. There are tall trees where I watch squirrels
play and gaps between the branches where I watch the Moon.

I spend a lot of time in bed. I watch squirrels hop from tree to
tree. They climb to the top, walk to the narrowest edge of a limb,
crouch back, and then propel their lithe and fluffy bodies over
to the next tree, flying with their own limbs outstretched for a
moment before landing on the next branch, which droops down
with their weight and then flings them forward as it bounces
up again. I wonder how the squirrels feel each time they leap.
I wonder if they worry whether or not they'll make it. I wonder
if they are impervious to fear.

If we are dangerous, then capitalism and patriarchy are in
danger. When we cast spells against capitalism, what alternatives are we building? How do we dream of living? Where? With
whom? What alternatives have we created in the meantime?

Squirrels are scrappy creatures, too. Like us, they must find
rest and refuge. They must build homes, find somewhere to
sleep. Squirrels build their nests in the crooks and crannies
of trees, foraging for leaves and moss. I watch them from my
window, enveloped in my faded and tattered thrift store patch-
work quilts, protecting myself from the cool draft whispering
through my entrance. The trees where squirrels build their
shelters arch towards the hundred-year-old building I rent my
apartment in, branches casting crooked shadows across my bed.
The leaves cushion their delicate bodies against the bark, and the
stems tickle their furry limbs. My own blankets keep me cosy
and sheltered, providing a small sanctuary, the loose threads
of the ragged patches tickling my tattooed limbs. Sometimes

the holes the squirrels move into naturally shape themselves in the trunk of a tree as it grows. My own home shifts with the trees, the warped floorboards gathering dust and dirty laundry, the doors becoming misaligned with the frames, exposing me to chilly air and unwanted cracks of light. I imagine if a human carved a small hole into the side of a tree, a squirrel might show up and move in.

Lacking adequate crevices in trees, squirrels build their own nests, collecting leaves and other little scraps of nature to gather into the corners of branches where they fork, building safe and cosy spaces for themselves and their families. Other squirrels burrow underground. They scramble through parks and alleyways. They find what they need.

Unlike us, squirrels and raccoons don't have to pay rent. The trees and garbage already belong to them, and they know that they belong with the trees and garbage, too. They don't need to contact anyone before moving in, don't need to ask for permission, don't need to sign papers, prove their identity, earn cash. They don't have to worry about noisy neighbours or eviction notices. They don't have to cast spells.

When my social assistance income was cut off due to misfiled paperwork during a review, a process that happened during Mercury Retrograde in Taurus, after crying on the floor for a few hours, the next thing I did was burn green candles. Cheap unscented candles are my favourite, especially for money and abundance spells. If squirrels and raccoons could cast spells, I think they'd choose the cheapest candles, too. (I crowdfunded rent, meds, and food. And my income was reinstated, an apology issued. Witches in poverty are powerful.)

All of these animals are foragers. They've got serious coping skills. They're creatures I've been observing and been fascinated by for a long time. When I began researching more about their lives recently, I found yet another affinity we share: The first result for squirrels and raccoons is not *how they live* but *how to get rid of them*.

How to get rid of squirrels and raccoons. Rake leaves and collect acorns, nuts, and berries. Confiscate their main source of food. Use sealed trash cans they can't unlatch or chew through. Squirrel-proof your birdfeeders. Deprive them of access to found food. Install a wire fence around your garden. Make sure it's deep enough and tall enough that they can neither dig under nor climb over. Spritz black pepper and cayenne around your garden, trees, and home.

To encourage squirrels and raccoons, to invite them into your life, to connect with them, do the opposite.

The same thing happens when I research borderline personality disorder, when I research chronic illness. How to cope with us, how to care for yourself while we deprive you of your energy. How to get rid of us. The city produces immense amounts of garbage, inaccessible structures and transit, unmanageable schedules and demands, and then retaliates and punishes those of us who find other ways to survive. The crazy, the poor, the witches, the unwanted.

It's as if this capitalist ableist misogynist racist classist madphobic culture has attempted to cast a banishing spell. But we're the real witches, not them. We know how to fight. We've got unretractable claws. We've got signs. We know.

I think about the word 'coping' a lot. *Coping* and *survival*, those infinitely dynamic words that carry so many meanings—negative to some, positive to others, neutral to yet more, and meaningful to me no matter which category they fall under. Coping and survival are what witchcraft has given me. Each moment of my life, from the mundane to the magnificent, feels like ritual. Prayer and ritual are entwined throughout each day, each action, each object and surface. Even my bed feels like an altar.

I watch the animals from my window, encounter them when I'm out dumpstering. We watch one another. I wonder about them, ask questions about them. In what ways are squirrels and raccoons dangerous? Dangerous to others and dangerous to the order of things? In what ways are they kind? To each other, and to us, the abandoned, the feared, the magical, the dreamers? How do they care for and protect themselves and their families? What do their markings mean? What art have they inspired? How do they resist? What can we learn from them?

⌒

One of my altars has the skull of a squirrel. Although mostly bare, teeth rotted out, a few whiskers remain. Bones fascinate me, and I'd dreamed of finding the skull of a squirrel for a long time. I felt like it would make so much more magic possible, that talisman or safety object. I know you can buy bones on the internet, but I wanted to stumble into one on my own, wanted it to find me.

Like so many of my possessions, like so much of what I eat, like so much of what nurtures me, I found it in the trash. And I didn't have to go too far, didn't have to dig too deep.

I found my squirrel skull at home, buried underneath Amethyst Cathedral.

My building contains twelve apartments, plus the family of raccoons residing on the rooftop. The corner where the garbage bins are contained is a perpetual mess. I'd tried organising it myself, tried leaving aesthetically pleasing but curt notes, tried passive-aggressively discussing the nearly unbearable garbage situation in shared hallways and near open windows. Nothing changed. One day, a friend who lives in the building and I decided to put on some gloves, gather some plastic bags, and clean it up. Almost nothing was in the bin where it belonged. Trash was scattered all over the yard, the pathway leading to the door, the sidewalk, the road. It was embarrassing. Witches don't leave garbage on the ground.

After most of it had been picked up and disposed of, I saw one more piece remaining. I bent down and reached towards it, but couldn't pick it up. I realised it was buried. There were tiny bones around it that I'd mistaken for take-out leftovers as I scattered them away with my fingertips. But once I noticed they hadn't been cooked and slobbered all over, had no meat or fat remaining on them, it became clear that this creature had died here. Died here and remained hidden under garbage long enough to rot into nothing but bones.

I cleared the dirt around the smudge of white and unearthed a skull. It felt fragile in my hands. I gently dusted it off and brought it home, put it on a shelf with branches, crystals, and books. I placed it near the plastic dumpster on my altar, an object acquired because I thought it was cute, not realising how much trash-magic it would bring to me.

꙳

My disabled body is inherently anti-capitalist. I cast spells from bed. I'm writing this essay in bed, listening to witchy albums on a stereo I found on the sidewalk. More milkcrates surround the stereo, with plants—ivy, aloe, lavender, prayer plant, spider plant—growing over the edges and a glittery purple Toronto snow globe I turn upside-down as I wish for city-magic before going outside. A junk store statuette of Saint Dymphna, Patron Saint of Crazy People, watches over it all.

Learning histories and legacies of my blood family is a form of resistance, an intention and action against forgetting, against abandoning, against erasing. I think of my mom, who collects crystals and talks to ghosts, and her mom, who also talks to ghosts. I think of multiple generations of my family who lived in the same city, who once resided in the same neighbourhood as me. I remember their psychic premonitions. I think of our ongoing histories of depression and alcoholism, poverty and chronic pain, migraines and suicidal ideation. I think of all the doctors who wouldn't believe us, all the non-believers-of-witchcraft who won't believe us. I reclaim everything I've been told is fake and irrational.

I think about the magical and revolutionary possibilities of housebound and cripple witchcraft and art, writing, and resistance. As I perform my loner rituals, I remember there are other mad, broke, crazy witches performing rituals, too. I imagine us all in our homes, what we've managed to scrape together, lighting candles and casting spells, resisting messages that tell us we are not enough, rejecting the world that wants to have us cast out. I think about my lineages, blood and otherwise: poor, crazy, borderline; witch, cripple, writer; queer, non-binary, hysteric; survivor of incarceration and abuse, psych wards, poverty and violence; high school dropout, zinester, multiple suicide attempt survivor. I write affirmations for us. I name us again and again. Nobody else will.

Each morning, in bed, I drink coffee and draw my daily tarot card, write it into my diary. I imagine myself within the cards, my body-life-psyche portrayed in magical decks, disability and madness as an integral part of my witchcraft, not something to overcome or transcend, not something to hide or feel ashamed of, not used as a metaphor for lack. I like the cards where the figures hold canes and crutches.

I read tarot for others, write a tarot column. I ask questions.

When your friends feel inadequate for not being able to attend protests, what cards will you show them? When your friends are worried their art and writing are not good enough as resistance, what cards will you show them? When your friends feel left behind, what cards will you show them?

Where are our sick and disabled bodies in the cards, in the spell books? What do our magic and resistance look like when we're puking? Crying? Fighting? Dreaming? What does it mean to see our mad minds and crip bodies in rebellion? To know that our sick-witch bodies and psyches are not rebelling against us, but against individual and systemic trauma, against capitalism, against complacency and complicity?

What does it mean to cast spells as resistance from bed?

What does it mean to be dangerous and in danger at once?

What does it look like, feel like, when our spells come true?

⁓

On Halloween, I booked a WheelTrans ride to take me to the other side of the city, to a place that felt even further away; a place where the Moon's glow reflected on the water, where the Moon was the only light, bright enough to see our shadows. A place where I could pretend I was in the middle of nowhere.

I wanted something to happen. I didn't know what. I worried there'd be no signs. I worried there'd be a sign but I wouldn't know what it meant.

A long, meandering ride, multiple pick-ups and drop-offs before reaching my destination, driving in the opposite direction at rush hour. Nausea. Reading in the backseat anyway. And then in the time it would've taken me to return to my hometown, I was on the other side of the city, driven to the edge of land.

'Are you sure this is where you're going?' the driver asked.

'I'm sure.'

'There's nobody here.'

There was a dirt path, a closed gate.

'I know. My friends are late. They'll be here soon.'

He seemed hesitant to drop me off. I didn't know if he was being protective or conniving. It's hard to tell the difference between intuition and paranoia.

But after he left, my friends arrived.

At thirteen, I had a coven. Since then, I can count the friends I've practiced witchcraft with on one hand. Much of my witchcraft is internal and difficult to share. We gathered at the gate and followed the path as the sun began to set, walking through the trees and dead brambles, scattered milk pod seeds, purple asters, pineapple weeds, and dried wildflowers for nearly an hour. I held my cane and they walked their bikes. We turned at a few forks in the path, skirted deep puddles, arrived at the edge of the lake, and chose a spot to build a fire.

We created an altar, placed offerings along the surface. Each of us, without coordinating beforehand, had brought a different variety of apple, which we took a single bite of before setting down. I'd brought small sunflowers and gerbera daisies in various shades of pink and purple, pale pink roses, three slices of bread with plenty of nuts and seeds, an eggplant, and a small chunk of amethyst. Aside from the crystal, everything was salvaged from dumpsters.

My crip-body can only do so much. While my friends created a border for the firepit with thirteen broken cinder blocks and wandered off to gather fallen branches, I sat down on the ground and looked up at the sky. The Moon was glowing between drifting grey clouds and stars were slowly appearing, glittering. All I could hear were the waves of the lake against the empty shore. All I could see was the night, my back turned to the lit-up city skyline.

At first I thought it was a shooting star. But its tail traced its flame through the sky for longer than usual—I have the strange luck of looking up just in time to see shooting stars and other oddities in the sky—and as it flew and then slowly burned out, I realised it was a meteor. I watched in awe as I always do when these things appear.

And I wondered what it meant.

With my friends off in the semi-wild, I had space to contemplate. I thought about how I was alone when I saw the meteorite, but I knew its message couldn't only be about being alone. I wouldn't have gone out there on my own. I wouldn't have been there without having first found the courage to apply for WheelTrans, without the driver, without my friends compromising by walking alongside me instead of riding their bikes, and without them understanding that although I wanted to, I couldn't gather firewood with them. I remembered the raccoon family I'd observed when I moved to the city, the way they helped one another learn to navigate with their imperfect bodies.

I have difficulty balancing solitude and friendship, careening between existential loneliness and social burnout. But I created equilibrium that night, and I realised the meteor was a sign of interdependence, a reminder of the magic I've been able to create in times of distress and despair, and in times of joy and contentment, too.

~

'It's like finding a flower in a dumpster,' someone said to me, walking together after midnight.

We were talking about trauma. About the terrible things people do to one another. About the unavoidable, seemingly insurmountable legacies of trauma—that which we've endured, and that which we and/or our ancestors have perpetrated. Colonisation and land theft, slavery, rape, genocide, war, torture. Misogyny and sexism, racism, ableism and madphobia, transphobia and transmisogyny, poverty. Devastation. The scope of all this pain and the daily mundaneness of it, too. Inescapable.

We were trying to find the good in the world, the flower in the dumpster.

The conversation began when I mentioned how often men catcall me, how often men approach me on the street, hit on me, harass me, take my photo. How often they refuse to ignore me, refuse to leave me alone. How often they refuse to hear my *no* when they try to ask me out, try to get my number. How often they follow me, follow me home.

I was talking about how I like meeting strangers, like talking to people on the street, sometimes even—gasp!—like talking to men, but that with all the trauma they've caused me and my friends, caused so many, caused the world, everything

I can't know about a stranger and their intentions makes this feel impossible.

All the devastation.

I don't think it's impossible, though. I'm a witch. I don't think anything is impossible. I've cast impossible spells and watched them come true. I've survived too much to refuse belief.

And I find signs. I find signs everywhere. I slink around the city collecting what I need from the trash. The sandwiches, the salads, the desserts, the fruits and vegetables, the flowers: they belong to me as much as they belong to the city, as much as I—with my black cat stare and crooked-body, my claws and my spells, my friends and my art—belong to the city.

As I prowl through the streets searching for food and treasure, those black cats who appear as symbols of my own strength, luck, and survival, don't just cross my path, don't just share a furtive glance and saunter away. They come right up to me, their paws tickling my toes, nose sniffing my ankles. Their tails spiral and swirl around my body and then around my cane, and I realise my cane is my own tail, too: the magical fifth limb giving me stability and presence, giving me access. Like the brazen squirrels and gutsy raccoons, those underappreciated misfit creatures that cultivate a sense of belonging wherever they go, we each have our fifth limbs holding us steady.

I've never found a single flower in a dumpster. That's true. But after that conversation with my friend, through the devastation, flowers began to appear. But not single flowers, not loner flowers.

Entire fucking bouquets.

Uncensoring My Ugliness

Laura Mandanas

On the day I was released from the hospital after being shot in the face, the outside world felt like my last trip to the Vegas strip. Although in theory I was happy to be there, everything seemed much too bright, much too loud, and much too crowded. There were blurred waves of heat visibly rising from the asphalt; I stuck to the grass as much as possible. In the chaos of the shooting, my flip-flops had somehow been lost, so our first mission after checking out of the hospital was to locate a drugstore and replace them.

With my dad in charge of driving the rental car, my job was to read the map on the GPS to get us to the Walgreens 3.2 miles away. Maybe the streets had changed, or maybe the Garmin was badly in need of an update; whatever the case, we made wrong turn after wrong turn. The supposed ten-minute drive took us at least twice that long. Weeks later, my dad—a family practice physician—confessed that he'd been testing my spatial skills to try to figure out if I'd gotten a concussion when the bullet hit me. My poor performance didn't provide him with a clear answer; both of us had always had notoriously bad senses of direction.

After picking out the world's ugliest plastic sandals, my dad and I got back in the car for a three-and-a-half-hour drive to Austin. There was a brief reunion in the parking lot with the two friends who had been in the car with me during the shooting, then we all headed to Amy's Ice Cream for dinner. At checkout, the cashier cheerfully asked our group, 'How was your Memorial weekend?' I felt my friends hesitate. After a long moment, I pulled the gauze from my mouth to speak. 'We were in a shooting,' I said bluntly. The cashier looked shocked. I pressed the gauze to my mouth again. Outside in the parking lot, my friends and I erupted into deep belly laughter about the expression on the cashier's face. In many ways, what had happened still felt like a hilarious joke. It didn't feel like real life yet.

Back at the hotel, I tried to eat my ice cream, but the sensation of salted caramel brownie against the raw insides of my mouth quickly became too much to handle. The stitches in my left wrist throbbed. *One, two, three, four, five, six, seven, eight, nine,* I counted them. *One half, two, two and a half, three...* I attempted to count my broken and missing teeth, but the terrain was too foreign: too much swelling, too many new bumps and sharp edges. It would be another few days before I arrived at the final count: *a dozen.* I never counted the stitches inside my mouth and crawling across my face. Fully quantifying the damage felt both morbid and impossible.

I looked at my friend who'd driven the car during the shooting and wanted to curl up inside him, envelop myself in his hug, hold tight and never let go. I looked at the other passenger and felt overwhelmed with relief that I'd been the one who was shot and not her, my most beautiful friend, the one all the boys had wanted in high school. I looked at them both and felt every feeling I'd ever felt with them or about them crackling across the surface of my skin, electric. I wanted to connect with them, ask if they felt the same, *make* them feel it, all of it, every feeling I was feeling. Instead, we returned to the hotel room and I laid my head on the driver's shoulder and closed my eyes. Instead, I cracked a lot of jokes and avoided looking in mirrors. Instead, I slept.

We flew back to upstate New York, and when my girlfriend wanted to see me, I resisted. Early on, I'd overheard a well-meaning female relative on the phone: 'Sue them! She's young, and it's going to be much harder to find a husband with her face like that.' I didn't say anything. Part of me knew that she was correct—even if her assumption about what I wanted in life was not. Luckily, my girlfriend seemed not to care. ('I thought that you were going to look way worse, from the way you described it!' she told me later. 'You know that you don't actually look like the Joker, right?' Right.)

Following another relative's advice, I began taking daily photos to document my recovery. I didn't even look at the results during the early days, just pointed my camera phone in the direction of my injuries, pressed the button, and dragged the unseen images into a folder on my desktop in case of a lawsuit. 'You look like Angelina Jolie,' my dad joked one day as he walked by a haphazard selfie in progress. 'Some people pay a lot of money to get their lips blown up like that!' I cracked a smile, then winced; the stitches were beginning to pull.

As the swelling in my mouth went down and I began taking phone calls, I repeated the story of what had happened to me over and over. After having to comfort the first few people who started sobbing mid-tale, I learned to breeze through the highlights, adopting the same tone I'd use to talk about, say, a rude seatmate on my morning commute, or an unusually long line at the grocery. *Oh, you know. Two friends and I were road tripping through Texas. A truck pulled up acting weird and the driver started firing. There was a car chase and a bullet hit me and knocked out a dozen teeth. We got away by hiding in a used car parking lot. The shooter hit a bunch more people, but the sheriff found him and killed him in the end. I feel really great! How have you been?* Well-wishers marvelled at how lightly I seemed to be taking it all, saying things like 'You're so brave' and truly meaning it. I certainly did not feel brave—but does anyone, ever? How does one reconcile 'bravery' with an overwhelming feeling of uselessness?

As I shuttled between appointments over the next few weeks, Flowers By Mr John visited my family's house two or three times a day. Friends sent books that they thought I would like. An acquaintance gave me their parents' HBO GO password. A member of my father's fraternity commissioned a monastery to include my name in their prayers for the next calendar year. I was astounded. Even more astounding, my boss called to inform me that I'd been promoted at work. I began making preparations to return to my life in New York City. But everything had shifted slightly while I was away. And I'd shifted slightly too.

Aside from the immediate and obvious effects of the gunshot wounds, weeks of sitting on the couch sipping smoothies through straws had also changed my body. My favourite clothes no longer fit, and when I went to the mall to replace them, the items I instinctively grabbed off the rack were too large.

'I wish I could lose fifteen pounds that quickly,' a friend quipped. I burst into tears, a blubbering mess. 'I really liked my clothes. I didn't choose this,' I tried to explain. I'm not sure they got it. I should have explained it like this: seeing my clothes hang off me served as a reminder that I couldn't get enough food down my throat to stabilise my weight. Compliments only reinforced how little control I had, both over my own body and the beauty standards it was (and is) being measured against. I never wanted to be told that I was 'still pretty'. I wanted it not to matter.

On my return to New York, I resumed my daily commute from Greenwood Heights to West Chelsea. This included an eleven-minute walk from the subway exit to my workplace—a stroll I'd previously found energising, as it gave me a chance to shamelessly scope out the city's 8.4 million inhabitants. In affluent Chelsea in particular, I'd marvelled at how effortlessly gorgeous everyone seemed to be, how fashionably put together. I'd peered at my own reflection as I passed shop windows, idly wondering if this haircut or those boots would make me as beautiful as other passers-by. It was a game I'd been playing my whole life, seeing myself as others saw me. We all know the rules; there is no win condition. There is, however, plenty of feedback provided on one's performance.

Walking the streets of Manhattan again as I shuttled to and from work, I now avoided looking at my reflection. My clothes fit weird, and my own face was startling to me. On top of this, I found myself flooded with white-hot rage on a daily basis as strangers weighed in on my appearance. This is something I'd grown used to in my life; I've been regularly catcalled since the time I was in tenth grade. At fifteen, my friend Sarah and I used to count the number of honks we'd get walking down the main street in our small town. It seemed harmless at the time, even a bit thrilling as we felt the charge of a power dynamic we associated with sex and, consequently, adulthood. But a decade later—on the receiving end of one to three catcalls per day, even with a large open wound on my face—I was through with it.

'ARE YOU FUCKING KIDDING ME?!' I roared at a man attempting to follow me down the stairs to the subway. 'I HAVE NO TEETH. I WILL END YOU.' He reflexively put his hands up and backed away.

Unfortunately, this small victory didn't actually make me feel any better; instead, my mind reeled with thoughts of what could have gone wrong. What if he'd had a knife? What if he followed me? Vibrating with adrenaline and unspent fury, I pulled out my conspicuously pink plastic earbuds, jammed them into my ears and blasted Beyoncé. The comfort was fleeting. Although I couldn't hear men on the street for the rest of my commute, I could still see them. I thought back to my teens, Sarah and I feeling flattered by their attention, and felt sick. Simultaneously, some twisted, tiny sliver of myself felt relieved that I still registered as attractive. My insides churned. Once again, I felt utterly helpless.

That night as I photographed my injuries, I turned my frustration towards the lens. I sneered and wrenched my face up, contorting my features with exaggerated anger. The results were off-putting and absurd. I laughed and felt slightly better. The following day, I repeated the experiment. And the next. And the next.

Taking purposefully ugly photos is such a small thing, but it feels subversive in a world that values prettiness in girls and women above so many other traits. You can be smart and interesting and successful—as long as you look good while doing it. This is how we're trained to receive women: visuals first, second, and third—then maybe we can move onto other topics. Get the aesthetics wrong and your infraction will over-power anything else you do or say. A brilliant woman runs for president, and before we can focus on the substance of her platform, we all weigh in, real quick, on her pantsuit. I'm as guilty as the next person; feminism has not saved me from craving compliments or making snap judgments about other women's appearances. It's just given me the tools to recognise the pattern, think through my participation, and strategise on how to get free. Reminding myself that beauty is not the only option is a good place to start.

Three years later, this is my ritual of resistance: I delight in taking deeply unflattering, hilarious photos of myself—double points for posting to social media. Sometimes I set up a tripod, DSLR, and remote shutter, but mostly, I stick to cell phone self-ies and my laptop webcam. The equipment isn't the important part. What matters is how it makes me feel: like I have agency over my own life and body. Because I do.

I am in charge and I get to choose how I want to be. I choose to be dangerous, a force to be reckoned with. I am not decorative. I photograph myself across a whole range of expressions because my double chins, frizzy hair, and scars are all weapons I intend to keep razor sharp. If my belly looks unexpectedly round and flabby on the beach, great; I'm going to find the angle that plays that up the most and capture it. If my eyes look tired and crazy, cool; I'm going to zoom in and take twenty more shots. There's power in a pretty face, yes, but there are also so many other ways of being. Bodies are funny and weird and awkward and ugly. I embrace and celebrate that, too.

By now, all my wounds from the shooting have healed nicely and my (fake) teeth have no remaining gaps. People who are just meeting me for the first time often don't notice the scar on my face—or at least if they do, they're too polite to say so. I frequently feel like I look good. And even when I don't, anyone with negative things to say about my appearance will be taken down swiftly and mercilessly. This has very little to do with my personal relationship with my body; as a feminist, it's simply a matter of principle. I'm not here for other people criticising women's bodies. On the flip side, I'm also not here to march in the 'all women are beautiful' parade/Dove ad campaign. Not for myself, and not for anyone else.

Here's the thing: I don't want a world in which all women feel beautiful. I want a world in which physical beauty is irrelevant to women's self-esteem and self-worth. It's nice to feel attractive, sure. But I don't buy into the idea that attractiveness is an essential trait in women, or that all women must strive for it. I feel an overwhelming indifference when I look in the mirror on most days, and that's fine! Beauty is not a mandatory requirement for me or any other woman. Neither is liking the way that I look.

I'm not a failure as a woman if I experience emotions outside of the socially approved script of unrelenting public positivity. Anger is an okay thing to feel and express, too. And sadness. And dissatisfaction. All of my feelings about my body are valid, and I refuse to stamp out my own ugliness; it's an indispensable part of who I am.

(I'm also very, very bad at directions. But that's a story for another time.)

Femme as in Fuck You:
Fucking with the Patriarchy
One Lipstick Application at a Time

Catherine Hernandez

'And you? How do you identify?' my lover asked while we lay supine and naked on *their lumpy mattress. I attempted to prop myself up onto my elbows, the pokey cushioning of *their second-hand bed giving way to the pressure. I finally repositioned myself so I was tall enough to look *them in the eyes. I realised that despite several years of being a visible part of the LGBTQ2S community, I had never been asked that. People often assumed I identified as a lesbian.

The word 'lesbian' didn't sit right. To me, it connotes a very particular sect of the community that still connects to the idea of gender binary. I wanted a more fluid identity that transcended body parts.

'I'm...' I let the word sit in my mouth to see what it tasted like before spitting it out. 'I'm queer and...' Then another word found its way to my mouth and I wasn't sure what exactly it meant, but it felt right. 'I'm a queer femme.' It was a profound moment for me, lying naked, feeling beautiful with my body recently pleasured, discovering my identity. I felt reborn and new, like I had finally chosen a home in which to live—this home that is my body.

My lover and I made love again immediately, the exoskeleton of my past tossed aside amongst the flower-patterned sheets on the floor.

I had to accept the clumsiness of being newly reborn, though. The process of learning and unlearning the fine and gross motor skills around the complexities of femininity was an exercise in humility and bravery.

I hadn't the faintest clue what being femme meant. In my outdated politics, I had assumed it meant I was queer—as in body parts didn't dictate who I fucked—but I 'dressed like a girl'. As my politics progressed thanks to the generosity of my fellow queer community members, I realised that while the act of self-adornment was absolutely an essential element of femininity, its most important tenet was, 'Femme as in "fuck you".'

Through trial and error, I realised that no matter what my gender presentation, femininity is a dangerous thing. Throughout history into present day, us femmes survive poverty, rape, slut-shaming. And as a queer femme of colour, I can tell you racism and homophobia are daily realities. The threats of our powers of intuition and of our sexual prowess topple colonial structures of ownership and gender in ways that society must silence.

Around the world, thanks to colonisation, acts of body celebration (from belly dancing to twerking), adornment (from makeup to jewellery), and agency (from sex work to child care) are seen as invitations to victimise the very bodies that dare to be feminine.

But that is the point of being a femme. We are daring all the damn time. To be a femme is to care unapologetically for oneself. It is to accept the divine presence one has in this world, to listen to one's intuition, to foster community and support the beautiful ways in which femininity manifests (such as parenthood, loving sex, story sharing).

Getting to this place of understanding took a great amount of time and patience in my unlearning. One of the most challenging aspects for me was the element of the divine or magic. Sure, I could easily adopt regular self-care and makeup application as part of my femme manifesto, but spiritual practices were difficult for me to accept without thinking to myself, 'Whoa. This is some hardcore granola bullshit.'

A year into identifying as a 'queer femme', I was sitting on the floor of my kitchen, surrounded by a circle of other queer femmes of colour I was hosting in my home for a retreat. It was my turn to speak and I gulped hard.

'Um...' My eyes searched the cabinets. My eyes searched the walls. I rolled my eyes from side to side. I bit my lip. 'I'm a Scorpio.' My fellow femmes had their eyebrows turned up and their mouths open, waiting for clarification. 'A Scorpio...Sun?' They all smiled the way one does when a toddler says their first words, only I was finally speaking Astrology-ese. The others chimed in with their full astrological identities.

'I'm a Leo Sun, Capricorn Moon, Aquarius Rising.' I nodded, pretending I knew what this meant. I did not. When the femmes offered to do my chart, they told me I was a Scorpio Sun, Cancer

Moon, and Taurus Rising. I nodded again, pretending I knew what this meant. I did not.

'Wow. All the feelings,' one femme said.

It's not that I didn't know that magic and the divine existed. It's just that being a colonised brown woman, I have been taught that neither existed except through the bible. And being Catholic, I was taught that the divine existed in the form of carefully authored rules, most especially around policing feminine bodies.

What I did know, deep down in my most secret places in my heart, was that I was, in fact, holy. I am a theatre practitioner, and when I have performed and part of my costume was a headdress, the act of placing the headdress on my head and pinning it into place awakened something inside of me. I knew for a long time, without words brave enough to exit my mouth in the face of Christianity, that in a past life, I was considered holy. Wearing a headdress that was heavily beaded, I was turned to for blessings, for guidance, for counsel.

So, when that retreat occurred with several femmes of colour taking up space in every corner of my home, it unlocked so many truths within me. In the kitchen, one femme was teaching the art of tarot card reading. In the living room, another femme shared techniques for self-massage. In the bedroom, two femmes languished on the bed, delighting in the act of unapologetic rest.

It was in those moments shared between us that I began to compile these elements of Femme Wisdom. These understandings were not rules to live by, which I was accustomed to in punitive Catholicism, but rather concepts I could adopt to enrich my life.

SELF-ADORNMENT: *To paint, pierce, cover, or uncover oneself in a way that refuses to be invisible.*

Oftentimes, femmes call this 'femme armour'. The idea is to challenge society, which often shames us for being sluts or being expressive in the interest of conformity. With every lipstick application, we are saying, 'I am happily offending you with my presence.' With every set of fake lashes we adhere to our lids, we are saying, 'I have complete control over this body I call mine.' With every ensemble the status quo may call 'too much' or 'too little', we are saying, 'Rape culture has no power over my body.'

Coinciding with the subversive nature of self-adornment is ritual. All over the world, adornment is essential to preparing for ceremony. The divine people of a community, be they shamans, witches, or priestesses, prepare themselves for the act of ceremony by adorning their bodies with objects that are rife with symbolism in order to assist them in dialogue with the spirit.

Since regularly reading or performing my work around the world has launched my career into public figure status, my ceremony, my convening with my congregation, happens when I speak at events. While a Catholic priest understands the order of each ritual that makes up a mass, I understand what is expected of me at each speaking engagement: I know I will be introduced. I know I will read my work in an engaging way that breaks the ho-hum conventions of most literary readings. I know I will then be asked questions by the audience, who will undoubtedly be majority white folks who want to confront my anti-oppressive beliefs. I know I will then calmly, with the grace of my ancestors, de-centre their whiteness by challenging them to think progressively by first tracking their oppressive behaviour in their own bodies. I know I will then leave the event and self-care, to allow my body to be soft and vulnerable after fighting a war against the machine of whiteness.

To prepare for this ceremony, I take my time. I consider the energy that will most likely be in that room; I consider the battle I am about to fight as I look into the mirror. Reminding myself that I am holy, I apply my foundation, eyeliner, and lipstick as my mask. I do my hair until it feels like my headdress, the same headdress I know I have worn in my former life. I clothe myself in ways that make me recognisably holy—ready to do battle with racism, homophobia, and sexism with my heels, my loud colour choices, and 'suggestive' silhouettes.

COMMUNICATION WITH THE DIVINE: *To communicate with spirit as a way of resisting Christian supremacy.*

'Here you go,' said my theatre professor as he handed me a manila envelope. Inside were photocopies of monologues from the plays featuring an Asian woman that he, as a white man, was actually aware of, such as...well, anything by David Henry Hwang. That was as far as his research went, it seemed. 'This is for you. It's a bunch of monologues that have *you people* in it.' This about summed up my theatre school experience. I spent three years in that school being taught that I as a brown woman had no place in theatre. I could learn how to be white, talk with an American or English accent and, fingers crossed, aim to be Pauper #3 in Stratford's millionth production of *Henry V*. It was disheartening, to say the least. I graduated the programme working in film and television as a two-line day-actor, feeling empty and lost.

Then I read about the T'Boli dreamweavers. This Indigenous tribe in the Philippines has sacred women who, after they receive a dream from their ancestors, proceed to weave their dreams into intensely intricate textiles. Being a colonised brown woman of Filipino, Spanish, Chinese, and Indian descent and having survived a diaspora, I had to actively decolonise my work. I had to return to the act of dreamweaving myself.

I tossed aside any former notions of artistic practice that the white institution of theatre school taught me. I refused to create work that sought critical and community acclaim for its adherence to colonised ways of storytelling. I refused to put pen to paper based on a 'good idea', but instead put pen to paper based on ancestral messages. I began writing as if I were simply notating what my ancestors were telling me to write. I began experimenting ways in which I could distract my colonised ego to allow for the ancestral messages to become clearer and the work to be more genuine.

This decolonisation of my practice became essential to my being. Listening to my ancestors every minute of every day has been part of my healing process as a survivor of many traumas. The most glaring and tragic mistakes of my life were decisions that were made when I was most at odds with spirit. The most wondrous successes of my life stemmed from moments when I allowed spirit to take the wheel and for my work to come forth, beautiful and true.

USE OF TOOLS FOR PROTECTION AND MANIFESTATION: *To use objects we deem holy to protect us from harm and to envision a world in which we are safe.*

An ongoing challenge of mine is sharing space with my perpetrator. I was raped around the time I came out of the closet. My perpetrator is someone with whom I share space regularly due to logistics and obligations. Before I began practicing Femme Wisdom, I would often find myself shaking, sweating, and disassociated after having seen him. I felt that since seeing him was beyond my control, my reactions to him were beyond my control as well.

When it became unbearable, I posted on a private Facebook group for LGBTQ2S folks who have disabilities and mental health issues, asking for their strategies around similar experiences. I assumed they were going to offer the usual poultices for such situations: a sense of mindfulness or a positive reframing. Instead, the majority of femmes offered the use of crystals and spells as a form of protection. I had never done that before or even considered that as a possibility. Despite some hesitation on my part, I decided to give it a go.

The next time I had to share space with my perpetrator, I held a rose quartz wand in my hand. While he conversed with me as he always does, making small talk to replace the big trauma he caused, in my head I repeated the mantra, 'I have complete control over my body. My body is mine. I am protected from this person. I will not be harmed.' I felt invincible, as though a shroud of protection surrounded me that was impervious to his desire to destroy me. Since then, I have relished in my own power.

SKILLS SHARING, LABOUR SHARING: *To understand that in order to survive as femmes, we need to join forces.*

In a colonised society, we are taught that survival demands us to get what we can, keep what we have for ourselves, and work towards goals of success dictated by the status quo. Femme Wisdom teaches us to gather for the collective using our best strengths, that each person must teach another, and to celebrate each person's individual goals.

Some of my most dear moments have been in the presence of femmes who have taught me lessons in life. I have learned dance moves. I have learned languages. I have learned mental health strategies. In turn, I have taught the decolonisation of artistic practice. I have taught parents how to effectively chest feed. I have taught parents how to sleep train their newborn babies.

In a colonised society we are also taught labour stratification, which often demeans the work commonly given to women, such as sex work and caregiving. Femme Wisdom fights against this by celebrating such labour, asking for fair wages, and encouraging the sharing of work.

CONNECTION TO SEXUALITY: *To reclaim agency over one's body by giving it pleasure.*

I do not feel I truly came into my queerness until I accepted my own overt sexuality. The catalyst for this learning came in the form of burlesque.

Back in 2012 I became fascinated with this art form. This awakening in the form of entertainment seemed to me to be the best manifestation of Femme Wisdom in action: when I put tassels on my nipples, I'm self-adorning; when I allow the music to move my tassels while I perform, I'm communicating with the Divine; and when I teach my colleagues my favourite strategies for pasting on tassels without having them fall off mid-number, I'm engaging in skill-sharing.

I wanted to embody this art form. I began learning from a few select people and I started performing myself. It was profoundly powerful for me. As a survivor of rape, physical abuse, and emotional abuse, reclaiming my body by exposing it to audience members was life-changing. When I removed a glove, I told the audience that this hand, this hand that was forced to touch, was mine. When I peeled my bra off, I told the audience that these breasts, these breasts that my perpetrator refused to let go of before he raped me, were mine. When I danced in stiletto heels, I told the audience that these legs, these same legs that ran away from my string of abusive partners, were mine.

UNAPOLOGETIC REST AND SELF-CARE: *To know that caring for your body is a radical act in a world that seeks to shut it down.*

In 2015 I was finally diagnosed with two chronic illnesses. One, called Red Skin Syndrome, I acquired after thirty years of using topical steroids. The other, Chronic Fatigue, stems from my many years of sustaining trauma.

Admitting that I had these issues felt, in part, like a relief. I could finally put a name to what I was feeling. In part, it felt like a failure. I could no longer be the multi-tasker I once was as a single mama with the wage of an artist and home day care provider. I had to make some major changes in order to survive and continue writing.

I had to learn to ask for help in a healthy way.

I had to learn how to receive help in a healthy way.

I had to make self-care my job.

Thanks to being partnered with a loving and supportive person, I was encouraged to rest whenever I could. I allowed myself the luxury of receiving help from my partner and community members to help me parent my child. I developed a care regimen that involved yoga, lymphatic drainage, acupressure, meditation, and marijuana self-medication.

As one fellow femme once said to me, 'When you rest, you

must get zero tasks done and you must give zero fucks.'

In my learning about self-care, I have said the following to my sick body over and over again in its healing process.

I will drink more water. I will sleep more. I will laugh more. I will eat better.

Self-care is a radical action against a world that seeks to shut my body down.

I aim to do only work that fills my soul. That includes work for money and work in a relationship.

I will not fill hearts that have holes. The real estate in my heart is occupied by the energy that the universe has bestowed upon me. Therefore, that energy does not deserve to be tossed aside in the fringes of another person's confusion.

My femininity is Church. Worshipping at the temple others throw spit at, throw side glances, throw away.

I break bread with my brown skin.

Pray prayers to my hard-loving heart.

Kneel at the foot of my humility.

My sway, my swag, my gait, my songs are a hymn dedicated to the goddess of me.

These aren't just heels.

They are blades slicing through my own shame.

May these words guide others towards their truth.

Before I Was a Woman, I Was a Witch

Avery Edison

An all-boys high school is no place for a young girl.

Of course, nobody knew I was a girl yet, including me. A conventional narrative (and a self-perpetuating one, since any doubts or deviations from society's expectations of trans people's experiences are weaponised as excuses to deny us treatment) is that transgender women feel their real identity from birth or soon after. In my case, that wasn't necessarily true. I didn't know I was trans. But I knew I was different.

Other people knew, too. Especially other kids. Children are attentive to differences and vicious once they notice them. Throughout early and middle school, I'd been bullied by my classmates, who made fun of my size, my devotion to reading, my perennial teacher's pet status, my refusal to play football during morning break and lunch, and, most of all, my tendency to burst into tears. My name then was Kyle, which was all-too-easily adapted as 'Cryle'. It wasn't intentional, but maybe it's no coincidence that when I picked my new name, I chose one you can only turn into 'Bravery'.

I'd hoped that Poole Grammar School would be a learning environment in which I could finally feel comfortable. The school seemed like a potential escape because you needed to pass a test to become a student there. One part of my identity I'd always been confident of was 'genius' (yes, I'm yet-another millennial told she had limitless potential). I was sure both that I'd get in and that since my fellow students would also be a bunch of nerds and boffins, we'd create a more gentle and under-standing learning environment. I figured that I was headed for a school full of people like me, and I'd be safe from bullying, fear, and loneliness.

I was wrong.

After years of the harsh real world deprogramming my millen-nial delusions of grandeur, I know now that I wasn't a brilliant student. The test to enter Grammar School wasn't even that hard. And my classmates and I? We weren't some rarefied breed of super-intelligent diplomats. We were a bunch of children thrown into a competitive, testosterone-heavy environment, and so the bullying only got worse. I was teased and taunted; my possessions were torn and broken, even thrown from the top of the building; they beat me, choked me, and, on one occasion, held me down and forced me to eat food from a rubbish bin. I've suffered from depression my entire life (even, I think, as an infant), but those initial months at Poole Grammar were the first times I ever considered suicide as a solution to my problems.

I tried other coping methods first, though. I tried to pretend things weren't so bad, and that I could defuse the situation by becoming friends with my adversaries. That led to them setting me up on a fake date with a girl from our sister school so that they could find out personal details about me and hone their jibes. I tried to limit my exposure to the worst of my peers by hiding, at every opportunity, in the library. But they merely waited to ambush me on my way to and from it, or else distracted the librarian on duty and used the books to beat me. As a last resort, I went to my teachers, even though experience had shown me that they only ever made things worse by punishing the bullies in a way that made them angrier or else just ignored the problem, making me feel even more alone and vulnerable.

At Poole, it was the latter. The school had long had a problem with abuse among students, and the party line was that it was just 'boys being boys'. When I wouldn't stop asking for help, begging the head of my year to do something, the school nurse referred me to outside counselling so that I could 'grow a thicker skin'. (It didn't help, but my sessions with the therapist were the first times I ever vocalised that I didn't feel like a boy, which was an essential first step in my eventual transition.)

It seemed hopeless. I resigned myself to trauma. I dreaded school, I cried constantly (which did not help at all with the bullying), and I began to consider suicide. But before I could take such drastic action, my body's internal systems engineered an escape for me: in the late spring of 2000, I started suffering from constant, debilitating diarrhoea. All my stress and anxiety stopped pouring out of me as tears and instead flooded out of me as shit.

Nobody wants to read too many details about my bowel movements, so I'll try to be brief. Every single day, for six weeks, I needed to go to the bathroom at least five times an hour. I was in intense pain, sometimes dull and prolonged, occasionally sudden and sharp. Despite a history of crying wolf, my mum could see that there was something seriously wrong with me. When I didn't get better after two weeks, she called our doctor (visiting the clinic was impractical, because our car didn't have a toilet in it), who referred me to a gastrointestinal specialist, who scheduled me for an endoscopy to find out what was happening inside me.

The working theory was coeliac disease, the inability to process gluten. The presence of shortened villi in the small intestine confirms coeliac diagnoses, but after I woke up from sedation with a Polaroid of my insides (I'd asked for a souvenir), my doctor told me that my gut was perfectly healthy. Clean, naturally, but sturdy. They found nothing. If they didn't have my mother's assurance that, yes, our downstairs toilet was my bedroom at this point, they would've sworn that I was making it up.

I'd been hoping for a solution, an end to the discomfort and annoyance of my illness, even though I knew it would mean going back to school. The exchange of peer-led suffering for self-contained pain was a grand bargain at first, but as my condition persisted and my time away from the classroom grew, I began to forget just how horrible it was there. I was bored of daytime television, and I missed the enormous school library and the few friends I had among my fellow students and, yes, teachers. By the sixth week of my illness, I was needing to excuse myself less and less, and over the weekend I felt completely normal. I went back to school, healthy again.

All I'd needed was time. Time away from the stress and torment of a school environment to which I wasn't suited. But that's something I realise in hindsight. At the time, there was a less nuanced, more obvious solution.

Magic cured me.

My Aunt Agnes has always been into holistic medicine and New Age philosophy and practices. My early memories of her are of visits when she'd make me swallow disgusting-tasting aloe vera supplements, or talk me through my astrological chart, or explain to me the law of attraction and how I should use it to have a perfect life. I didn't buy into any of it, but I appreciated the attention (and the gifts she would bring, usually a book token I could spend on a new Roald Dahl). She was adamant that I was an 'Indigo Child', an ill-defined term that indicated that I was special. (How many of us limitless-potential millennials heard this moniker growing up?)

When I got sick, Agnes was ready with a list of possible reasons and remedies. Perhaps the microwave oven was upsetting me. Or the fact that we lived below power lines. There was a good chance our house had a ghost, probably a poltergeist. And I'd been spending time on the school computers — that couldn't be good. She recommended solutions like acupuncture, urine therapy, and even exorcism. My mother, who is more cynical and averse to spirituality of any kind (even the pomp and circumstance of a standard funeral is too much for her: 'When I die, put me in a cardboard box!'), vetoed anything extreme or invasive. But she did let my aunt arrange a visit from a psychic she'd recently met, a crystal dowser named Sarah.

Sarah didn't fit the stereotypical, cartoonish idea of a psychic. No flowing robes or gaudy jewels in turbans, and indeed, no crystal ball. She was simply dressed, an ordinary mum of a girl two years below me at my previous school. The only mysterious thing about her was the slight tingling feeling she gave me when she talked (something I now know to be ASMR), but I'd experienced that with my optometrist, too, so it wasn't that strange.

Sarah calmly explained that she worked with a small onyx crystal suspended from a chain. She would talk to me, asking me questions while swinging the crystal back and forth, gaining insight from its movements. It seemed silly but no sillier than anything my aunt had previously endorsed, and I wanted to hear more of her calming voice. We talked about my interests, my family, my school, and, of course, my illness, all while the pendulum swung at varying speeds. Sometimes it was slow and lazy, but occasionally it would whiz around in circles impossibly fast.

I couldn't discern the connection between the specific points of our conversation and the activity of the crystal, but Sarah assured me that she was cleansing my aura and that I'd begin to feel better in the next few days. And I did already notice a small change—either her technique had calmed me, or the conversation had allowed me to vent some of my frustration and anxiety in a way I'd been unable to before. Whatever the reason, I felt calmer and less fragile. My aunt paid Sarah her fee and set up another appointment for a week later, asking if there was anything we could do in the meantime to maintain or even bolster the positive effects. Sarah recommended meditation, and also, perhaps, purchasing a crystal of my own.

I was well enough, a few days later, to go crystal shopping with Aunt Agnes. She knew our local New Age store owner well, and after they helped me pick out a rose quartz pendulum and chain, they stood at the front counter and caught up on the latest holistic trends and conspiracy theories. I hovered nearby, browsing the bookshelf, as I preferred to do in any and every store. My mum used to say, '[She's] always got [her] nose in a book.' Sometimes she even said it like she thought it was a good thing.

A bright yellow and blue box drew my attention to the bookshelf. It was a starter kit for teen witches, which included a booklet on the history and practice of Wicca, a couple of candles, a pentagram necklace, a few small gems, and a pack of salt. I've always been a sucker for instructional packages; despite having a supposedly-prodigious intellect, I've often found learning too dull and time-consuming. The promise of the all-in-one beginner set is that it's everything you need to know to achieve some level, even a small one, of expertise. Even the act of owning it grants you a little more status in the field—after all, you have both the information and the tools.

I stared at the box. I picked it up and turned it over, put it down, read the blurb over and over, turned away from the shelf entirely, and then back to check it out one more time. I was performing my interest in the set, for the audience of my aunt and the store owner.

After what felt like forever, Agnes finally asked me what I was looking at and put on her very own performance of not being sure if she could buy it for me. I never doubted she would, though, because this was the first time I'd shown any unprompted interest in her world, and there was no way she'd quash that. Even though her lingering childhood Christianity made her wary of witchcraft, as she would warn me on the drive home. 'Be careful with all that. You don't want to attract something unpleasant by accident. I'm not saying it would be the Devil, but you never know...'

Somehow, the two small candles and pinch of salt didn't end up summoning the Dark Lord to my bedroom. They didn't end up doing much at all. On reading the guidebook, it seemed that Wicca was far less exciting than I'd hoped. Growing up on comic books and superhero cartoons had primed me for an easy acceptance of extra-normal powers and abilities. The feelings I'd experienced during the session with Sarah and the irregular movements of her pendulum, along with the starter kit's talk of magic, had me hoping for grand spells and hexes to change my life and ruin my enemies.

Instead, I found meditations on nature and respect for all people, and a description of spellcraft as gentle requests that worked a subtler, less noticeable power. A glamour spell wouldn't let me change my appearance; it would, at most, make me feel a little more confident in myself. There was no incantation to bring people back from the dead, but there was a ritual for acceptance of loss and help with grief. Even the passages on working with spirits to generate money were just reiterations of the same law of attraction stuff my aunt had told me a dozen times before.

But there was still power for me in the identity. If I knew I was different, and everyone else did too, then the least I could do was try to harness that difference as protection. I kept an altar and started saying 'Merry meet' to people so I could tell myself I was doing enough to call myself a witch. I wore the pentagram necklace and carried my rose quartz and gems with me so that other people, especially my bullies, would know that I was one. I hoped that they would be, if not scared, then at least cautious.

I was not subtle about it. Every morning before our first period, my class would gather in our form room so that Mr Partridge, our tutor, could take attendance and read announcements. Then we had twenty minutes of quiet reading time, which, in practice, were twenty minutes of chaos. Full of kids laughing and joking, running a black market for copied CDs and beating up the weakest among them. I dreaded these early mornings and hoped every day that my classmates would be distracted by their conversation or another victim, or that Mr Partridge would be paying enough attention to my safety that I could get a few moments of peace.

One morning, soon after I returned from my illness — 'We hoped you were dead, Cryle!' — I pulled out my bag of charms as the announcements finished and dealt out a pack of cards in front of me. Then I swung my pendulum over each card, focusing intently on its movements. I was playing a game I'd devised as 'practice' for my dowsing abilities: I would pick a card and ask 'yes' or 'no' questions of the crystal, using process of elimination to determine the card's value.

'Is this card red?' I muttered.

The pendulum started swinging counter-clockwise.

'Is this card a spade?'

Clockwise.

'Is it a face card?'

Clockwise.

'Is it the king?'

Counter-clockwise.

'Is it the queen?'

A final swing clockwise.

I turned the card over.

Five of diamonds.

Apparently, the crystal didn't always get it right. Or, instead, I didn't get it right. I knew enough about the autonomic nervous system to figure out that the movements of the chain were down to small adjustments in my wrist and hand, rather than some mysterious force. But that's explained by thinking of the act of dowsing as a way of manifesting and making clear one's own psychic or clairvoyant gifts. I just needed to hone the power that was in my head and I'd get my ratio of correct guesses to false ones up.

And, in the meantime, there were small victories—whenever I correctly discerned the colour of a card (a 1-in-2 chance), or its suit (1-in-4 chance), or if it was a face card (4-in-13), I knew I was on the right track. In those moments, I would let out a small, knowing smile, trying to convey the confidence of hidden power. I knew that making my bullies cower was out of the question, but I wanted the vibe around me to be uncomfortable enough that they would give me some distance.

Mr Partridge was a devout Catholic and watched me with curiosity and worry. He usually spent the mornings reading or cutting out Far Side cartoons from the Sunday paper and pinning them on a noticeboard at the front of class. But when I huddled over my deck and dangled my crystal, he craned his neck to close the small gap between my desk and his (sitting close to the teacher had never protected me, but it didn't hurt to keep trying). After I'd spent a few minutes whispering to myself and turning over cards with a smirk on my face, he finally spoke.

'So what's the belief system behind what you're doing there?'

'Oh, um,' I responded, 'It's sort of nature-based. There's a lot of—The environment is important, and Gaia and stuff.'

'And who's the god? Who do you pray to?' His tone was sceptical, now.

'I'm not sur—For me, it's not about a god. Or goddess. I'm thinking of the universe as its own thing, rather than... Uh...'

I trailed off and looked at Mr Partridge vacantly, searching for the right words to convince him that I was genuine. They didn't come, probably because I wasn't.

I hadn't thought a lot about the theology behind Wicca. The starter kit had been somewhat evasive—there was plenty of talk about the tone of magic practice and the general mood and vibe, but none of the mythology of the more common religions. I wished for an epic work to describe, like the Abrahamic texts, or a pantheon of gods to reference.

'Well, as long as you're getting something out of it, I suppose,' he concluded. Then he went back to his book, leaving me stumped on the subject of my own faith. The bell for first period rang, and I packed up my works, sullen and obviously dejected. That knowing smile vanished from my face, and the aura of mystery I'd been trying to cultivate was demolished. I don't know if my classmates had even been slightly threatened or unnerved by my magical demonstration, but if they had been, that was over.

I still remember that conversation with Mr Partridge because it destroyed my confidence and conviction in practising Wicca. I went through the motions for a few more weeks, doing drills with my playing cards, maintaining my altar, and parting the invisible curtain I'd put around my room whenever I entered or left it. But the bloom was off the rose. Failing to adequately describe my relationship to Wicca, let alone its fundamental tenets, made me confront the reasons I was experimenting with it at all. I'd put aside my corrupt motivations until then, but I had to face it: I was faking my faith so I could take on an identity.

I left Poole Grammar the next year. I'd stopped wearing the pentagram necklace, and I'd not touched a crystal for a long time (although I still had sporadic sessions with Sarah, who my aunt always credited with my recovery, even as I had occasional relapses once I was back at school). My witchcraft period had become yet another thing for my bullies to taunt me with, and on my last day, as the final bell rang and everyone filed out of the building, I heard Jason Langham-Green tell Charlie Hunt, 'Punch the witch'. One final blow, a goodbye goose-egg.

I transferred back to my local comprehensive school and the friends I'd left behind when I took the grammar school entrance examination. They were (understandably) a little cold at first but soon welcomed me back into the clique. I still got occasional jibes from rougher classmates, but nothing anywhere near as bad as what I'd previously suffered. My friends didn't know about my attempt at being a Wiccan, and one of them even invited me to check out his church's youth group. I went along to the weekly meetings and became a member, now identifying as a Christian. I wasn't a fervent believer, but I liked the feeling of community, and attending a Church of England elementary school—as well as, obviously, growing up in the UK's Christian culture—meant I was well versed in the Bible and associated figures, practices, and stories.

I didn't stay Christian for long, though. A year later, I was a militant atheist, devouring Richard Dawkins books and regurgitating Christopher Hitchens talking points. Then I calmed down and tried to shirk my nerd status by failing all my classes and approaching everything with an ironic distance, putting on the outdated but still powerful 'slacker' identity. Then I bought a unicycle and learned to juggle while riding it, sinking into a bizarre clown phase. Then my mum finally paid for internet in our home, and I became obsessed with upgrading my computer over and

over, rebranding as a tech geek. Every teenager has to reckon with
finding themselves, and my inability to confront and deal with
my gender dysphoria only exacerbated that. By the time I came
out as a woman, my friends and family were tired of my trying-on
and discarding various personalities and assumed that 'trans' was
just the latest in a long line of temporary phases that I'd soon
abandon. I'm sure that now, ten years into it, some of them are
still expecting me to mass-email a de-transition announcement.

I've never entirely abandoned any of those identities, though.
I remain an atheist, although I long ago disavowed Dawkins
and his ilk. I enjoy riding my unicycle, even if I refuse to do it
here in London; I don't want to die and/or get laughed at. I still
keep a close eye on tech and computing culture, although my
Apple partisanship would be anathema to my former dedicated
PC-builder self. And I work as a comedian, which is only slightly
more respectable than being a full-on clown.

We keep parts of our past selves. And even though I was never
a real witch, I still remember and hold dear those early feelings
of confidence and power. I don't believe in the supernatural,
but I believe in the placebo effect. So I believe that casting a
spell won't change the universe around you, but will help you
approach situations with an insight or perspective that's just
as good. I believe that carrying a few crystals or gems won't
give you supernatural abilities, but will give you confidence
and a feeling of safety. And I believe that meditating on your
intentions and creating a sigil won't magically make a problem
go away, but will focus your mind on it in a way that merely
being pre-occupied or worrying about it won't.

That's the part of my practice that I actually still practise: sigil
craft. Back when I was playing around with Wicca, sigils were

merely silly doodles to me. But one thing that's been consistent about me is my love of comic books, and they led me to a talk by writer Grant Morrison in which he spoke about the importance of sigils in his work. He discussed the radical effects they've had on his life and gave instructions for creating them.

A simple (and reductive) version of his method: pick something you want, write it down as if you already have it, remove the vowels and repeated letters from what you wrote, and use the remaining glyphs to make a symbol. There's your sigil. You can do something like writing it on paper and burning it or crafting it onto a piece of jewellery, but I find it motivating enough simply to create the thing. So much of our brain-space is taken up by the clutter of keeping track of tasks we need to complete, and one of the principles of internet to-do list culture is that getting that jumble of tasks out of your head and onto paper will make you less distracted and more able to actually do the work. And what's a sigil if not a beautiful, personally encoded item on a to-do list? Or, since sigils predate task management culture, perhaps it's better to ask: what's a to-do list if not a tedious attempt to reduce the complexity of sigils?

I don't use sigils for everything in my life (in fact, I probably use to-do lists more than sigils, because I am boring), but I use them for important things. I made a sigil when I moved back to the UK from Canada, to acknowledge the importance of the trip and release some of the anxiety around it. I made a sigil when I was getting ready for a significant stand-up gig and hung an enlarged version of it on my wall, to remind me to put in the work and attention necessary for a good performance. I made a sigil before I wrote this essay and used it as the centre of the mind map I used to plan it. The trip went well, the gig was great, and this essay, you can judge that for yourself. Maybe the sigils had nothing to do with those results. But they certainly made me feel better, and in this nightmare world, I'll take all of that I can get.

I'm a sceptic and an atheist, and I'm kind of a bore about it sometimes. But I've done extraordinary things in my life—like surviving my awful school experiences for one, and changing my entire gender—and I like to leave a little room for the extraordinary outside my life, too. I'm not going to guzzle turmeric to ward off cancer or perform an exorcism when I move into a new apartment, but I'll happily draw a little picture. It always feels good to move your hands and make something.

The Avery who was a witch still lives in my head. She may not have been the person I wanted her to be, but she's part of the person I am. She was there before I was a woman, and that kind of service deserves a little input now and then. Just as long as it's more nuanced than clockwise and counter-clockwise.

Undressing My Heart

Gabriela Herstik

When I was seventeen years old, I walked into Northpointe Mall in Alpharetta, Georgia, and paid five dollars for a 'bang trim' so a hairstylist could shave off the left side of my hair.

This was the first time I had done anything drastic to my appearance and the first step in my initiation into fashion magick.

Just shy of seven years later, my shaved side has taken over half my head. I like to keep it shaved to the skin, which I did for the first time when I was twenty. The barbershop is always full of men who avoid looking at me, or look through the side of their eyes. I'm disruptive just by existing, and shaving my hair is a ritual to honour this. It may seem silly, but having a freshly shaved head makes me feel sexier than nearly anything else. It's like wearing my favourite black lace bra at all times. And now, in the era of Trump, it's my way to disrupt binary fashion while flipping a double bird at all the men who think I'd be beautiful if I had long hair.

Looking back, I see shaving my hair off for what it was: the first real step I took into my practice of glamour magick, something that continued on through college and continues to this day. While I take credit for my own personal style, in truth, my relationship with fashion is in my bones, and it's my favourite way of honouring my ancestors.

Both my paternal grandparents, Grandma Rose and Grandpa Harry, spent over three years in concentration camps during the Second World War. Rose just happened to have the same name as the head seamstress of Auschwitz's niece. Since she was also a seamstress, she was able to live in their quarters, with a real bed and showers, and help sew uniforms for the Nazis. My grandpa had just become a master weaver in Prague when he was shipped off to the camps. He was an instructor for the Haganah, what would eventually become the Israeli Defense Force, in Czechoslovakia. And one day when he was teaching cadets to load cannons, he said his first words to his wife-to-be: 'If you don't mind me telling you, soldier, your fly's open.'

I grew up with the stories of my family and their survival in the Holocaust. Since I was five, I have known what the numbers on my Grandma Rose's arm represented. And I also knew she was a seamstress, that my Grandpa Harry was a weaver, and that fashion had caused them to meet, not to mention that it saved my grandma's life. Unconsciously, I carried this with me, feeling the presence of my grandma in my relationship with clothing. Although she passed away my senior year of high school and my grandpa passed away before I was born, I continue to honour their memory through the way I merge fashion and magick.

I was eighteen when I decided to wear whatever the hell I wanted. I decided I'd pretend I was living in New York, hitting the pavement of the city of eccentricities every morning instead of my reality: the streets of Columbia, South Carolina. While New York welcomed weirdos and those who choose fashion as a form of self-expression, Columbia's biggest fashion statement was oversized t-shirts and Nike shorts, with the occasional pearl necklace thrown in. But for better or worse, I was stuck in the small Southern town for the next four years while I studied at the University of South Carolina. So I decided I would just lower the amount of fucks I gave to a negative number and wear whatever I wanted no matter the amount of side-eye I got from old Republican men.

I remember walking out of my dorm room freshman year after making this decision. Suddenly the air felt lighter. My heart felt lighter too. It was as if I had given myself permission to be whoever I wanted, simply because I pretended that the environment I was living in was conducive to my fashion evolution. Columbia turned into my New York, and for the next four years, it helped me foster my fashion, magick, and self-love.

Although I had already been a witch for about six years, it wasn't until I moved to Columbia that my style and magick started to mingle. I started paying attention to the energies of the clothing I was wearing and how the pieces made me feel. I started seeing my tarot cards as fashion and beauty inspiration. My magick naturally grew more powerful as I continued to find my own style alongside my voice and spirit; as I continued to come into myself unapologetically, my magick reciprocated, growing in strength. I started connecting my ancestry to my magick through my clothing. I started buying more vintage. I started to wear more lingerie, honouring my body as a temple for myself and no one else. I created a signature look for myself (hello, cat eye and orange-red lip), and I cut my hair short. I started to incorporate both fashion and magick into my writing, penning pieces on how the Death card was my style muse and styling a series of nine looks, each inspired by a different tarot card. More than anything, I started curating my own glamour.

While we may associate the idea of glamour with looking beautiful, in truth, glamour is rooted in mysticism and faery lore. A glamour is something that veils what lies beneath. This is how faeries and beings from the other realms can appear to us as something other than their true forms. According to legend, when a faery baby, known as a changeling, replaces a human baby, there is a glamour cast on the faery baby so it appears human. We too can veil our true selves with this same magick.

My first memories of glamour come from the women in my family. My Grandma Rose, my mother, and her mother all wore lipstick every day. Growing up as a five-year-old in Los Angeles, I would visit my Grandma Rose every Sunday, always looking forward to seeing what makeup and classic floral perfume she would be wearing. Rose had an air of elegance about her, and always had her nails immaculately painted in reds and pinks, even when she was simply giving my sister and me strawberry candies or drawing superheroes for us on tracing paper. I remember feeling entranced as I searched through her medicine cabinet, finding nail polish in auburns and mauves and perfumes with names I couldn't pronounce, occasionally trying them on to help embody the energy of my beloved grandma.

My maternal side of the family carries the same stylish essence. Growing up, I was always entranced by my mother's rosy pink lipstick. It's something she picked up from her mother, who I call Tita. Both my mother and maternal grandmother were born and raised in Mexico City, a place we visited every year while I was growing up. Once I was older I realised how much of my maternal family's glamour comes from their home country; I started to appreciate it more. Mexico is a flurry of bright colours, where bold lipstick is the usual and arched brows are a must. Though my family belonged to the city's Jewish community, I was still able to see the emphasis Mexican women at large placed on the ritual of makeup. Looking good wasn't for other people, but for yourself. The ritual of getting ready and putting makeup on every morning was sacred time spent in solitude, a time to find solace before the day began. Looking back at my mother's own morning routine, I realise that this is something she carried with her even after moving to the United States.

Though my mom doesn't consider herself a witch, she was my introduction to energy, spirituality, crystals, and more. She was also my introduction to the power of fashion. She always taught me that the most important thing was feeling good, and that confidence and self-assurance could help you pull off any look. This was one of the first glamour spells I learned, and alchemising energy externally into a killer outfit is still one of my favourite forms of magick. Now when my mom and I go shopping, especially when my Tita is visiting from Mexico, it's like we're all casting charms of glamour together, bonding over how we feel and how we choose to present ourselves through highly stylised outfits and bold lipsticks.

The women in my family were my first style icons. When I bought my first lipstick at seventeen, a red Revlon hue called 'British Red', I was unintentionally tapping into my lineage, one that embraces glamour as protection, as self-love, as magick.

And now, every time I put on lipstick, I'm channelling those women, all while casting a glamour on myself.

When we wear something that alters how we look, whether it be latex, a suit, or lipstick, we're casting a glamour. We're taking back our autonomy by deciding how we should present ourselves, and then we're forcing others to see us in that light. And when we create a ritual of putting on our makeup or of getting dressed, when we embody who we want to be unapologetically, we're casting a spell with our glamour. Whether it's wearing a leather jacket for protection or a rose quartz necklace for love, the little glamours we cast hold power, and when we pay attention to them, they can become a deep practice.

I use glamour to create a ritual out of my morning. I wake up; I glance at my altar and appreciate how the light dances across her surface. I stretch my body, feeling my limbs awaken, and then I crawl out of bed. I check to see where the Moon is, and then I start my day. If I don't know what to wear or how to do my makeup, I'll pull my daily tarot card before I get ready and base my look off that. But sometimes what I wear is simply guided by a feeling; when I'm anxious, I know I need to wear something black, something dark, something powerful. When I want to honour Venus and open my heart, I'll wear pink. Sometimes I base my outfit around a lipstick, sometimes around a pair of shoes or a purse. There's a little magick woven into most of my wardrobe; the pins that adorn my beloved silver leather jacket double as talismans, the gold necklaces I have from my family double as amulets, and the sharp cat eye I draw doubles as a weapon. But the biggest thing my fashion witch ways have taught me? Listening to your intuition is everything. Recognising where I am energetically in the moment, trying to have a feel for what I *need* that day is the most powerful magick of all—and it's vital, especially because this is a way in which I connect with my own heritage. Being intentional and honouring the clothing I wear is like celebrating family, because if it weren't for this medium, I wouldn't be here.

Glamours can be cast in various ways. Your intuition will guide you, letting you know if there's something that you need to listen to above the surface, like through clothing, or beneath, like through lingerie. The power of lingerie is intense; it's transformative, and sometimes it can be the little secret you need to walk powerfully throughout your day no matter who catcalls you or what's on the news.

Ever since I was little, I've been fascinated by the power of lingerie. I would buy bras in second grade, even though I was nowhere close to sprouting breasts or developing at all. But I'd still wear them to school, walking down the hall as I pulled my shirt taught, imagining the line the band of the bra made as breasts. This obsession became more apparent as I got older, even though I never grew past an A cup. I have always had an affinity for lingerie, for feeling sexy and sultry in my body. Even before I was comfortable with my sexuality, lingerie helped me learn about myself, my desires, and my body. It shifted the way in which I perceived myself, creating a new space for my soul to inhabit. The process of putting on lingerie is almost as sacred as the process of taking it off.

When I strip off my clothes, I strip off my mortal essence. With every layer of mesh, leather, cotton, silk, and polyester, I remove who it is this world tells me I should be. When I slip on a strappy, kink-inspired black bra, a lacy red thong, or a sheer vintage onesie, I slip into my inner goddess. I am both Venus and

Hecate—the ultimate lover or dark mother, ready for pleasure and ravaging alike. My lingerie alone has the power to control who and what I channel. And I use this to my advantage in situations that require me to strip even further.

There is sex magick in dressing for sex. There is magick in dressing for pleasure, for getting laid, for hooking up, for masturbating. There is magick in getting dressed period, but there's something extra powerful about dressing in lingerie. Want to really cast a spell with your negligee? Place it on your altar and lay rose quartz and selenite on it. Then light a pink candle and call to your favourite deity of love. Ask for their compassion and blessing. Ask that you embody their essence. Let them know that this clothing is an offering in their name.

Lingerie helped me connect to my own inner love goddess too. It's what gave me permission to find the slutty flame of my soul and unleash it in full force. When I started collecting pieces when I was eighteen, I didn't realise that I was curating my glamour, crafting my magick, and igniting my own soul, but I was.

When I was in college, I really started to build my lingerie collection and I started to take sexy photos in it. I used my body as a political device, drawing hearts with 'not' and 'yours' in them, pasting them to my palms and covering my breasts with them. I started using my sexuality as a political force. I started to take more and more photos, documenting my love for my body, for myself, and for whoever was lucky enough to earn it. Taking portraits and photos has always been a powerful spell for me—both in lingerie, in clothing, and in nothing at all. The photos help me to see myself as a goddess, as a queen embodied through whatever I wear, and to document it so I don't forget it.

My favourite lingerie magick memory is the first time I had sex. Day to day, I wear underwear, but for this instance, I decided not to. I slipped on a mesh bra that I got from a market in London, thigh-high black stockings, a garter belt, and a black dress with a flared skirt and bell sleeves. Using lingerie as a way to help me remember this experience only made it more special. And each time I had sex with this person, I performed the same ritual—dressing in something empowering and sexy, all while nixing the underwear. I even left him a couple of nude Polaroids I'd taken in self-appreciation, passing on a piece of my magick to someone I wanted to remember.

I still continue to work with glamour and fashion magick in a similar way, except now I use it not only as self-worship, but as goddess worship too. In late 2016, I started to work with Venus, the Roman goddess of beauty, sex, love, and desire. When I was just beginning my practice with witchcraft, I had a dream that Venus told me she was my matron goddess. At twelve, I wasn't quite ready for her. But ten years later, I was. Besides my personal magickal practice, which is sacred and private, one of the ways I honour Venus is through art. I started a series of work called 'Love Letters from Venus' that act as both an offering and a way for me to channel the Goddess. I photograph myself in lingerie, with flowers coming out the seams of my underwear, bra, or tights. I then accompany this with a poem, usually to myself, sometimes to the Goddess. And when I find myself incorporating roses into this practice or into my Venus worship, it's like I can smell the floral perfume my Grandma Rose always wore.

When I started to work with Venus regularly, I had one goal besides connecting and worshipping her, and that was to keep my heart open. It's one thing to open your heart; it's another to keep it that soft and vulnerable. Through a practice of glamour magick that incorporates lingerie, art, and writing dedicated not only to Venus, but to myself, I gradually started to feel my heart grow and grow and grow. Now I weave this worship into my wardrobe, channelling the Goddess on Friday, the day ruled by her planet. I'll wear sparkly pink pants or a rose quartz necklace, or I'll match my makeup to a rose. When I feel the petals of my heart curling up, I unfurl them with some pink eyeshadow from my Lime Crime Venus palette, a prayer to my ancestors, and an outfit in red, pink, and silver. Venus has not only become my matron goddess, she's a part of me as well.

Fashion is my resistance for many reasons. Because I love dressing up. Because I live my life in clothing. And because it's in my blood. It's how my family has survived and it's how I continue to survive. It's how I show up into the world, how I cause chaos, how I disrupt the heteronormative patriarchal society we live in. It's how I honour my body, how I honour my ancestors, how I honour myself, and how I dress my magick. Columbia, South Carolina, gave me the strength to believe in my own glamour, but it is the women in my family who give me the strength to carry this glamour with me no matter where I go. And it's with the blessing of my ancestors that I continue to carve out my path—a witchy, rebellious path of resistance that wouldn't be complete without my shaved head and some black lingerie.

Garden

Marguerite Bennett

One.

A garden is an altar.

Two.

Blood and bone meal and shit and decay—the gardener must clear out the dead, the dying, the withered, to make room for new life, cutting and cleaning and slicing, all sap and saplings and seeds, digging a graveyard steaming with rot and heat to feed the roots of something stronger. She nurtures what she pleases. She cuts down what does not earn her favour. She controls sun and shade, wind and water. Poisons and potions, elements and herbs—her hands are the scales of life and death.

Here, she is not only gardener, but guardian. Here, she is witch and priestess and god.

A garden is an altar.

Three.

I rise before the dawn to tend my garden.

It is cool in the grey light, the last chill of the day before the desert heat ascends. The clouds still gather on the mountains to the east, and to the west, the cool, the wet, the morning glories and the gloom — the garden, before the rising of the sun.

Four.

Come and see them, my familiars, my little creations.

Here are the succulents, overflowing as the Nile overflows its banks. Here are the purple stars of *Echeveria*, spiny as shells, and the rosettes of stonecrop, moss green in little branched bouquets. Here is the explosion of yellow-striped *Aeonium*, proud as Lucifer fanning his wings, and the little *Cotyldedon*, snuggled together like baby rabbits in the hutch. Here is the glossy green jade plant and its little flowers, pale as constellations; here are the golden barrels, like barbarian warlords with spiny crowns.

Beyond them are the silver-blue stalks of *Senecio* and the dusty *Dudleya*, like a matron in a grey-watered silk gown. Beneath them are the feathery *Sempervivum*, fat hens surrounded by clusters of chicks. Beside them are little firestorms, plump as the paws of kittens, and the red pencil shrub, like a reef of flaming coral, with its poisonous sap that sears the skin. Above them all is the ruthless and towering agave, its blades serrated as bread knives, its veins as stiff with toxic sap as a hard-on gorged with blood.

The wind blows off the mountains; the wind blows from the sea. The orange trees stir, heavy with fruit; the lemon trees bob in the breeze. The kumquat and calamondin are still beside the single pomegranate teeming with bloody seeds.

Look, there. Look, as the sun rises.

Beneath the winding stairs that curve around the swell of the house on the hillside, there are the seven princesses, my pride—a wall of roses, red as the lips of sly women, orange as koi in deep ponds, yellow as the eyes of stalking cats.

When the setting sun hits them, before the gloaming and the gloom, the white stucco wall blazes with the light of each blossom, until the house seems to be burning with them, red and yellow and orange as flame.

Five.

This is the life I have created. This is the life I have nurtured.

Here is where we live and laugh and scoff at death, surrounded by what grows in defiance.

Would you like to learn a spell?

Six.

A garden is a holy place, if you wish. Only the blessed may enter. Only those you have blessed may enter. Only your guests, your friends, your lovers, your kin—only those you have welcomed and entreated to come.

They will drink what you have brought them, liquors and libations, under the little twinkling lights strung from the loquat tree. They will eat what you serve, in the breaking of bread, as they run their hands over the heads of the stone dogs and the ears of painted clay foxes. They are under your aegis, pilgrims at your wayside shrine. You have power here.

'How do you keep them so healthy, in all this heat?' the blessed say, gesturing to the ocotillo and its tongues of flame, to the bougainvillea swallowing the arbour whole. 'How do you manage all this, in the desert sun?'

Grace is the answer I wish I could give those who come and eat and drink and ask me, but one should not lie in holy places.

Spite, I think, and maybe that is true. I cannot bear to lose something so dear ever again. I lost enough before I came to the desert, fleeing ghosts, fleeing death, fleeing old shadows in a distant city.

But this place, this sacred place where the blessed come, this is where I look at death with sidelong eyes and scornful smiles. Death has no power here, not here where I can start again. Look — look at all the life I have fostered and raised.

But a garden is an altar, and on altars, sacrifices are made.

Seven.

You, too, will love your garden, as its witch, as its protector. It is your queendom, your realm, your little Eden — your firstborn in the creation of a new world.

And though you love it, and because you love it — and in loving it, covet it, smother it, resent it, neglect it, adore it, despise it — one day, you will lose this garden.

Even the first garden was lost — by Eve and by Adam, who knew too much, and against whom a flaming sword was set at the gates of paradise; and by God, who perhaps did not know what it meant, until then, what it is to love and to lose.

If God cannot keep a garden, what chance have you?

Eight.

I have a spell to teach you — a spell to laugh at death.

Nine.

The flaming sun will stand like that flaming sword at the gates of Eden, trying to cleave you from your garden.

Your role — caretaker and curator, witch of blood and bone — is to tend this place and keep it holy. The garden is in your power: this world, this place of life and death and life again.

The sun will knead its fingers up your spine in the heat of the day, knuckling up each knob of bone until you can feel the sweat run behind your ears, down your neck, beneath the brim of the grand old straw hat you bought in the store, though the story would be better if you had found it at some roadside yard sale.

Your nails will cake with black grime, chipping and splitting above hands that will roughen with muscle and callous, until it is pain to even fumble at the laces of your apron. Your sinews will creak and crack like some terrible lyre; your head will throb in the heat and the blinding summer sunlight. You will lie awake for hours into the night, aching in every limb, trying to save the garden.

How dare you think you were stronger than the sun, and heat, and time. How dare you think you were stronger than gods.

Though salved like a prize hog under a smear of sunblock, thick and white as lard, you will burn as your flowers burn, shrinking with the sun. You race against the sun each week, moving the painted pottery as your muscles seize and strain, shepherding blossoms into shadow, shading leaves from the scorching desert sky.

The hydrangeas will die first, and the delphiniums will shrivel like the trumpets of angels turned to ash on Judgment Day. You will find yourself losing. You will not be fast enough, strong enough. Some things cannot be kept. Some things were never yours to keep.

If God cannot keep a garden, what chance have you?

Look. Listen.

Ten.

Here are the tools of your craft. Look how they shine, even in the grey before dawn, when the city and the desert sleep.

Here is the chalice, a watering can. Here is the cauldron, a red clay pot. Here is the pentacle, a fresh garden bed. Here is the sceptre, a spade.

Here is the scythe, forever and ever unchanged.

Eleven.

Look, there—a glossy garden spider sits in the January mist. The rains have come to the desert and to the red brick and white stucco of your garden. Beads of crystal hang from the spider's web. A tug at this gossamer thread, to feel what is to the north. A tug at another, to feel what is to the south.

In this way, you will sit in your web. Threads and channels will connect you from your garden out into the world, and back again to you.

This is the spell of life and death.

Twelve.

Here is the sack of soil, rich and stinking even before the rising of the sun. Where did it come from? Not the warehouse, not the nursery—where did it come from?

It came from cows the colour of rust and cream, or white as

magnolia, or black as coal, licking their calves in April sunlight, in sweet clover — cows with their thick dark eyelashes and great wet eyes. It came from the cows rending shoots of grass coaxed up by the sun, showered by the spring rains. It came from the cows taking life into their bodies, bodies that once came out of some Cambrian sea eons and eons ago and evolved from scales to feathers to fur to hair. It came from their bodies drinking and draining away what nutrients they can from the grass, expelling what was not needed, what was not used.

Even shit has its purpose. Even shit has its reasons for being. Reclaimed, what it is left from the earth and passed through the bellies of beasts comes to rest here in your garden, rich with nitrogen and potassium and carbon for the soil. Life is death is life again.

Here is the bag of gravel that lines the pits, the pots, the beds. Where did it come from?

It came from eternities past, when the earth was a molten, swirling miasma of minerals and stardust, cooled and concretised into mountains and valleys and strata of stone. It came from the crash and crush of the moon colliding with the earth, from the kiln in the guts of the planet, heating and belching and cracking and breaking. It comes from the hills, where machines with teeth like dinosaurs split open the earth, from dynamite blasting through cliffs where black roads will one day run. Life is death is life again.

Here is the bone meal that salves the soil. Where did it come from?

It came from the slaughterhouses, where the beasts that walk on four legs go to meet their ends. Their skulls are crushed and their bodies are carved, meat stripped from skeleton frame, cleaned and rinsed and weighed and wrapped in plastic and foam and sent to markets across the wide meadows, to distant cities and distant towns, where bread will be broken and libations drunk with those we love. And what of the bones of the butchered dead? Their bones, filled with marrow, calcium, and phosphorous, are ground fine and come to rest in a graveyard that is a garden. Here the bones of poor beasts are buried. Here the bones of poor beasts endure in the roots and fruit and leaves of things yet living. Life is death is life again.

These are the lines, the channels, the web.

Once, it was another thing, in another land, another time.

But now, it has come to you, and it is part of your garden, your Eden, the thing you love and the thing you will lose.

These things have their place, their purpose, and their meaning, as you have yours. They have their story, their birth, and their death—their beginning and their end.

All things have their beginning and their end.

In the garden, you will sit among death, and the knowledge of death is everywhere. Life will teem around you, made possible by all that came before.

In the garden, I sat among death.

Spite, I thought then. I could not face another loss. So I nurtured life, frightening off the spectre of death like crows from a cornfield, planting, tending, growing—growing, always, in defiance.

I must make more life, I thought. I must make a better life.

Thirteen.

A garden is an altar, a house of God, and may be glorified accordingly.

Here, there are clay pots as intricate as the wings of birds, of as many colours as Joseph's coat. There are clay coyotes and rattlesnakes and pomegranates, ceramic cows and chickens and crows—red, yellow, orange, green, blue as the blue of the sky the moment after the sun has gone.

Here are also paper flowers and plastic hummingbirds, scattered amid the purple succulents and grey-green cacti, grafted to the surviving plants. There are little pinwheels that spin and catch the light, feeders for the finches, suet for the scrubjays, and houses for the bats. The garden is a place of aid and rest—the struggling sparrow sleeping on the bright red birdbath, the ailing aloe trimmed and coaxed until it raises a flag of mango-coloured flowers.

Fourteen.

A garden is an altar, where life is consecrated accordingly.

There were days and nights when my garden was a place of barbecues and cookouts, days and nights of lying in the hammock with the little grey dog under a sky so fiercely blue that it stung my eyes to watering. The garden was a haven of recovery in those long, Orphean weeks, staggering back to the land of the living. The garden was a place of stolen kisses, of drunken friends and melted marshmallows around the firelight, and candles on the steps leading up to the lighthouse sanctuary of the back door on the hillside. The garden held the scent of meat, heavy with fat, wet and crackling on the grill, of the smoke rising to the sky, of the chocolate sucked from fingers caked with graham cracker crumbs. The garden was in casks of cider, of beer and of wine, bottles slick and dripping in the hands of witch-women laughing over the flames. It was in the light in the eyes of the creatures that watched through the darkness from the trees.

How will you consecrate your own garden?

Fifteen.

You must tend your garden, or you will lose it. And you will lose it one day, no matter what you do, but that cannot trouble you. You will lose all things, one day, and that must not trouble you, either.

When you lose your garden, it may be for you to decide if you would plant another. Can you risk your heart again, under such conditions? Can you labour in the sun, against the sweat and stink, against the strain in your back, the pain in your bones, coaxing every tiny bloom, treasuring every cactus thorn? Can you watch your hands coarsen until the one you love laughs and shies away at their touch? Can you sell the labour of your body and your mind, earning the wages you must earn, to turn them over to the maw of the garden that will one day leave you? Can you nurture and create to be betrayed? Can you watch all of your love buried in the earth?

You may love another person, and that person may turn from you. You may bring a child into the world and live as that child goes out of it. You may surrender the years of your life to the thing most honoured and most beloved, and watch that thing burn high into the pillars of the clouds in the night. All things that are loved may be lost. Their loss may destroy you. All joy carries the price of pain.

If you survive a loss, do you begin again?

Sixteen.

How did I begin again, after all that I had lost?

I planted a garden.

And I lost my garden, the first year in the desert.

And when I lost the garden, after all I had lost before, I knelt in the gloom before the rising of the sun, too tired for tears, too tired for anything anymore. I remember the stone beneath my knees, the aching in my hip, the emptiness in my body, hollow and torn. I beheld the loss, the garden burned, the roses brown and seared to ash, the oranges gone, the thorns the only things that thrived. In the garden, graveyard and altar and centre of so many threads, lay the loss of all the things I had never had the chance to mourn.

I mourned them then, in the dark and gloom, before the sun rose.

I mourned the loss of the one I loved. I mourned the loss of the life that wasn't to be mine. I mourned the loss of dreams and youth and ideals and illusions, all the thousands of miles of running, all the silent years.

And as the sun came over the mountains, I rose to my feet, over the ache in my hip, the throb in my belly, the pain in my back.

I picked up the shovel, and I began again.

Seventeen.

A garden is a spell, as well as an altar.

Blood and bone meal and shit and decay—*I* clear out the dead, the dying, the withered, to make room for new life, cutting and cleaning and slicing, all sap and saplings and seeds, digging a graveyard steaming with rot and heat to feed the roots of something stronger. *I* nurture what I please. *I* cut down what does not earn my favour. *I* control sun and shade, wind and water. Poisons and potions, elements and herbs—*my* hands are the scales of life and death.

I am the gardener witch. I am the guardian of this new Eden.

Eighteen.

I will lose my garden again, as will you. We all lose everything, in time.

The garden may survive a year, or ten, or thirty, and perhaps it will pass from our hands to another's and live still, but it will live without us, and in this way, we will lose it.

We will die. All things have their beginnings and all things have their ends. A witch can hold the scales of life and death—but only for so long.

Perhaps we will be buried in the earth, strange seeds sleeping through the winter. Perhaps we will be burned to ash and sail upon the winds.

All things come from somewhere. All things have their channels.

We made an Eden, if only for a little while. We made life and nurtured it, and it was a place where our loved ones came, and kissed, and ate, and laughed, and drank, and danced amid the firelight. All Edens are only for a little while.

All things came from somewhere. All things, I think, live on.

When we die, all that we were—kindness and compassion, atoms and air—goes forth. As all that made the garden came to you, so all that you were will return to the world that lives. Bodies decay and return to the soil. All the air we ever breathed is there still, touched with the memory of our lungs, held for a moment in our bodies, above our hearts.

Every moment of sweetness, of kindness, of joy, lives on in those who came to us, who knew us, who lingered for a night in the garden.

As the atoms of your being remain in the cycle of creation, so does the best of you. Your breath endures in another person's lungs. Your kindness lives in another person's mind.

The seeds of your soul will bloom in another person's garden.

This is the spell to laugh at death.

I think it is enough.

Reddit, Retin-A, and Resistance: An Alchemist's Guide to Skincare

Sam Maggs

Let's start with things you need to know about your new path to skincare alchemy:

- It's going to feel overwhelming. Don't get overwhelmed! You can do it! And it's so worth it, I promise!
- You don't have to start getting up at 5 a.m. like you're getting into crossfit or whatever. Your morning routine is an abbreviated version of the whole massive shebang you do before bed.
- Instead of using one super-heavy cream on your face and calling it a day, this kind of routine relies on piling up multiple thin layers of different products. It's far less likely you'll end up feeling weighed down by moisturisers that are way too thick for your skin, while still delivering the same amount of moisture. Plus, you get to enjoy the benefits of a bunch of different ingredients this way!

- Layer your products thinnest to thickest for best absorption.
- You get to customise your routine based on products that contain ingredients that work best towards whatever your personal skincare goal may be (acne, preventative anti-aging, dryness, etc.).
- pH balance isn't just for vaginas anymore. Knowing the pH balance of your face is incredibly important. Most cleansers (especially American ones) have a very high pH (9+!), which strips all the moisture from your face (bad) and damages your skin's natural moisture barrier. What you want to look for is a cleanser with a pH of between 4.5 and 5.5.
- Whenever you think you have put the weirdest thing on your face (snail secretions), you will find something weirder to put on your face (donkey milk).
- You have to wear sunscreen every day. I'm sorry! I don't make the rules! You gotta!
- You're going to need to try one new product at a time, with a two- to three-week buffer between new products. It is super tempting to open all those beautiful new packages simultaneously and start slathering up all at once—but if you do that and you break out, you'll never know to which ingredient you had the adverse reaction. Patience pays off. Your face isn't going anywhere.
- I am not a dermatologist or an expert of any sort. This is just what I've learned from my time experimenting with skincare, using it as a focus to distract from the horrors of being a woman in the modern world.
- Snail goo will change your life.

~

'Don't touch your face.'

It's what we were all told growing up. 'Don't touch your face—that's how you get breakouts.' I've always struggled to find my way to clear skin, and not just as a teenager; they never tell you that you're going to be dealing with acne and wrinkles at the same time, but they really, *really* should. Underlying all the brands and ads and articles was the same idea: your face is untouchable. You use cotton balls for toner, the barest brush of your ring finger for creams; hell, even those idiotic face wash commercials had girls splashing water at their face from a distance of approximately three feet (remember the first time you tried that in the bathroom? Because *I* sure do, and it *sure doesn't get any water on your face,* FYI).

Why did we put so much emphasis on a zit-free face growing up? I always heard it had something to do with evolution, with biological selection—that the brain developed to look at someone with pimple-y skin and think, 'That person looks gross and probably has a garbage immune system; I shouldn't procreate with them.' So we tried Clean and Clear, we tried Stridex, we bought heavy-duty ultra-concealers probably at least two shades darker than our actual skin tone in an attempt to appeal smoochable to the boys in our class. Boys who (surprise, surprise) never felt the same pressure to get their skin lookin' right, never agonised for hours the morning before the school dance over the fresh pimple that had sprouted on their chin just moments earlier, in what was probably, had to be, retribution for some past sin. The onus was, as usual, on the girls to look their very best, in the hopes that some underwhelming, unapologetically-zitty dude would grace them with the opportunity to awkwardly grind in a gymnasium.

And so I bought my first Proactiv kit, found boyfriends, and never touched my face.

As time went on, I came up with reasons to rationalise my choice to use a brutal system like Proactiv. I was on camera, at conventions, in the public eye; I couldn't *afford* to have bad skin. But I couldn't ignore the fact that harsh exfoliation and the slathering of multiple layers of benzoyl peroxide all over my face twice a day just wasn't very good for me. Besides the fact that they tell you not to use it while you're pregnant (always a good sign!), BP is a chemical probably better known for its use in hair bleaching and tooth whitening (RIP my towels). I mean, hell yeah, it worked for my acne—but it also gave me horrifically dry and scaly skin, and lead to *many* conversations with *many* makeup artists about how I'd look like the crypt-keeper by thirty if I didn't figure my shit out.

Of course, the makeup artists were all correct about peroxide and skin damage. The thing is, I was scared. I *liked* my clear skin. I'd gotten older, louder, queerer; I'd been hired and published and torn down and lauded. But there's something so pernicious that lives in the subconscious of women in today's world. It's not our fault—we're bombarded from birth with annoying, terrifying, contradictory messaging at every turn: don't dress too sexy—but not too prudish, either!; we'll make fun of you for not playing video games—unless you do, in which case we'll harass you!; always be smiling—but we'll blame you if your co-worker misinterprets it! That vile idea that if you don't conform to men's expectations, you'll never work again, never find love again, never have value again lives in your brain, and it's hard to dislodge.

I am a researcher by trade, a gravedigger in literary non-fiction with anxiety-driven obsessive-compulsive tendencies. Very few things in the world are as satisfying to me as the moment I can unearth a piece of information about a long-dead, relatively unremarkable historical figure that either no one else has found or everyone else has misreported. And this (sometimes unfortunately) carries over into my non-work life, as well; I fall headfirst into fandoms and exhaust every single piece of information I can about them until my interest burns out and I move on to the next thing. If I love a video game, I'll play it sixteen hours a day for months on end until I get sick of it. One time, in the midst of what I would later come to realise was a crippling depressive episode, I watched ten seasons of *Supernatural* in thirty-five days. I smelled awful, but I could name every single Destiel-heavy episode off by heart.

That fateful and honestly kind of disgusting *Supernatural* marathon was the immediate predecessor to a trip I took to Japan. I was alone in a Tokyo Airbnb at a weird and terrifying crossroads in my life: I'd finished my second book and my five-year relationship was crumbling. I was adrift, and not even getting halfway through two seasons of the Winchester Bros. for the second time was helping.

That's when I discovered Korean skincare.

⌐

So why do we do this with Korean products instead of American products? There's a few reasons: first, K-beauty brands focus way more on skincare, while American brands put the majority of their resources into makeup. If your skin is already flawless, the thought goes, there's no reason to cover it up with heavy foundations and highlighters if you don't want to—you get that glow from the inside out. Combine that with a more wearable approach to sun protection, a competitive market that makes higher-quality ingredients available at a lower price point, and different regulatory standards that make new ingredient experimentation more readily available, and Korean-based (and some Japanese-based) products just provide a different kind of skincare than US brands.

~

I was on an internet hunt in my tiny Tokyo rental for the top cult beauty products in Japan, and I kept finding references to the 'K-beauty regime'. The more I dug into it, the more I realised this was not something I could casually learn about it one sitting, consuming information selectively and incorporating things into my bleach-filled current routine. This thing was *serious skincare business*, and it usually involved twelve steps *or more*, with wait times and specific product orders and chemistry-sounding ingredient names and—no cotton balls.

Wait, I remember thinking. *This skincare routine is an hour-long time commitment, and you have to apply everything... with your hands?*

It was too much for me. I didn't understand any of it—and I suddenly *had* to understand it all.

~

The best way to pick new products you'd like to try is by choosing ones with ingredients that work best for your skin issues—and there are a lot of different ways to improve the health of your skin. Here's a quick breakdown of some of the most popular current skincare ingredients.

Hyaluronic Acid

This is one of those new, hot ingredients you see people loving lately, but a word of warning: hyaluronic acid is a humectant, constantly trying to balance the water level between the skin and the air. In a humid environment, that means that it draws the water from the air into your skin—great news! But in dry environments, that means it will pull the water out of your skin and into the air—very bad news. So your mileage may vary. The nice thing about the Hada Labo Gokujyn Hyaluronic Acid Cleansing Foam is that it contains hydroxypropyltrimonium hyaluronate (gesundheit), which forms a protective film on your skin that stops it from losing water while also creating more water-storage space. Science!

Arbutin

You get this goodness from wheat and pears for evening out skin tone.

Niacinamides

Vitamin B3 is pretty great for redness, anti-aging, and skin brightening. It can also help repair your moisture barrier and fade your acne scars. Some folks say you should use it at opposite times of day from your actives, just to be safe.

Ferments

Tons of stuff can be fermented, like fruit, rice, and yeast. It's supposed to be great for brightening, elasticity, and anti-aging.

Green Tea

Apparently super for anti-aging, it also controls oil production!

Snails

My best friends! The heroes of skincare! Put snails on your face! And no stress: the snails are fed and treated well, their goo is ethically harvested without doing harm to them, and all the goo is purified before going into a bottle. Snail secretion can help retain water and soften skin, it's antimicrobial, and it's full of antioxidants, collagen, elastin, and more. It might even heal wounds (like popped zits) or reverse sun damage. It looks like stringy hot cheese when you use it.

Ceramides

Punch out dry skin and strengthen your moisture barrier in one shot.

Sea Cucumber

Packed with peptides to promote collagen, which skin loses when it ages.

Donkey Milk

????

Propolis

Bees harvest it from tree resin to varnish honeycombs, and now you too can benefit from bee glue all over your dang face. Antifungal, antimicrobial, barrier-forming, acne-preventing... bee glue.

Bee Venom

The key ingredient, melitten, is supposed to be an anti-inflammatory that increases circulation and collagen production, reducing fine lines and wrinkles. And no harm comes to the bees in the harvesting process! You can also find similar 'syn-ake' products made of synthetic snake venom.

Honey

Bees are good and honey is naturally antibacterial. It's perfect for acne-prone skin.

Rice

Products with rice water or fermented rice contain a punch of antioxidant vitamin E for anti-aging and skin brightening.

Starfish

The new snails. Research is still preliminary, but it seems to have a lot of the same benefits, like wound healing! It's very bouncy.

~

I was committed to learning everything I could about this new skincare life—but there were, as in all worthwhile things, some obstacles I had to overcome on my journey to embrace healthy skin. First, it was all about knowledge: though it was tempting to just start purchasing pretty packages wildly, I knew it wouldn't do me any good if I was completely ignorant to what I was putting on my face. There are tons of sites with great info out there, mainstream Western beauty sites and niche K-beauty blogs. But to my *great* astonishment, nothing was as helpful—or as comforting—as r/AsianBeauty. A *subreddit*.

Now, Reddit is not exactly known for being a feminist bastion of kindness and rationality. But in that one small corner of this otherwise often-toxic website, I found a community of women who had dedicated themselves to sharing the gift of good skin with their sisters around the world. With new Q&As, product reviews, and recommendations going up every day, it's a constantly evolving centre of knowledge with someone always ready to dispense invaluable advice at a moment's notice. I used r/AsianBeauty to start carefully planning and curating my own compendium of K-beauty products, rows of boxes and bottles that started to look like my very own potions collection, an assortment of alchemical wonders I couldn't wait to try out. Though I'm mostly a lurker, I started to view this subreddit as a kind of coven: powerful women around the globe advising each other on how to be their best selves, putting nothing but positivity out into the world in the hopes that they might visibly get it back on their faces times three.

⁓

1. Oil-Based Cleanser

It's time to embrace the double-cleanse. Forget your harsh, eye-burning, cotton-pad-requiring makeup removers—what you need is an oil-soluble cleanser. With just a couple pumps, you rub this stuff all over your dry face. The oil in the cleanser bonds to all the gross dirt and oil on your face and in your pores (makeup included), and it comes out and off in one easy rinse. Don't worry about putting more oil on an already-oily face; you're not clogging your pores with more oil, but actually using good oil to get all the bad oil out (as opposed to oil-free cleansers that strip your face of natural oil, causing you to overproduce oil afterwards in response—that's where those pimples come from). You will look like the Joker for a hot minute before washing it off, but it's kind of delightful to see all that goop sliding off your face. There are tons to choose from, and you can pick yours based on what kind of oil your skin likes best—I'm fond of olive oil (good for sensitive skin), but other people swear by kukui nut oil, sunflower seed oil, camellia oil, and more. Oh, and did I mention that essential oils are antibacterial? It's wins across the board. Try: DHC Deep Cleansing Oil, Kose Softymo Speedy Cleansing Oil, Banila Co. Clean It Zero, It's Skin Green Tea Calming Cleansing Oil

2. *Water-Based Cleanser*

Okay, all that being said, you now have to properly wash your face. It's time for the second part of the double-cleanse: a water-soluble cleanser! This is where you want to be pH conscious, keeping that acid mantle right. There are foaming cleansers, cleansing sticks, milky cleansers, cleansing gels—the world is yours to explore. But the key here is to make sure that its pH level is between 4 and 6.
Try: Hada Labo Gokujyun Hyaluronic Foaming Cleanser, Su:m37 Miracle Rose Cleansing Stick, CosRx Good Morning Gel Cleanser, Tosowoong Enzyme Powder Wash

3. *Wash-Off Exfoliators*

Despite how good it might feel to scrub your skin raw with the roughest shit you can find, this is in fact very bad and can cause a lot of damage to your face. Typically, it's suggested to limit exfoliators to about twice a week in the evenings (obviously trial and error will help you find what works best for you here, as with everything else!). Some exfoliators are physical, sloughing off skin with things like sugar or salt, and some are

chemical—rubbing it on your face until your own dead-ass skin balls up and falls off (it's magical).
Try: SkinFood Black Sugar Wash-Off Mask (twice a week), Cure Natural Aqua Gel (twice a month)

4. Actives

This is where your Serious Business Skincare comes in. Actives are products you put on your face to change the structure and function of your skin. Depending on what you want from your skin, there are a bunch of different kinds you can use. You may want to consult with a dermatologist before incorporating any of these into your routine if you're not sure if they're right for you—and since some of these are regulated by the FDA as 'drugs' as opposed to 'cosmetics', you'll definitely want to if you're pregnant or nursing. Wait about twenty minutes between each product to give your skin time to return to its proper pH level before applying the next thing.

a) pH-balancing toner: For actives to work, your skin needs to be at the proper pH. To speed up the process of getting your skin balanced right after cleansing, one of these can help.

b) Vitamin C: Most commonly formulated as L-ascorbic acid (L-AA), vitamin C products are antioxidants that can help with acne, aging, hyperpigmentation, and even sun protection. They can oxidise, so keep vitamin C serums in the fridge and use them in the morning.

c) AHA: A big help with taming and preventing breakouts, preventing fine lines, and healing dry skin. Glycolic acid, lactic acid, and mandelic acid are three water-soluble, humectant alpha-hydroxy acids you'll likely see a lot, and they help to remove dry and dead skin while increasing collagen production.

Be warned: AHAs cause photosensitivity, so use them at night, and sunscreen the next morning is a must.

d) BHA: If the AHA just isn't enough for your oily or acne-prone skin, you could consider an oil-soluble beta-hydroxy acid to bust through those blackheads. We're usually talking about salicylic acid here, an anti-inflammatory aspirin derivative that digs down into your pores to dissolve gunk. They can be a little drying, so make sure you're layering lots of moisture on top. Like AHAs, this is probably not a daily thing for most people—if you're going to start, once a week is more than enough off the top.

e) Retinoids: These vitamin A-based products are for people who are really serious about acne treatment and aging prevention. There are over-the-counter retinoids, but they're usually too weak for actual skin improvement. Strong retinoids (like Tretinoin) are available through a dermatologist with a prescription. These also give you photosensitivity, so again, sunscreen is a must. But you were going to use sunscreen anyway, so it's fine!

Try: Mizon AHA & BHA Daily Clean Toner, OST Original Pure Vitamin C20 Serum, Mizon AHA 8% Peeling Serum, Stratia Soft Touch AHA (10% Mandelic Acid Gel), CosRx BHA Blackhead Power Liquid

5. First Essence and Toner

Unlike alcohol-heavy astringent American cleansing toners that can rip the moisture right off your face, K-beauty toners are designed to start putting moisture back into your skin as a step to prep your pores to best absorb all the fun stuff you're about to stack on top of it. A first essence is similar, but it's usually made of fermented yeast filtrates (like galactomyces or saccharomyces) and gets your skin all bright and glowy. Some are very, very, very prohibitively expensive, but they use a lot of the same key ingredients as the more affordable ones, so, you know. You do you.

Try: Hada Labo Gokujyun Super Hyaluronic Acid Lotion, CosRx Galactomyces 95 Whitening Power Essence, Missha Time Revolution The First Treatment Essence, Kikumasamune Sake Skin Lotion High Moisture

6. Sheet Mask

Surely by now you've seen those all-over face masks that make you look like a horror-movie serial killer while you wear them? Those are sheet masks, covered in a highly-concentrated version of your favourite facial essence to deliver a blast of benefit all in one go. There are a ton of different kinds for whatever your skincare issue of choice, and you can use them for about a half-hour twice a week in the evenings. If you want to Treat Yourself, I've really grown to love hydrogel masks, made out of essence hardened into jelly instead of the soaked cotton sheet masks you typically see. When you peel it off, just gently tap your skin to get the rest of the good goo to absorb.

Try: Freeset Donkey Milk Skin Healing Mask, Nature Republic Aqua Collagen Solution Hydrogel Mask, Petitfee Black Pearl & Gold Hydrogel Eye Patch, Tony Moly I'm Real Sheet Mask

7. Essence, Ampoule, and Serum

Here's where all the sweet stuff comes in. These products pack a big punch in a small package. Again, there's a ton of different stuff out there for all different kinds of skin priorities (anti-aging, hydrating, healing, brightening, etc.). Though they're all usually pretty watery, you layer these up thinnest to thickest (essences being a little less intense than serums and ampoules), taking the time to let each one fully absorb into your skin before applying the next one.

Try: Benton Snail Bee High Content Essence, CosRx Advanced Snail 96 Mucin Power Essence, Banila Co. Miss Flower and Mr Honey Essence Oil, Mizon Original Skin Energy Placenta 45 Ampoule, Scinic Honey All-In-One Ampoule, Missha Time Revolution Night Repair Science Activator Ampoule (it activates science!)

8. Gel, Emulsion, and Cream

Now that we've got all those good, good treatments on your face, it's time to make sure you're all moist on top of that. Again layering from thinnest to thickest (emulsions and gels being lighter, creams being heavier), pick the products that work best for the level of hydration you're looking for in your routine—this usually differs from summer to winter, or if you live somewhere very humid or very dry. Make sure you get these into your routine to prevent water loss.

Try: Mizon Snail Recovery Gel Cream, Benton Snail Bee High Content Steam Cream, Mizon Black Snail All-in-One Cream, Stratia Liquid Gold, Rosette Ceramide Gel

9. Eye Cream

Your eyes need love, too. Get that collagen going ASAP.

Try: Etude House Moistfull Collagen Eye Cream, Sulwhasoo Concentrated Ginseng Renewing Eye Cream, Whamisa Eye Essence

10. *Sleeping Pack or Sunscreen*

You've layered about seven billion products onto your face and you want to make sure they aren't going anywhere. Lock everything in at night with an occlusive sleeping pack, a final step that will make sure you wake up looking fresh (even if you barely got six hours in). You can pop any spot treatment on just before bed, too. In the day, every day, no excuses, you'll be finishing your pre-makeup routine with a sunscreen. Luckily, Japanese sunscreens know what's up, and they're not gloopy or breakout-causing like the facial sunscreens you might be used to. Plus, Japanese sunscreens have two ratings systems for sun protection: you'll be looking for ones labelled SPF50+ (that's your UVB protection for sunburn), and PA++++ (UVA protection against aging and melanoma).

Try: Tony Moly Intense Care Dual Effect Sleeping Pack, Innisfree Green Tea Sleeping Pack, Laneige Lip Sleeping Mask, CosRx Acne Pimple Master Patch, Biore UV Aqua Rich Watery Gel, Shiseido SENKA Mineral Water UV Essence

~

Once I'd started purchasing shiny new products with complicated names, there was the moment I had to decide to ditch my Proactiv and start testing my new skincare regime in earnest. I put it off for ages, waiting until the end of one con season only to have another sneak up on me before I knew it. If I'm being completely honest, it happened mostly by accident—a first-time camping trip meant I was relegated to makeup wipes and sample-size moisturiser and not much else. When I got home, I decided it was a sign. And, frankly, I just... decided not to care anymore. About what other people thought of my face. About what I'd look like in photographs. About what the male-gaze-driven media told me it expected my face to look like. I prioritised the health of my own skin over the expectations of others; and, though it was anxiety-worthy, it was liberating, too.

The final mental hurdle — and, full disclosure, one I still struggle with sometimes — is the time commitment necessary when incorporating this routine into your daily life. Depending on the person, it can take over an hour some evenings to get all the goo going on your face in the right order. It can feel selfish — egoistic, timewasting. But it's become clear to me that such dedicated and laborious self-care is a radical act in the face of a patriarchal society that expects women to consistently place the well-being of others above themselves. Taking the time to prioritise your own health and well-being is essential, especially when the news and the needs of family and friends constantly drain you.

There was a time I might have shrugged off my extreme desire to learn as much as I could about K-beauty and skincare with the acknowledgement that it was just another of my micro-obsessions, like *Supernatural*, or that time I decided to try *Diablo III* and then forgot to put down my PS4 controller for three straight months. But I realised I was doing myself a disservice by thinking about K-beauty that way; indulging in an extreme focus on something like skincare might actually be the only way to survive in the world today without sacrificing your mental health entirely. An embracing of body positivity and positive self-image can and should manifest in different ways. We spend so much time absorbing information about the collapse of the world around us — why shouldn't we devote some of that energy to keeping ourselves feeling good, and healthy, and as vibrant as we possibly can? If everything else continues to fall apart, at least our future selves will be able to look forward with glowing faces. We are allowed to want something good for ourselves, no matter how small or seemingly insignificant or selfish. We are allowed to have that.

Now, I sit on my couch while I watch TV before bed and carefully line my potions up in the right order. I unstopper the first one and use the attached eyedropper, three clear, cool dots landing in my palm. I take deep breaths, remembering that I don't owe anyone my time or my emotional labour. I rub my hands together, spreading the product, letting myself enjoy the strange texture. I repeat to myself, as many times as I need, that I can only do so much, and that this small moment of self-care in and of itself is an act of defiance. I take my hands and I smooth them across my face, over and over, memorising the planes of my cheeks and my forehead and my eyes and my chin. I think about all the other women in my life who I love, who support me, who I would kill for and feel like, these days, I very well might have to. I tap the tips of my fingers over my face, knowing that I'm stimulating blood flow to the most important areas. I feel everything. I'm not afraid to know myself anymore. And neither should you be.

The Future Is Coming for You

Deb Chachra

At about ten-thirty on the night of the 2016 United States presidential election, I closed my laptop and got up from the sofa. I carried my half-drunk glass of whisky to the kitchen and set it beside the sink. I got ready for bed, set my alarm for early the next morning, and went to sleep.

When I woke up, I went to the gym.

I worked out with a heavy bag until my arms felt leaden and slow, and then went through a powerlifting workout: squats, bench press, deadlifts. At the end of it, I was sweat-soaked and drained, but I had placed one more brick into a foundation of strength. I already knew that this would be the first of four years' worth of mornings of waking up with the sure and certain sense that I needed to be strong.

~

Set the Olympic bar on the floor, loaded with full-sized bumper plates so it sits at the proper height for deadlifts. Stand behind it, carefully lining the bar up with the laces of your shoes. Reach down for the bar, pushing your butt out behind you in an unladylike way, and let your shins come forward just until they touch the bar. Grasp the bar with both hands, one overhand and one underhand to keep the heavy load from slipping. With your arms straight, raise the bar just slightly to take the slack out, so the next millimetre of movement will be off the ground, and brace your body against the weight. Check the angle of your back, your hips. Take a deep breath. Then push all of your thought into your legs and lift, keeping the bar level and directly over the centre of your feet until your legs are nearly straight, your hips are forward, and the bar is as high as it can go. Reverse the motion in a near-drop, so the plates hit the floor hard but still under control. Exhale. Shake it out. Do it again.

~

There's a meme going around the internet. It consists of two photos. The first, of someone calm and happy: ME IN 2016. The second, ME IN 2017.

Winona Ryder as Veronica in *Heathers*, first perfectly groomed and dressed to play croquet, and then from the end of the film: dishevelled, soot-streaked, a cigarette dangling from her lips, a picture of exhaustion and defiance.

Willow Rosenberg, first red-haired and smiling in a fuzzy pink sweater. Then black-haired, with eyes like pools of ink, black veins showing against her pale skin, the visible manifestation of the dark magic that she's summoned to avenge the death of her lover in the sixth season of *Buffy the Vampire Slayer*.

Sarah Connor in *The Terminator*, soft and scared. When we first meet Connor again in *Terminator 2*, she's doing pull-ups with newly-muscular arms in the asylum cell where she's been consigned, punished like Cassandra for telling the truth about the future and transforming her mind and body to face it.

A 2014 Pew Research study asked people how they felt about technological changes over the coming fifty years and found that women were significantly less confident than men about the positive impact of new technologies. Given the historical differences in the outcomes of past technologies for men and women (and other marginalised groups), a greater degree of generalised anxiety about the future might well be justified. But on the night of the US election, that low-level dread crystallised into a certainty that 2017 has only confirmed: as a woman in the United States, especially as a non-white immigrant, I knew as surely as Sarah Connor that the future was coming for me and many of the people that I know and love. It was time to prepare, and I immediately realised that the rituals and lessons of boxing and lifting would become part of this.

⁓

Pick up the soft cylinder, pull apart the fastener with that characteristic rip; let the wrap unroll in your hand and cascade its full length to the ground, revealing its centre. Put the loop over your left thumb, then wrap it around your wrist twice, then across your palm twice, then around the base of your thumb and around your wrist again. Then through your fingers: beside your little finger, around the wrist, ring finger, wrist, middle finger, wrist. Twice around the palm again, around the base of the thumb again, around the wrist again. Then crosses: diagonally across the back of your hand, across the palm to the thumb, then diagonally across the back of your hand in the opposite direction. Again. Again. Finish with a wrap or two around the wrist, and then carefully smooth the fastener patch down so there are no free edges to scratch or catch. Then repeat for your right hand. Do this often enough that you don't consciously think about wrapping your hands or even look at them when you're done, going straight into your workout or pulling boxing gloves over them. But then one day, find yourself looking down, and see for the first time the striking herringbone pattern on the back of your hand made by the wrap crossing over itself again and again, the left hand mirroring the right, echoing the practiced complexity of a double-Windsor knot, a sari, or an obi.

～

By last November, I'd been boxing and lifting for more than a year, gradually getting more serious. I'd started with boxercise-style aerobics classes at my suburban gym, where I was once called 'killer' for, as far as I can tell, treating the punching as more than just choreography. I bought a pair of fingerless MMA-style gloves and began to discover how therapeutic it was to work out on a heavy bag on a morning when I was frustrated or sad. I also learned that, contrary to what I had always thought, padded gloves are not just to protect your opponent. Boxing gloves are to protect *you*, and specifically the twenty-seven small bones in your hand that allow for the precise articulation of digits. Even with my fingers folded into the blunt weapon of a closed fist, I didn't have to get much better at putting my weight behind my punches to start feeling it in my hand. Protecting yourself and protecting your opponent are inseparable. I bought proper boxing gloves and hand wraps and learned to transform 180 centimetres of cotton ribbon into a support for the delicate phalangeal bones of my hand, bracing them against impact.

I signed up for classes at my local fight sports gym and began to work on my form, learning how to move more and more effectively. After a childhood mostly spent in libraries, I started exercising and training seriously in my early twenties, and I generally think of my workouts as falling into two equally worthwhile categories: there are the workouts where I have long uninterrupted stretches of time to think about whatever is happening in my life, like runs, hikes, or long swims. And then there are the workouts where I am entirely focused on what I'm doing and I *can't* think about my life for the duration. Boxing falls into the latter category. I spent each class thinking hard about my form, about getting the combinations right, about hitting the heavy bag as hard or as fast as I could. Generally, beginners train for at least a year or so until they even begin to think about sparring, so my workouts were comfortably theoretical, like learning and refining dance moves.

～

A new instructor. Set the clock ticking: how long will it be before 'You think too much', 'Stop trying so hard!' Ding! Check the time: twelve minutes, a new record.

～

I have tattoos on both my wrists. The one on my left wrist is a bracelet of three stylised neurons. I had it done shortly after I got into graduate school, and it represented my membership in a scholarly and intellectual community.

I didn't get its mate until a decade and a half later. That tattoo is a short stretch of the chemical structure of collagen, twined around my wrist and reaching up my inner forearm. I decided on it because I'd been researching and teaching about collagen since I was a teenager. It was only after I made that decision that it occurred to me that collagen was a good metonym: it's an important component of almost every tissue that plays a structural role in the body, including bone, tendons, blood, vessels, skin, and muscles, and it's the single most abundant protein in mammals.

Together, of course, the tattoos represent mind and body, and it's telling that it took so long to realise that they were *both* important, and that they could work together.

Every boxing trainer that I've ever had has told me, usually within the first half hour of a session, that I think too much. Sometimes they also tell me that I'm trying too hard. I'm used to hearing this. As an engineering professor, people have been telling me this since I was a teenager. Women don't choose to go to engineering school, much less get advanced degrees or become faculty, as a default option. Given how few women there are in these fields, it would be fundamentally impossible to do what I (and my female colleagues) do if we weren't seriously committed to it, not least because the data suggests that the attrition of women from the field is directly attributable to the male-dominated and -coded environment. I suspect a similar commitment on the part of women training at a boxing gym, for much the same reason. Any woman who shows up every day is there because she means it and because of that commitment to learning.

I've spent two-thirds of my life immersed in engineering education and research, and I've learned all sorts of new skills as an adult, and I really have no idea how to do so without thinking too much or trying too hard. There's a popular notion that it takes ten thousand hours of practice to become an expert in any field, and although it seems implausible that there is a constant amount of time that's required to become highly competent across a wide range of domains, there's no question that putting in the time is a key component of developing new skills. But time alone is not enough—if it were, the world would be full of *really great* drivers. Improvement comes with *reflective practice*, which means thinking hard about what you're doing and continuously incorporating feedback. This is why I find workouts where I'm learning new skills fully absorbing, even if I'm terrible. I frequently remind myself that there is exactly one way to get better, which is usually precisely what I'm there to do.

There is an enormous amount of pressure on women to make our bodies look a certain way. The list is lengthy, but it includes: shave your legs; wear makeup but not too much makeup; dress just right; and above all, don't be fat. I have what I think of as a Punjabi peasant body—sturdy and muscular and curvy. After a lifetime of being told, both explicitly and implicitly, how my body fails to live up to societal standards, I've learned that trying to make my body look a certain way is an endless source of frustration. For most of us, there's only a weak correlation between what our bodies look like and what we can do. I look about the same in the photo of me finishing my first marathon as I did in those taken before I started training for it, and you'd have to look quite carefully at my arms and shoulders to see how they've changed over the last year or two. But if I try to get my body to *do* specific things by committing to practice, it's an endlessly satisfying source of reward, a constant positive feedback loop as I get better and better. Not only is the ritual of going to the gym and learning new skills a constant reminder that I can defy the constant societal pressure about how I look in favour of expanding what I can *do*, it's a continual development of my ability to *learn*.

~

This ritual lasts the length of three breaths.

When the buzzer sounds, go to the corner. Try not to sag onto the ropes as your heart pounds and your arms burn.

Bite down onto the mouth guard, close your lips, and inhale deeply through your nose. Hold. Exhale. Feel your heart rate slow.

Inhale and exhale twice more.

~

I started sparring by accident.

At the end of January 2017, I moved to London for six months. I joined a fancy gym in Holborn that had lots of squat racks and plates and would be good for lifting. It also had a boxing ring.

For the personal trainers in the gym, I was fresh blood, and many of them seemed to use the strategy of 'negging', telling me what I was doing wrong as a way to convince me that I should work out with them. Instead, I began working with a trainer who started by asking me what I wanted to do and why, and who listened carefully to my response. One of the things on my list was to continue to train for boxing, which turned out to be his focus. He had a group of clients who met twice a week to practise, and I joined them.

I went to the first session, where we warmed up as a group, then paired up to work through drills, and then it was sparring time.

I know how prevalent violence against women is, and I've seen domestic abuse close up, so I consider myself fortunate that no one had ever hit me since I became an adult. I'd certainly never hit someone else. And now here I was, with my hands up to guard my face, circling around my opponent, trying to see their punches coming and to figure out how I could make one land. The first time I took a hard hit to the head, I was shocked and almost reflexively indignant. I knew objectively that I was fine—that I could step out and shake it off—but part of my brain was still going, 'What the hell?!' It's almost impossible not be angry and afraid, in varying proportions, when someone is trying to hit you, especially if they've already succeeded. It's that 'fight or flight' impulse—either lash out or run away. Every sparring session, I work to master both of those impulses in order to be able to respond effectively.

Over the course of the next few months, I slowly got better at blocking incoming punches or slipping out of the way, and at finding an opening and landing my own punches. But there was one person in particular, a former black belt in karate, who was fast and strong. He landed on me again and again and *again* and I couldn't even see the hits coming, much less move fast enough to keep them from making hard, painful contact. There were a few weeks that I couldn't hold back the tears, less of pain than frustration (but of course, the pain made it easier for them to come out).

That was when I wondered what the hell I was really doing there. But I kept coming back, and I gradually got to the point that I could face even him with some equanimity, even if I still couldn't block his punches fast enough to keep them from landing.

And then I realised that it was that *calmness* that mattered. It's often said that boxing is like chess—moves, countermoves, finding your opening and driving through it. I needed to be able to think clearly and to be open to opportunities when they arose, and those are both hard to do in the grip of fear or anger. The lesson that waking up early, going to the gym, wrapping my hands, practising my drills, and sparring was teaching me, week after week, was how to think and respond effectively even when I was—on those mornings, quite literally—under attack.

∼

At the end of the sparring session, go to each person in the ring in turn. Shake their hand or give them a sweaty hug. Thank them by name, and wish them a good day.

∼

It wasn't a coincidence that the trainer I started working with was the one who listened to me; his commitment to community was evident in the group. In the training sessions, we rotated through drills and sparring with every other person there, whether they were seasoned boxers or utter newbies. You tapped gloves to start, introduced yourself to the people you didn't know, and you reduced your power—or raised your game—in response to the ability level of your partner. And you thanked (and hugged or high-fived) everyone at the end of the session.

There is a feminist concept of emotional labour—that the creation of pleasant social environments and communities is work, and highly gendered work at that. These rituals of rotating through partners and of social niceties, session after session, were a structured form of emotional labour for our mostly male group. It was how we did the baseline work necessary to create and sustain a community.

A recent study has documented a jump in hate crimes in major American cities since the November 2016 election, particularly against Muslims and transgender people, which is consistent with anecdotal reports. As a woman of colour and an immigrant myself, I've found myself keeping an eye out for other women, particularly those who might be from targeted groups, on subways and in other public spaces. I think of this as 'soeurveillance' (from the French *soeur*, sister). The May 2017 tragedy on Portland light rail, in which two men were knifed to death and a third injured as they stood up to a white supremacist shouting at two women, is a reminder that just standing up to this kind of hate may be a tragically inadequate response to someone who is armed and dangerous. But in many other cases, a willingness to stand up might be enough to make someone back down.

I saw this deterrence in action on the community scale at a march in Boston in August 2017, a counterprotest to a 'free speech rally' that included a number of speakers associated with white supremacist movements. This was less than a week after the Charlottesville clashes between counterprotesters and armed white supremacists and alt-right militias at a rally, which culminated in a hate group member ramming his car into a crowd, killing one person and injuring nineteen others. Every single person who showed up at the Boston counterprotest march knew that there was a possibility of another attack. The protest signs were unusually sweary, even for a protest in the US in 2017; one of my friends said that she had decided to use the word 'fuck' on her sign because she (correctly) anticipated that the risk of violence meant there would be very few children present. A careful observer that day might also have noticed that all the marchers were holding their signs in their hands—the Boston police had issued a warning that anything that could be used as a weapon, including posts for signs, would not be allowed onto Boston Common, the site of the 'free speech rally'. About fifteen thousand people showed up for the march and counterprotest, and almost every one of us had made a conscious decision to not only face the possibility of physical violence, but to face it unarmed. Only a hundred or so people attended the 'free speech rally' itself, and the organisers cancelled the entire series of events that they had planned.

Feeling physically strong and able to face violence as an individual enables you to stand up for yourself, but that only goes so far. Ultimately, change comes from standing with and for your community, and especially for those who can't stand up for themselves. Community and solidarity are the key to not just resistance, but to holding ourselves together while we do the work.

～

Get into a left guard stance, your left foot forward, right back, weight balanced between them, gloved hands up to guard your

face. Then listen, and throw punches. One. One two. One two
one. One two one two. One one two. Triple-one two. One two
three. Add the four. Add the five. Add the six. Six three two.
Two three two. Boxer's rhythm. Shake it out.

Again.

Again.

Again.

~

There are two kinds of rituals in the world. The first is to do
something once, in a carefully specified way, with the goal of
effecting change in the world. The second is to repeat something
over and over again, in order to effect change in oneself.

A large part of training is about burning form and technique
into muscle memory—how to stand, how to move, how to
throw a punch or a combination, how to evade or block—until
it becomes utterly unconscious and all of your attention is on
higher-level decision making, not mechanics. This calls for drills,
like following along with a trainer's calls of coded numerical
cues for specific punches (one for a left jab, two for a right
cross, three and four for left and right hooks, five and six for left
and right uppercuts, and so on). While punching drills build
strength and endurance, they mostly form the foundation of
the ability to *fight*.

On learning that I was a professor, someone joked that I should
accidentally-on-purpose let my boxing gear be visible to my
students, so that they would know not to mess with me. While
he was kidding, we do live in a world where being physically
stronger is, at least implicitly, a way to command obedience, and
one where telegraphing an ability to defend oneself probably

does deter harassment, if not outright violence. Casey Johnston, who wrote about weightlifting from a female perspective in her 'Ask a Swole Woman' column for *The Hairpin*, quoted trainer Bret Contreras: 'If you think lifting weights is dangerous, try being weak. Being weak is dangerous.' It's a terrible consequence of living in a patriarchal society that this is true.

There is no question that lifting or boxing in the morning makes me feel better equipped to take on the world that day. I walk out of the gym with my shoulders square, my head held high, and my 'don't fuck with me' urban forcefield fully recharged. An experiment for women in dense urban environments is to walk around your city and be aware of every time you're about to step out of the way to clear the path of a man, and then don't do so. At least three female-presenting friends told me about being all but bodychecked by men, who were presumably expecting that they would get out of the way, even if only unconsciously. So I tried this experiment for a couple of days, walking around Boston and Cambridge, and not only did no men bump into me, but a number of men stood aside politely to let me pass.

The feminist journalist Laurie Penny has written about how the amount of anger that it's permissible for a woman to express is directly proportional to her social status. Like a lot of women, I am increasingly angry with the state of the world. I also have enough social power that I can often express it, especially when it's on behalf of other people, like my students. And I suspect that feeling physically strong is part of what allows me to stand up for what I believe in—and gives me a clear path on the sidewalk—in a patriarchal world.

～

The simplest and hardest of rituals:
Get up.
Do the thing.
Get up and do it again tomorrow.

~

For a long time, I thought that the main reason why women
(including myself) learned to fight and trained to become strong
was so that we'd feel better equipped to face or deter violence,
and by extension, be mentally and emotionally better able to
function in a patriarchal society. And the truth is, I do. I do
feel like I can handle the world better. But I was also deeply
conflicted about this. I don't want to live in a society where
physical strength is what matters. I don't want to join the win-
ning team—I want a different game. Even if my goal of learning
to fight was to resist violence, was I effectively endorsing that
system of values?

But just becoming a strong woman is an act of resistance
because it undermines the entire *premise* of patriarchy.

As species go, the degree of sexual dimorphism in humans is
slight (even compared to peacocks, never mind a species like
Osedax, sea worms that are almost entirely females—harems of
males can be found, in an arrested, juvenile state, attached to
the bodies of the female worms). But humans have taken these
tiny differences—that men are marginally larger and stronger
than women, on average—and turned it into an entire structure of control, in which strength is how you get and maintain
power. We can trace a direct path from feudal society where
people became leaders by being really good at inflicting violence on others while limiting, or just surviving, its impact on

themselves, to our present patriarchal political system, where men are more 'naturally suited' to be leaders. And it's not just politics—the same dynamics are at play in the domestic sphere, where for thousands of years, men could control women and children. Even when this control wasn't by violence outright, it was a result of creating a system that allowed men to deny them access to resources. But at the same time, many people have been working hard to create a world where power and violence *don't* define what you get to do and where more and more people have access to agency (in the form of money, education, healthcare, personal expression, and more). Five hundred years ago, one's right to govern accrued from one's capacity for violence. As this changed, so did the rationale for power. Not for nothing was there an eighteenth-century project to prove that white men were intellectually or emotionally superior to the people they sought to govern, including women: more objective, level-headed, intelligent. Even if might was no longer the requisite characteristic, somehow the men who had the might also (just coincidentally, surely!) had the newly-required skills of the post-Enlightenment era. Now we've arrived at a world where most of our serious political problems can only be solved by communication and collaboration, not by macho posturing, and still less by war. But we still mostly think that politics and leadership are about displaying or expressing dominance. The few women who have succeeded have often done so only by fitting that mould created by men, for men.

It's a measure of the progress of society that more and more of us can live our lives without a daily interaction with violence. But it's taught to us from the playground that deviations from binary gender norms will be met with physical or emotional violence in the form of bullying, physical or verbal. Once everyone is safely consigned to their gender boxes, the patriarchy still holds to itself the power to define who gets to do what. For example, 1950s-style homemakers were created as a direct response to end of World War II, where men returning home needed to displace the women who had worked in the wartime factories. And computer science was recoded as a male discipline in the 1980s, despite the involvement of women from the earliest days of computing, as the power of the field began to become apparent.

Given that physical violence is baked into our politics and society by the continuing existence of the patriarchy, if men are no longer capable of dominating the women around them by force, it undermines that whole implicit basis for their having decision-making authority. When women and nonbinary people become strong and able to fight, making the threat of violence much less effective, it destabilises the whole system by revealing its basic assumption: that male privilege is, ultimately, reliant on the ability to inflict violence. Lifting or boxing isn't just about breaking gender norms or being stronger as an individual—it's a subversion that reveals this moral bankruptcy at the heart of the entire system of patriarchal power. If the entire system is built on the evolutionary accident of men being stronger than women, and then women and gender nonconforming people decide to become strong, it's not that they are buying *into* the system—it's that they're showing that building a system of power with physical strength as its foundation is, ironically, fragile. And that it's long past time for us to collectively build a new system that's not based, whether distantly or daily, on dominance and fear.

The rituals of boxing that I've described—becoming strong, learning to protect yourself to protect others, remaining calm in the face of threat, creating and sustaining community, committing oneself to practice, learning, and getting better—these are skills that we need to build a better tomorrow for all of us.

We're not getting strong because the future is coming for us. We're learning to fight so we can come for the future.

My Witch's Sabbath of Short Skirts, Long Kisses, and BDSM

Mey Rude

'Do you want to make out?'

By putting those magic words out into the world, I had put something into the air around us. I had awoken something in me. I had transformed myself. Quickly we were all over each other. She was pulling my hair and biting my neck and breasts. She chewed on my lips until it looked like I was wearing purple lipstick. She made me feel more in my body than I had ever felt before. I could feel every inch of my skin; every pore and nerve in my body was singing. I was a goddess.

The first time I had casual sex, a one-night stand, I felt like I was entering a religious fervour, like a mystic or a whirling dervish. I was too afraid, too ashamed to try this until I was thirty years old, and when I released all that shame and fear into the air that autumn night, I finally became my true self. I opened my eyes to a new way of living that gives me more strength and confidence than I've ever had before. I realised that I'm a slut and I love being a slut and I'm powerful when I'm a slut. This is who I am.

Have you ever felt like you're something more than human? Felt like you were more powerful than you had any right to be? That night I felt like I was flying. I felt like we were playing 'light as a feather, stiff as a board', but it was only her fingers and tongue touching me and lifting me up into the air. I started screeching like a banshee and cackling like a witch. 'Be quiet or the whole camp will hear you!' I could barely get out the words 'I don't care' through my laughter. I shook those walls that night. I screamed and laughed until the room shook just as much as my legs did when I stood up afterwards. This is what power feels like.

Now that I've tasted that power, I never want to feel powerless again. I do summoning spells to call on partners to sleep with. I cover myself in magical runes and colours to strengthen my body and mind and heart. I conjure the sexuality that I want to have into being. I own my body and I own my sexuality. I'm a bruja. I'm a puta. I won't let anyone dictate my sexuality except for me. I'm made of magic, motherfucker.

As a woman I'm constantly told to be quiet, especially when it comes to my sexuality. I'm supposed to speak softly and never cause a commotion. I'm supposed to raise my hand and wait my turn to talk. I'm supposed to be demure and soft-spoken. No one likes a loud lady. Be quiet and let your husband do the talking for you. Don't talk back or interrupt. Loud men are assertive and leaders; loud women are only ever bitchy or loudmouths.

Back before I transitioned, I was told, 'Never go out with a girl who asks you out. Girls like that are tramps.' Because of that warning, and because I knew I was a girl, I didn't ask anyone out until my second year of college. I was afraid that if I talked about desire or sex, people would think I was disgusting and immoral. I held the garbage belief that wanting to have sex made me a bad person. We have to put up with men constantly talking about their sex lives, but when we do it, we're sluts. And when we're called sluts, it's not meant as a compliment, but rather as something the patriarchy wants us to believe we should be ashamed of.

I was even taught that women don't like sex. My church told me, 'Men give love to get sex and women give sex to get love.' Before I had sex, I thought that men could be loud, but women usually would just lie there. I really thought that. I thought that I was sick for being attracted to people and thinking and dreaming about sex. I thought that in order to be a good person, I needed to keep those thoughts and desires quiet. I thought I needed to be silent whenever the boys were talking about sex.

But fuck that lack of noise. Now when I fuck, I scream and I yell and I laugh my head off. I want the world to know how much pleasure I'm feeling. I want to scream so loud that the pastor at my old church hears me, and I want my laughter to echo down the hallways of the houses of the men who made me feel ashamed for wanting to feel pleasure.

This censorship doesn't just happen with the noise we make and the things we talk about. Men do all sorts of things to try to keep us down. They know that we're powerful. They know that magic lies in our skin and blood and spit and in our freckles and hair and stretch marks. So they try to make us hide it and be ashamed of it. They don't want us to show skin because it makes them too weak to control themselves. They don't want us to walk tall because it makes them smaller. They don't want us to be sexual beings in public because it neuters them.

Becoming powerful like this doesn't happen overnight or by accident. Sluttiness, like magic, is all about practice and intentions. You've got to focus on your spell and focus on your sex appeal. You've got to hone your craft and you've got to hone your skills in the bedroom. I can't even count the number of hours I've spent admiring my thighs in mirrors or taking selfies and posting them saying that I'm hot. I had to speak those things into truth. I am sexy because I say that I am and I have been saying I am and will continue to say that I am. My words are powerful and magic, and when I use them to build myself up, they're not just words, they're potions that touch my lips and make me stronger and braver than I ever was before.

I turn my affirmations into spells. I repeat them three times.

I love my ass, I love my ass, I love my ass. I love my thighs, my lips, and eyes. I love my thighs, my lips, and eyes. I love my thighs, my lips, and eyes. I look hot in this dress. I look hot in this dress. I look hot in this dress.

I've heard people say that the power in magic lies in the power that you put into the words. If you don't focus and if you don't put good intentions into it, the spell won't work. That's abundantly true here. You need to say these words until you mean them. Say them until they're the truest things you know. Say them until everyone around you believes them.

It took me literally thirty years to start liking my body, but girl, when I did, I started *loving* it. I'm a trans woman, I'm mixed race, I'm fat. There's so much about the way I look that is deemed unattractive by society, by men, by queer culture. When I look in the mirror, I don't see the type of person who is on magazine covers or billboards. I don't see the type of person who is hit on in queer clubs. I'm not androgynous or skinny or masc of centre, or the combination of skinny and masc of centre that so many people think has to define androgyny. I don't look anything like Tegan and Sara or Ellen Page or Kristen Stewart and I never will.

I'm not even the 'good' type of fat. My curves go in all the directions that they shouldn't. My boobs are small and my belly is big. I've got these child-bearing hips, that's true, but my waist is thick enough to disguise them. I'm so much lighter than most Latinos but vaguely ethnic to white people. I have the broad shoulders, big feet, and tall stature of the men in my family. I have a penis that feels like it doesn't belong to me. But, fuck, I love my body. I've worked hard to survive this long and be this cute and damn, I'm going to appreciate the vessel that's gotten me here. That's where I am now. That's where I've worked to be. That's where I'm going to continue to work on being.

For years I tried to make myself as invisible as I could. I would wear all blacks and greys and browns, I would cover as much of my body as I could, I would hope and pray that no one would give me a second glance. I would keep my head down and try to blend in. No more. Now I walk confidently through the world, hoping people look at me. I gain strength from their glances and their slack-jawed stares. They are paying attention to me and their attention is a valuable currency.

Think of yourself the way modern-day authors write about old gods. They get their power through worship. The more people who worship them, the stronger they are. According to these writers, the reason you don't see Odin and Bast and Quet-zalcoatl around as much is because not nearly as many people worship them. It's the same thing with you. Don't become like these old gods. Stay fresh and stay relevant and stay vibrant. The more people look at you, the more they stare, the more they want you, the more power you have.

One of my favourite rituals is to take walks and feel this praise washing over me. I'll put on a skirt that shows off the tattoos on my uppermost thigh. I'll get my favourite t-shirt and I'll cut off the sleeves and the bottom half and make a crop top that lets my body breathe. I'll paint my lips pink and draw the sharpest cat eyes I can. I'll put in some of my chola hoops and finish it off with a playlist full of songs that make me feel amazing. There's this thing where men think that we dress for them and walk down the street just for them. Turn that ritual around on them. If they want to stare, use those stares to become more powerful. The difference between being proud and in control of your sexuality and being objectified lies in the power, so if you have the power, you're in control. Keep in mind that they're your worshippers and that you are more powerful than they will ever be.

Now, this is something you need to be safe with. There are vile men out there, vile people. Society teaches men that they're allowed to control us and hurt us no matter how magical we are. It's on them to change that. Until they do, form a sex pantheon. Get a slutty mythology together. Walk down the street with a group of fellow goddesses all looking the best you've ever looked. You and your friends will be even more powerful. These men gawking at you think that they're objectifying you, but you're in power—you're using them.

Always remember, a goddess is above those who worship her. When a man stares at your legs and whistles, that doesn't mean you owe him anything. Use that attention to feel good about yourself and to feel angry about the patriarchy. Fuck these men. Fuck these 'catcallers'. They don't deserve you and your witchy divinity. They don't even deserve to be named after our familiars. They are just sticks and twigs that become fuel for your fire. They are throwing themselves into your flames to make you bigger and brighter. They're kindling. That's all they are. Don't give them anything more than that.

The world hates a slut, especially if she's powerful, especially if she loves herself and she loves her sluttiness. They'll applaud and holler and whistle, but they'll do it for themselves. The shouts aren't for you, they're for how they feel when they look at you. They'll stare. They'll stand in front of you. They'll grab you. The world will try its damnedest to hurt you. I'm sorry. I wish I were the kind of witch who could end this sort of thing. All I can do right now is tell you to use the hate you have for the people who would judge and hurt you to fuel your power. Turn that anger into pride. Even if they've hurt you, you've survived this long. You're better than them. You're magic and they are not.

There are other ways to use your sluttiness to weave magic around you. When we talk about witches, we talk about black hats and black cats and broomsticks and spells. As sluts, we have our own versions of those things. Our black hats are hankies in our back pockets. Our black cats are our purses filled with lipstick and our broomsticks are our sex toys. Our spells are our tattoos.

You may have heard of candle magic, where you get candles and the different colours are good for different kinds of spells. And you can combine multiple candles to get a more powerful spell. If I light a green candle for success and a red candle for strength, I'll go into a situation prepared to take control and do my best. Let's take those principles and apply them to the hanky code. Now we're working with slut magic.

So, you're flagging that you're looking for a daddy (you know, someone who's good at taking control and punishing you in all the best ways), that's hunter green. But you're also into fisting and being fisted. So you want to flag red. In candle magic, green, like I said, is good for success, money, and prosperity; red is good for love, strength, life, and vitality. So you're not only flagging for two things that you love, but you're also doing hanky magic to bring success and love. You're on fire.

There are just as many colours of hankies as there are candles. There are just as many ways to weave together spells. Even more, there's a strong magic of tradition in using the hanky code. For decades, queers had to use this code to communicate in secret with each other to avoid persecution. This is a secret language of symbols and colours and body language. Few things get more magical than that. The souls of the gay men and lesbians and bisexual people who went cruising every night in decades past live on in the hankies that you carry in your back pockets. These are your ancestors. They give you strength.

Strength also comes from the elements. Many witches use the elements to charge their crystals; you can use them to charge your sex toys. I want my sex toys to be as magical as I am. When you get a new toy, leave it under the light of the full moon, run fresh water over it, charge it with a candle or with earth. Since you need to clean your sex toys, you can charge them while you do that as well. Wash it with clear water. Water from a tap is fine. When there's a full moon, leave your plug or dildo or vibrator on your windowsill at sunset. Light some red candles for sexual energy next to it and surround it with citrine for self-esteem and garnets for vitality and strength. Put your intentions into it.

I will have mind-blowingly awesome sex this month. I will have mind-blowingly awesome sex this month. I will have mind-blowingly awesome sex this month.

In the morning, your toys will be charged full of sex magic and they'll be ready for you to ride them and keep them by your side.

There's a long tradition of magic tattoos in cultures that I can't speak to, as well as with modern witches who ink runes and symbols into their skin to give them strength and protection. When I do this, I get symbols of my fertility and sexuality permanently on my skin. I have a tattoo of a heart-shaped butt, with a bruise and a handprint and a cute bunny tail and the words 'Sí Papi' on the side. I know who I am, I know who I like, and now the world does too. This modern-day rune calls out to those I want to attract.

I'm a sub, I love pain, and I want dommes to know that. When I'm dancing in a club in my too-short skirt, people who know what my tattoo means will see it and they'll approach me. It's not an open invitation, but it is a sign in the window. It's an extension of the secret language of the hanky code. This time I can flash my thigh at my dance partner and if they understand my secret tongue, we'll get to share a lot more than a secret language.

There are so many right ways to be a slut. No matter what kind of slut you are, though, you can't control other people, and so there's a limit on what you can do. You're a goddess, but you still bow down to consent. Don't ever, ever, ever force your sluttiness on another. Learn to read the energy of a room and release your power only when it's appropriate. Meet other people where they are; don't force them to be at your level.

There are plenty of opportunities to be a slut. You don't have to try to make them where they aren't.

You should keep your sluttiness in check in certain situations, but you should be the only one who owns it like that. No one else owns your magic. Other people will disappoint you sometimes, but that doesn't make you less powerful or less sexy. Most of the world is still stuck under the control of the boring, old-fashioned, cis- and heteronormative patriarchy. They're caught up in what they've been taught they should find attractive. There will always be people who will leave you for someone thinner, richer, prettier, whiter, more cis. There will always be people who will sleep with you but keep you hidden because you're not enough. Those people are not on your level. They won't be able to make you float off the ground or shake the walls with your screams. They don't know how to worship you. They're twigs and they can only help so much. You need the people who ask for consent before dancing with you in the club, Tinder matches that result in orgasms for everyone, respectful one-night stands; you need branches and logs thrown onto your fire.

There's that Terry Pratchett quote from his book *Wintersmith*, 'A witch ought never to be frightened in the darkest forest, Granny Weatherwax had once told her, because she should be sure in her soul that the most terrifying thing in the forest was her.' Well, I'm a witch and I'm a slut and I am never nervous in the sleaziest city. I am sure deep down in my slutty soul that the sexiest thing in the city is me. I keep that in mind, and I keep that in my heart; I'll tattoo it on my inner thigh and on my ass. I'm a slut and I have all the power that comes with that title, and if that makes me terrifying to the patriarchy, so be it.

Buzzcut Season

Larissa Pham

Everyone, especially men on the street, called me 'blondie' after I bleached my hair one summer. 'Hey, blondie! Hey!' I had it in a bob then, short and swingy, the double-process I got done at a cheap salon in Connecticut leaving me towheaded and ethereal—a dandelion, an angel in the wilderness. I was a novelty to those who didn't know me, both blonde *and* Asian, the collusion of two fantasies that got me catcalled in all kinds of improbable configurations. As my bob grew out and my dark roots began to show, the nickname dropped off, but the long, blonde ponytail stayed.

I've always been attached to my hair. Asian girls are supposed to keep it long as a point of beauty and pride, according to every family member who admired mine when I was growing up. My hair grows fast, luscious and thick, pin-straight but soft to the touch; it keeps a wave in it if I put it in a topknot while it dries. It's pleasing when messy, has always fallen over my

eyes in just the right way. It was always something I could hide
behind when I was shy — there must be dozens of photos of me
in college, all from the same angle, where I'm peering out from
behind a waterfall of dark hair, holding a Djarum Black — and it
was always something that I could exploit, like the way I learned
to tangle my hands in it while fucking someone, on top. For all
my adult life I kept it long while it picked up scents like the reek
of cigarette smoke and the dry, woody heat of bonfires and the
sweaty, musky smell of sex. I liked that it was thick, that it held
my history. When I used to paint self-portraits, I used my hair
as shorthand — that was how everyone would know it was me,
and it was how I would know I was myself. It was shorthand
for my physicality, my desire; it was desire itself.

～

The itch to shave my head began suddenly. One hot summer
night, a full year after I went blonde, I couldn't stop thinking
about it. It was like a fever had caught somewhere deep in my
body and wouldn't let up. Soon it became irrational, like I would
die if I didn't do it. I started texting my friends things like, *what
do u think the shape of my head looks like? do u think it's cute?*
and *do u think it would be totally deranged if i shaved my head?*
and: *i rly rly rly wanna shave my head* and, mere hours after
setting my phone's lock screen to a picture of Zayn Malik with
a swamp-green buzzcut, *GUYS I THINK I'M GOING TO
DO IT TONIGHT*.

That night — late June, a breeze coming in through the open
window — I sat cross-legged on a layer of newspaper on our
kitchen floor as my best friend Santi cut off ten inches of bleach-
blonde ponytail with a pair of scissors — a keepsake I'd later lose,

find, and throw away when moving out of that house a year later. They turned on the clippers and ran them up the nape of my neck in long, clean lines.

And there was so much hair—an ocean of hair, a country of hair, blonde with dark roots. A kingdom of hair, a golden crown, a de-throned throne. We were sweeping for days after. Even as we worked it seemed impossible that I could go through with it, that I could change myself so completely—the clipper moving in slow tracks along my skull. The hot mechanical buzz of it shooting down my body, prickling through my lower back. Making my toes curl, making my stomach clench. My room-mate Clare documented the whole process, taking pictures of me with all the punk haircuts in reverse—undercut, Chelsea, mohawk, and then, with one final run of the clippers on my crown, a neat buzzcut, my hair as short and fine and even as newly-mown grass.

Freshly shorn, I was struck by how much of myself remained. It was like I was still me—of course I was—but without the armature of external self I'd developed over the years to hide behind, my face felt new even to me. Open. Honest. My head, it turns out, was perfectly shaped, because it was the shape of my head. I felt impossibly free, giddy and unburdened, unbearably light. I couldn't stop touching what was left of my hair, running my fingers over the velvety short fuzz. I'd catch myself moving as though expecting my hair to fall, but there was nothing there—just me, solidly in the mess of myself.

Shaving all or part of one's head is a common practice across religious faiths—there's even a word for it within that context, *tonsure*, from the Latin *tōnsūra*, meaning 'clipping' or 'shearing', which originated within medieval Catholicism but now refers to the religious practice overall. The logic for the practice varies from tradition to tradition, but the common theme is that ritually removing our hair might free us of attachments—from greed, from vanity, from other people's perceptions of us. Buddhist monks of all genders ritually shave their heads when they enter their orders and maintain it as long as they are practising, some shaving their heads as frequently as every two weeks. It was this aesthetic ideal I had in mind—and yes, Zayn too, though I suspect he shaved his head for the same soul-searching, monk-ish reasons as I—when I decided to buzz my head. I hoped that the asceticism of the decision would make itself immediately apparent to me—that it would manifest in my spirit as soon as it manifested on my head.

⁓

There were other reasons—there are always other reasons; it wasn't as spontaneous as I might make it seem, the way you can tell a story any number of ways to prove a point. I'd shaved part of my head before, when I was nineteen. That year, I buzzed half my head because my grandmother died and I needed a visual expression of my grief. I was crazy with sadness, smoking too much weed and drinking during the day, and one April afternoon I went to my friend Nicky's house and said, 'Please buzz it off, please.' I parted my hair and waited for the blade to come, running my fingers along my scalp. For days after, I'd run my fingers over the soft, bare patch of skin, measuring time with its slow growth. Eventually, it all grew back, just the same as any other patch of hair, the way flesh knits over a wound.

A few weeks before I shaved my head—all of it this time—I was at a party at a friend of a friend of a friend's house. By party, I mean it was very late, and I was in a group of men, and I only knew two of them, and I was a pretty, anonymous girl with a long blonde ponytail who seemed like something that someone could grab and fuck. When I closed my eyes for a moment as the sun came up, someone in the room said: 'Okay, someone tell me, whose girl is that?' There was a silence, and then one of the men I knew said, 'She's no one's', and though I'm grateful for that moment, I was enraged that it had needed to come to pass.

And I was tired of it, of everything—of being so visible in the world, like a flame or a dandelion or a lightning bolt; of being feminine in predictable ways; of being *desirable* in ways that were uninteresting and invasive to me. I had just gone through a breakup—there's always a breakup in a story about a haircut—that seemed to have no end, as my ex and I kept stretching back towards each other like the snapping of rubber bands. It wasn't that I thought I was going to totally disappear, to be replaced with some shining and pure version of myself, but that I hoped maybe some kind of metaphysical metamorphosis would take place. I wanted everything to change; I wanted to be delivered some different future, some alternative path that I could just take without asking and without having to think.

⁓

I've always questioned the utility of our concept of the self. Maybe that's not quite it—I know *why* we think the self exists, why we believe in individuals and identity, I'm just not sure it actually lives anywhere we can find it. Not anywhere *I* can find it, anyway, not when I haven't been able to strip every aspect of my own character away down to an empty nub. I've always been aware of the artifice I've maintained and developed over the years: the rotating cast of dramatic glasses frames, the septum ring, the clothes, the tattoos, the long hair I always found a way to hide behind. If you took all that away, I wondered, what would remain? Who would I reveal myself to be all along? I imagined pulling everything of myself apart, the way you can pluck the petals right off a rose by holding onto the pale green and stamen-wiry heart and twisting the flower in your fist. What would mine look like, once I had shed the velvety petals and let the colours fall away?

You don't shave your head without wanting everything to change. I wanted to run away from myself. Maybe it was me trying to channel the materialists, convinced that if my physical circumstance changed, the rest of me would too, and then I would have achieved nirvana, and then I wouldn't worry about anything ever again. What a dream that we would all like to believe is true—that the outside might ever reflect the in. But you already know what actually happened, and I suspect I already knew it too: of course we remain ourselves. Of course we are incapable of being anyone but whom we have been all this time.

A few days after I buzzed my head, I slept with my ex again. And again. And again. The short hair didn't change the way I was treated by men—the catcalls might have shifted in content, but the number didn't decrease; if anything, I got more attention. I still had the same anxieties; still had the same inexplicable, waterlogged depression; still had the same job and life and plans. I didn't become any more loving, or kind, or generous. I was still me, just with a different shadow, one that startled me when I saw it moving on the ground.

But it would be too simple to say that nothing truly changed. Of course I was different. It wasn't that a new life was handed to me, but that I felt I was capable of building one on my own. After the buzzcut, I felt tougher, harder—clean and useful, like a freshly sharpened blade. When you have no hair, especially if you're coded as feminine, there's nothing to hide behind. People look at you, even if they're not intending to; it's because they have nowhere else to look. It forces you out of being shy, makes you reckon with the white-hot gaze of the world. With my head shaved, I started wearing dresses again and experimenting with ways of presenting that varied from the usual routines I'd fallen into. Why not start looking in the mirror again, if what I had to look upon had suddenly changed and was now exciting and new? It seemed possible to be everything at once, even if I didn't know which part of everything was the part I wanted to hold. All of a sudden I *had* been presented with a blank slate—just not the blank slate that I was expecting.

For the first time in my life, I was strikingly, visibly queer. More than that, or perhaps more exciting to me, I was suddenly androgynous in a way that I'd only dreamed about before. The femininity that I'd been so proud of, the softness that I'd learned to treat as strength was also, I realised, something that had been chosen for me, never something that *I* had intentionally decided to make for myself. Now it was shorn away—how easy it had been, to remove a lifetime of being looked at as explicitly feminine, and how complicated the effects of it.

What I found myself presented with at this juncture was choice. I didn't have to look like a girl; I didn't have to be soft, or pretty, or easy to look at. I didn't have to be the messy-haired vixen that I had constructed myself as in my teens—in fact, I couldn't be that person anymore. I had removed something—not irreversible, but certainly not something that could

be repaired in an instant — and it was up to me decide, and to
continue to decide, what to do with it.

I think I was worried, then, and perhaps I am still worried
about it now — that in cutting away something that had always
been such an integral part of me, I would lose all sense of who
I was and tumble into the chasm of not knowing myself. After
the first cut, and shorn like a lamb, it fell upon me to maintain
my edge. More than the first, which didn't feel like a decision
so much as it felt like a verdict coming down, each haircut I've
had since then has felt like a conscious reification of my self.

~

At first I made my friends do it. It was easy enough — just
put the clippers on level 2 and run over the whole thing like
mowing a lawn. Santi did it a few times. Once, I made my ex do
it, in exchange for all the times that I'd buzzed his sides for him
before, in an interaction that was neatly circular but didn't help
my progress through our breakup one bit. I grew to anticipate
when it was time for a trim — when you've got almost no hair at
all, even a millimetre feels like fuzzy, prickly overgrowth — and
eventually I switched to going to a barbershop.

It feels naïve to say this now, but there was so much that
I had to learn. There was an entire vocabulary, a language of
becoming with which I had no prior history — aside from doing
my friends' fades in a pinch when they needed it, I had no idea
how to talk about short hair. I talked to friends with short hair
about what words to use, how to describe the self that I hoped
to etch out in every visit. I learned to say *high and tight*, to say,
keep the sides short, to describe the way I wanted the back of
my hairline to be shaped (*round, but clean, and can you please*

trim the sideburns too). I learned to think in numbers—at first a 2 all over, then a 1 on the sides and a 2 on top, then a 3, as I experimented with growing it out.

And I learned to love the barbershop itself, how beauty became business-like, how practical and streamlined it all felt. The dull buzz of the clippers—so similar to a tattoo gun, another device I've tried in vain to use to reify myself—the chatter of clients, the smells of soap and antiseptic and pomade and styling wax. I was never in the shop longer than twenty minutes; once, a particularly efficient barber had me out the door in just ten.

Every time it felt like an affirmation. That yes, this was the fate I had chosen. Every time it felt like I was saying to myself, yes, this is my life, this is the right one. I loved how clean it felt to leave with a fresh cut, feeling soft and new and reborn, a few little hairs clinging to the back of my shirt—I loved those too. After all, who are we without our choices? Who are we without the decisions we make? For those months, especially the early ones where I kept my hair short and velvet-soft and tight, it felt as though I was literally shaping myself. Making and remaking who I wanted to be, who could also be the person I am becoming.

~

Maybe it's funny that in making a decision I'd hoped was ascetic and internal, I ended up mostly considering and recon-sidering the way I present myself from the outside in. I wanted my interior to change, for my broken heart to un-break and for my resolve to strengthen; I wanted to become from within like something that turns blessed and holy and pure all on its own. Think a peony blooming in the spring; think a lotus growing out of mud. But instead I turned my gaze towards the way I move through the world, considering for the first time in a long time if I truly knew what I wanted.

There are a lot of decisions made for us. Some of them are things we didn't get to choose, like the circumstances we were born into or the people we're drawn to or what makes our hearts beat fast. But there are some that were made for us long ago, and some that we might have chosen when we were young—like how to move through the world, whether as dandelion or flame or smooth river-stone. And those, I think, are ones worth interrogating.

Recently I realised that since I shaved my head, I've gotten to experience something that I've never experienced before. I've had to consider what I hadn't considered before, now that something as simple as a hairstyle can't be accomplished without a lot of waiting. I set my slate back to zero, though perhaps not in the way I originally intended. But now what I have—the freedom I have, the freedom I have built and continue to build—is the ability to make decisions. To cut, to shear, to grow it out. To start at zero and question—and question deeply—where I want to go from this new beginning.

Now, my haircuts aren't quite as satisfyingly efficient as the barbershop excursions I used to pride myself on. I started growing my hair out again after the winter had passed, about six months after I'd first gone for the big buzzcut. It's not always a revelation, not the way it once was, and I still find myself grappling with whether I'm really happy with how I look or not. Sometimes I feel uneven. Sometimes I wonder if I'll wake up one morning and do it all again, shear the hair back down to the skin. But I know, now, that it is a choice to keep going.

When you turn on a light, a room stays the same. It's not as though anything in it has changed from when it was in darkness; it's that now you see where everything is placed.

You strip a girl bare and she's still who she was. There's nothing simpler than being yourself. Lately, I've been running into people who knew me four or five years ago. They never fail to recognise me, and that surprises me — that beneath all of this I had a face, that it hasn't changed, that I'm still subject to enclosure within that wire-thin loop of the self. That no matter how hard I try to escape, I'm still here.

But it makes sense. I was never an empty room. It wasn't that I had to leave it all behind — but how incredible to be able to choose, to say, this is who I am.

The Harpy

Meredith Yayanos

Picture a woman—naked, hairy, soft—standing at the centre of an intricate mandala of mirror fragments, shattered into thousands of pieces shortly after she was born. Sync your breathing with the rise and fall of her breasts. Myriad glinting shards, like feathers, like eggshell or teeth, rise and begin to spin around her. Up she rises with them. As above, so below, unsteady yet determined as she goes, delving the core of all that cleaving sharpness. Her spirit is restless. Her inner voice is polyphonic. We are, herself, the eye of a rapid cycling storm, peering out at the world through a cyclone of refracted memories, my identity a vast mental murmuration.

I am suspended in place at the centre of this constantly shifting, ever-changing twittering machine, and suddenly I can't breathe, there's an enormous hand clamped over m███████████████████████████████████

~

151

'Linear time is bullshit,' I often say. My snarky way of admitting something's difficult. I can effortlessly play passages from Cesar Franck's violin sonata, learned in childhood, from rote memory. I'm capable of communicating openly and affectionately with a diverse cross section of humans and animals. I can pluck ghostly melodies out of thin air with my theremin. I have a reputation for building and fostering communities with nothing but tough love and a laptop. Meanwhile, simply getting out of bed is often paralytically difficult for me, especially during times of great stress. This brain is full of broken glass. My memory is riddled with blind spots and bottomless pits.

Should I happen to falter and peer into, or worse yet, fall into one of these chasms, I'm beset upon by horrors. Flashbacks and intrusive thoughts about ███████████ that have the power to disrupt my sense of place and time for hours, days, weeks, months, sometimes even years. Gaping holes. Rips and slashes. At any given moment, she is four, they are forty, you are fourteen, it is ancient, we are here and now, he is more and more myself, and I am legion. In tandem, I endure excruciating chronic migraines that sometimes last for weeks, wreaking further havoc on my retention of objective reality. When my mental health isn't good, I become a bewildered, aimless swarm of self, wheeling loosely 'round to roost in a single human body.

(Like I said. Bullshit.)

My psychotherapeutic journey to a more cohesive identity could've started in earnest when I was still a toddler. Instead, it began about two years ago, when I first stepped nervously into the office of an MFT (Marriage and Family Therapist) expertly trained in a gentle, compassionate approach to shepherding people through the deepest, most frightening regions of their minds for the purpose of unearthing, cataloguing, assessing, and healing root traumas. I can give names to facets of myself here without feeling quite so patently ridiculous about it: The Poltergeist, The Wolf, The Pearl, and, most actively these days, The Harpy. On my therapist's couch, I've finally found a place where I can safely unpack all of these proxies without worrying a flock of men in white coats is going to show up, toting oversized butterfly nets and threatening ye olde Five One Five Oh.

While neither shaman nor doula, my therapist has entered my life for purposes of healing and birth. Since committing to this process, I'm finally starting to make sense of things I never could before. For one hour, at regularly scheduled intervals, we sit, and I mostly talk and she mostly listens while I cautiously reach into myself, pulling out fragment after fragment of memory like shards, holding them up to the light, letting them catch and throw rainbows. I will say, 'Look at this', and she will say, 'I see.' And somehow, that's some of the most powerful healing magic I'll ever know.

The daily reality of living with complex post-traumatic stress disorder and as-of-yet indeterminate dissociative issues isn't dissimilar from that of a confused child who has awakened to find herself abandoned at the centre of a scorched blast radius, mysteriously surrounded by wreckage and ruin, and having no idea how she got there. It's possible I'll never know precisely how I ended up like this. Many of us who have our mental development impacted by repetitive trauma early in life, and who continue to experience substantial trauma later on, never learn our sad little origin stories.

a cold, massive hand spreading across my tummy and
chest, his hot breath, reek of aftershave and ███████

███████████████████████████

I won't speak for others, but I've realised that for myself, knowing for certain whodunit (he's likely to be long dead by now,
anyway) doesn't matter half as much as finally pulling free of
decades of crushing, suffocating deadweight. For me, psycho-
therapy is chiefly about learning to live in the present moment
by accepting the current shape and depth of this adult-shaped
but decidedly atemporal human I've evolved into without any
sense of embarrassment or self-loathing. 'Fuck shame' is my
mantra, and dammit, I'm stickin' to it.

The therapeutic process is only beginning for me. It's been two
years of rigorous, often terrifying emotional and analytical work,
and yet I've realised I'm still only in the preparatory stages of
waging the battle not of, but for, a more wholly unified life. It is,
and will probably always remain, perilous work in interesting
times. But the rainbows are beautiful, down in these rabbit holes.

I've never been a religious person. But I confess that the regularly scheduled act of engaging in talk therapy, and my devotion
to several equally well-established mini-rituals that now spiral
out from that centralised act, is nearer to a consistent spiritual
practice than anything else I've tried. In recent years, I've discovered myself divulging long-buried secrets to my therapist
that, previously, I couldn't even admit to myself in my deepest,
most tranced-out automatic writing. While we're in session,
my therapist is simultaneously audience, witness, and guide
to any number of internal, fragmentary selves. I imagine that
the unburdening I feel in the aftermath of an especially intense
session is not dissimilar to the sense of having a curse lifted. It's

readily comparable to various descriptions of spiritual ecstasy or rapture experienced by human beings of various faiths for millennia. The only word I can come up with that comes close to describing it? Enlightenment. Not meditation, not orgasms, not even *music* get me there in quite the same way. Only self-acceptance through systematic acknowledgement, confrontation, and relinquishment of long-repressed trauma is granting me the release I've longed for.

As of now, Therapy Day is the only truly consistent window of physically anchored time I've been able to establish in my life in well over a decade, ever since having a nervous breakdown in the aftermath of an emotionally and sexually abusive relationship that occurred in my late twenties, and then falling far too soon into a subsequent series of co-dependent death spiral partnerships that never should have happened. I grieve every day about that particular life chapter. I'll likely spend the rest of my life recovering from ██████████████████████████ ███████████████████ and making amends to those I deeply regret harming as a result of not seeking help for my mental health issues much sooner.

Every bit of every Therapy Day, externally anyway, follows a concise and regimented script. I begin preparing myself hours beforehand with different forms of self-care and meditation in order to feel safe and present enough to do the work. I set multiple music alarms on my iPhone, usually with specific songs to bolster and insulate me. I take my meds. I get my customary 'morning constitutional' social media rantings and ravings out of the way early (often while taking my post-coffee crap, appropriately enough) before ditching the fast and dense gravitational pull of cyberspace for most of the day. I do this to carve out more psychological headroom around the therapy appointment. I make sure to eat a light breakfast (hardly my norm) so that my cortisol and blood sugar levels are in a good place. I spend a long time deciding what I'm going to wear, not out of anxiety or vanity, but because every item of clothing I choose on Therapy Day is consciously selected to pull up a particular thread of narrative. Every outfit I wear helps me to sort out what part of myself I want to invite to the front, to be most present and focused during the session. Sometimes I wear the cuddly knits, like long distance hugs, that my mother makes for me. Other times, like a berserker preparing for battle, I'm armoured up in spikes and leather. Then I get into my car and drive into San Francisco. While listening to a mix I made specifically for this drive, I try to prioritise what I want to talk about that day: fugues and flashbacks, my hypervigilant anxiety, confusing interpersonal friction, how to better manage certain triggers that still have the power to unleash my explosively terrifying dissociative rage and ███████████████████████████

That ecstatically furious part of myself is called The Harpy.

It was during a fifty-minute hour that I was first able to tell someone, safely and without worrying too much about scaring them off, about how and why this deep, seemingly ancestral rage that so many traumatised children carry all their lives feels like the manifestation of some kind of bloodthirsty, filthy, untouchable monster of vengeance. To admit that no matter what I do, there are always going to be these beastly parts of me that exist solely to protect me at all costs, even if it means tearing apart someone who inadvertently trips my reflexive internal alarm system.

I sing to myself. I breathe from the bottom of my lungs. By

the time I arrive at the session, mid-morning, I'm as ready as I can be. And when the hour is up, I keep going through ritualised motions. This somewhat exhausting, uncharacteristic laser beam focus upon commitment to self-care carries me through the rest of the day. I feed myself meals that I love, I text friends who I'm thinking of to remind them I'm grateful for them, I walk, I make music, I dance, I wander on instinct, I take notes on the session, and in the evening, when it's time for sleep, I drift off more peacefully than usual.

Every Therapy Day, at mid-morning, I drive into SF across the Bay Bridge, park in a carousel style garage on Mission, withdraw the cash for my session from an ATM on the ground floor, and cut through the ritzy Westfield Mall to get to the historic Flood Building on Market, where my CPTSDOMGWTFBBQ-specialising MFT keeps an office on one of the upper floors. I call cutting through the ground level Bloomingdale's 'running the gauntlet'. The last place I called 'the gauntlet' was a certain corridor of my high school, where the preppy kids hung out. Whole lot of the same sights and smells in Bloomie's: wealth, whiteness, arrogance, privilege. Upsettingly defanged feminisation. Images of airbrushed and sandblasted babysoft giantesses with cheekbones that could cut glass, baring impossibly even white teeth at me in supposed greeting from various display cases. Ugly designer purses like bling-encrusted bowling bags. I don't even pretend to browse. All you have to do is take one look at me to know I'm not here to buy $200 makeup palettes, but merely passing through. Breathing through my mouth, holding my head up high, tasting the miasma of basic beeyatch perfume, 'Fuck shame,' says I. It's a path that halves my arrival time to my MFT's office.

This particular Therapy Day, I'm not feeling social. I'm not feeling gentle. The Ghost Ship burned down a week ago, taking thirty-six comrades and friends of friends with it. From *The Daily News*: 'Before the Oakland warehouse became the site of a deadly fire during a late-night dance party on Dec. 3, 2016, it was a haven for artists—a labyrinth of makeshift studios and affordable homes. To others, the space was a disaster waiting to happen—featuring shaky staircases made of shipping pallets and outfitted with improvised electrical and heating systems.' Someone recently told me it took less than five minutes for smoke inhalation to pull all of those sweet, queer, gorgeous humans out of the world. *Could've been any of us.* Today, my internal world is simultaneously raw and volcanic. Today, I am The Harpy, clad in bedraggled feathers, a black jacket covered with patches and pins, and a brown waxed cotton Stetson hat, now dripping rain. I stomp the aisles in motorcycle boots, in warpaint, in headphones. I'm listening to the latest bounce of a nasty analogue synth ditty my current music partner just sent me, called 'Split Me Wide Open'. It's about as laid-back and retiring as the title suggests. Every last particle of me is awake, alive, and accounted for as I step out of that pristine tomb of prettification, jaywalking across steaming BART grates to get to the Flood Building on the other side. Realising that I've still got a few minutes to kill before my appointment, I wander into the Anthropologie on the ground floor, asking after leg warmers. No dice. Guess *Flashdance* isn't in this season, for once. But I do find a five-minute hourglass full of glittering silver sand, and The Harpy cackles with delight, remembering the reference to an hourglass in another song I've been working on. *Time's up, young man, time's up.* Snatching the bauble up in a scarlet talon, I speed through checkout, bouncing back out onto the street again briefly, cold drizzle welcome on my face, before looping back through the tall, heavy atrium doors that lead to The Flood's grandiose lobby.

The Flood Building stands where the Tenderloin verges with the Financial District. Old school. Elegant. Hardy. Survived the 1906 earthquake. One of the only structures downtown that didn't fall, didn't burn. Right now, its lobby is about as intensely and traditionally decorated for Christmas as anything west of Macy's in NYC, circa 1945. Walking in off the street, it's like immediately entering the depths of a pine forest. The heavenly scent cleanses the last remnants of Bloomiestench from my nostrils. Breathing deeply, I wait for the elevator, listening to a demo of the aforementioned 'time's up' tune, called 'Mother Tongue'. It's a perky pop song about our impending apocalypse. *You know, the one we can blame entirely on Abrahamic zeal-otry and hegemonic patriarchy.* Stepping into the posh, gilded elevator, pushing the button to the twelfth floor, I listen to my own voice, in Harpy mode, singing, *Here she comes, up she rises, rises like a firestorm.*

Stepping out of the elevator, pausing in the hallway, now, thinking, *This is church. This is a temple sojourn. This is a sacred space in which to bear witness to myself.*

My therapist is a graceful woman of indeterminate age with a quiet radiance about her. She opens her office door and smiles warmly, then more quizzically as she notices the bulbous manic pixie dream toy in my hand. 'Bought it on a whim,' I tell her, setting my cash for the session on her desk, turning to peer out of her office's enormous window with its dazzling view of neighbouring skyscrapers, wintry afternoon sunlight filtering through fog. 'Let's put it to good use. I'm giving myself five minutes to discuss the emotional fallout of the Ghost Ship, and then we have to move on. Some of my most upsetting mental dumpster fires keep flaring up, recently. I'm having fractalised flashbacks about ████████████████████████████████, which roll right into some of the childhood horror shows, 9/11 in NYC, that mugging at gunpoint, the car accident, the ruptured appendix, all of this ████████████████. Matryoshka of trauma. Seven-layer Inception burrito flashback fuckshow. It's *bullshit*.' She's calm (*Unflappable!* crows The Harpy) as she settles into her chair, clipboard at the ready. 'Tell me what's on your mind.'

Deep breath. Stay present. 'Here we fuckin' go.' I place the hourglass on the end table beside me, and the first grains of sand begin to tumble down. Turning back to face her, I swiftly work my way through unpacking the more awful and heartbreaking emotions that accompany looking after devastated loved ones, traumatised in the wake of the Ghost Ship. Time enough. The glitter sand runs out, then she and I proceed to spend forty-five minutes of our fifty-minute hour talking about

bleeding out on the side of a highway, screaming 'GO BACK FOR THE REST OF M█████████████████
████████████████████████████████████

The scars all over my arm that was nearly severed in two places in a car wreck, long ago. 'They're twenty years old, now. I love them.'

The brutal damage done to my crooked jaw during the re alignment process when I was four and the subsequent barbaric orthodontics that messed up my jaw and teeth, resulting in this hatchety hag face and tongue

████████████████████████████████████

'Breathe, stay in your body,' both she and I remind me. That trauma's not something I'm pleased about. But I love my monstrous organ. My very own mother tongue. More powerful, more versatile by far than the soggy prick I'm about to remember being raped with in a few moments' time. And I'm learning to love my witchy yiayia hatchet face.

'Fuck shame.'

The circular scar on my outer left wrist where I burned myself with a Djarum, years ago, to keep myself from spiralling into full bore psychosis during a ████████████████ flashback and jumping off a roof. (Bullshit. Bullshit. Bullshit. Bullshit.) Precious to me. Glad I don't resort to spontaneous ██████ or any of that other seemingly self-loathing shit anymore. But still, every time I look at that little white lump of scorched tissue, it feels like a stern, loving kiss from myself. Because that branding kept me alive and

> it's 2004 and I'm getting raped by my drunk boyfriend while lying on my stomach unconscious. I come to, feeling him digging his pointy man-in-the-moon chin and nose into my back between my shoulder blades. He's as blotto as I am.
>
> Waves of low, sinking, limitless horror wash over me, not only about my current state, but peering, quite suddenly, into a deep, black void of memory, from which emerges, faintly, the voice of a tiny little girl, screaming 'get away from me ████████████████████████████
> ████████████████████████████████
> ██████████████

It'll be several years before I dare admit to *myself*, let alone verbalise it to anyone else, that I'm being raped, and that I am not simply recalling, but entirely reliving other, much older violations as it occurs.

I go numb, frozen against the mattress. *This'll teach us to try to keep up with his binge drinking.* And yet, blotto as I am? I am still not okay with the events that are unfolding currently.

Nope, this is *not* fine, dog.

I decide to make it all go away ████████████████

████████████████████████████████

Ain't no body that can hold me yet, sings The Harpy, almost wistfully, suspended, incandescent, above the void.

Where am I? What time is it? What's happening? I'm suffocating. Help. My therapist's face, through the quicksilver murmuration of ███████████████ and other terrible memories, like a lighthouse beacon. Oh, thank goodness, it's not happening all over again. None of it is real. Not the way this couch is real, or her kind eyes, locked with mine. 'Let's pause for a moment, okay? Deep breaths, Mer.' Tears running down my cheeks. 'It's okay. You're safe.'

I nod, grabbing a tissue from the end table beside me. Gotta keep going. Plundering onward, deeper, weirder. 'I'm pretty sure I must have blacked out again, eventually? Maybe I blocked the rest entirely out of my memory? I don't remember him finishing. The next morning, after shuffling to the bathroom to pee, and sitting down, I wasn't thinking about anything except my hangover, until my pelvis started... vocalising. Not hyperbole. That happened. Holy shit, that really happened. I've never forgotten the sound of my own frickin' vagina, literally yelling at me. Imagine if you heard Joan Rivers herself, piping up faintly from down below, like out of some eldritch PA.'

Through the waterworks, I bark out a laugh. My therapist doesn't join in; she's quietly watching me. 'This is not me speaking woo. My vagina was groaning. Felt sore and bruised. Like a separate country from the rest of me. As my muscles shifted, it began literally gurgling, rattling, as though trying to expel something...'

Bullshit. Bullshit. Bullshit. *Stay on target, grrrl,* The Harpy growls from somewhere behind my back molars. *Here she comes, up she rises. Take a deep*

breath, reach in, pull out a condom. Forget to exhale for a long time. Hold the slimy rubber up in the light. Stare at it. █████████████

'This was still pretty early in our relationship. But it definitely wasn't the first time that he'd left a condom inside of me. I'd already had to take the morning-after pill at least once before because of his rummy's habit of lazily overstaying his welcome. This was just the first time he'd failed to notice it. Or, apparently, that I was blacked out.' Christ, he never even *saw* me, let alone cared about me, I remember how he'd stare right through me while he ████████████████████████████

My therapist has set aside her clipboard. She is leaning slightly forward, entirely focused on what I am saying. 'It's okay. Keep going.' I continue.

'I didn't consider it rape at the time. I tried to reassure myself that it had been considerate of him to wear protection before using my unconscious body like a gym sock. I just kept telling myself, "I love him so much. I know he loves me. He just doesn't know how to say it, yet."' Bullshit.

Ugh. This is terrifying. I don't want to say any of this out loud. Someone will punish me for it. No one believes me. It's all gone

so dark, I can't breathe ▓▓▓▓▓▓▓▓▓▓▓▓ No one cares. No
one ever listens. *Fuck 'em. Fuck fear and FUCK SHAME. Burn,
witch, burn,* The Harpy cajoles.

'I remember I left his place *so* fast, without waking him up,
without saying goodbye.'

> I take a super long, hot shower once I'm back in my own
> apartment. Take aspirin, try to wash it all down the drain,
> sing to myself, caress my body with soap, the same way
> I used to when I was just a tiny ▓▓▓▓▓▓▓▓▓▓▓▓

'I remember he called me later that day to say, "Whoa, we were
both so drunk last night! I'm, like, so hungover! Did you have a
good time?"' *Well, did we? DID WE HAVE A GOOD FUCK-
ING TIME?* 'I don't for the life of me remember my response.

'I stayed with him after that happened for over a year, dying a
little more inside every day.' The rape *and IT WAS RAPE you
doubting fuckers* was my Boiled Frog Moment: the experience
that set the parameters for our entire relationship, wherein
I compartmentalised like a champ while this man continued
to assault me and lie to me, and I kept right on loving him.
WHY THE FUCK DID WE DO THAT? Because it's what
good girls do.

He used me like a meat puppet. Cracked me like a safe.
Climbed me like a ladder leading to richer clients, bigger celeb-
rities. Some of whom he still works with to this day. None of
whom are a part of my life anymore. I still miss them.

*In her heart, in her body, so many black holes. All of this rot
and ruin.*

'I still miss me.'

Disassociation cam, from above: watching myself looking out
the window at sunlight shifting through thick fog. 'You know, he

never did tell me he loved me. Not once. Seemed almost oddly proud of it. Decided it was important, when he dumped me, to make sure I acknowledged that he had never lied to me.' *Not about that particular thing, anyway. He lied about everything else.* Trailing off, staring at the tiny silver mountain inside the hourglass. Might as well be peering down at Mount Everest from a great height.

'Where are you, right now?' It takes me a second to figure that out. *Get back in your body, honey.* The Harpy squeezes my leg above the knee, digging in with long red nails, and I'm back, safe in my own skin. My therapist is murmuring similar affirmations. 'Your body isn't anyone's but yours. You're reclaiming space for yourself. This is so important.' Nodding, gratefully drinking in the assurances, looking back down at my lap at what's probably half a box of wadded Kleenex, torn to shreds between my viciously manicured fingers. *Keep going, grrrl. Magic hour. Get it all out. Burn it all down.*

'He's most likely the one who gave me HPV. That guy's abuses definitely destroyed whatever was left of my sense of wholeness and personal agency for a very long time. Couldn't bring myself to go to the gyno for nearly ten years after that relationship, which recently resulted in my nearly getting cancer and having most of my cervix LEEP'd away. That was right before I started coming to see you. That's the health scare that woke all of my most loving monsters up.' Rising like leviathan, Grimm and Greek and grinning, shrieking together in one terrible voice: *FUCK SHAME.*

FUCK YOUR SHAME IN A WELL-LIT PLACE IN FRONT OF EVERYONE

The Harpy tips her hat to Jenny Holzer. 'I think that's when

I finally knew I wasn't gonna let some mediocre dick be the spiritual death of me.' It was during the cauterisation of my cervix, a procedure performed free of charge, minus anaesthesia, at Planned Parenthood, that I somehow managed to hold my ground, heels pushing hard into the cold steel stirrups, clinging to the hands of a blessedly compassionate RN while a lady doctor in a headlamp leaned forward between my knees, murmuring soothing words as she pried me open and nuked the site from orbit. Somehow, through all of this, I did *not* fly out of my body into the festive poster of hot air balloons pinned directly above my head. I stayed put, for once. 'It was one of the most powerful healing experiences I've ever had. And...'

I look up at my therapist, astonished. 'So is this.' She stays quiet. My cue to continue. 'I'm burning him out of my body right now. I'm burning it all out. Mentally, physically, ancestrally. I'm carving my birthright back into myself with fire, with breath, and with loving intent. I'm doing it in broad fucking daylight. That's what this is.'

Ritual of rage. Ritual of flame. Ritual of healing. 'I've never said all of this out loud, before. Not to anyone.'

A sudden, rudely startling burst of raucous male voices from out in the hallway. Couple of oblivious dudes getting on the elevator. It breaks the spell. She sets aside her clipboard. I glance at the clock on a low bookshelf behind her chair, just in time for the two of us to smile together, saying in unison, 'Time's up.'

Gathering my things to go, I unsuccessfully attempt to not apologise to her for doing precisely what I pay her for, then I apologise for apologising, and then I thank her profusely. Rain pouring down outside the window. 'Don't forget your hourglass!'

Laughter like liquid gold. I'm trembling as I leave, but not with fear. It's relief. Release.

The ritualised space holds steady as I descend in the elevator. Grinning back at the lobby concierge behind his huge, wreath-bedecked desk, a man who is by now quite used to seeing me emerge from the elevator with a puffy red face. Ravenous. Time for my customary post-therapy ramen back at the mall. The steam from it hot on my cheeks, more effortless tears salting the thick broth. Then I let myself do a dérive through the Financial District with my headphones on, wandering in the cold mist warm-bellied, on autopilot, the hourglass tucked into my jacket above my heart, listening to a sublime piece of music called 'To See More Light', composed and performed by a long-lost lover I think of often, who I'm unlikely to ever see again. More tears falling, then, grateful ones, for the recently dead and for the even more recently resurrected. Droplets pattering on the brim of my hat. A deep, low thrum, some kind of kundalini feeling spiralling through my entire body, circulating from the base of my spine to the crown of my head in languid figure eight patterns.

So far, so good. Here and now, just like we should be.

Whenever I find myself in these moments, I'm always more certain than I've ever been, am further convinced on deepening, ever-strengthening levels, that my body and my life belong entirely to me and no other. In these moments, I am entirely without doubt or fear. Melting with love and gratitude. These are the moments I have survived for.

I put on The Harpy demo for 'Chains': *Goddess help you if she ever gets her tits together. Saints and angels keep ya cuz she's finding ways to work the chains that bind her.*

Bliss fugue. Around 4 p.m., a frantic text comes in. I am urgently needed back in Oakland, because ███████████

██

██

██

██

██

████████████████████████████

And now it's pitch black, clammy night time—seated behind the wheel of my battered car in a Wendy's parking lot in Fruitvale, rain pattering lightly on the roof. Staring across the street at the blackened, charred husk of the Ghost Ship warehouse. I turn off my headlights and gaze beyond what few bright and tiny candle flames are somehow still lit in all this rain, beyond the mourners and neighbours gathered in small clusters by the chain link fence that city services erected to keep people out, which has since become an elaborate, rain-soaked shrine. Nearby, a trio of ladies converse in hushed Spanish, discussing when to bring fresh candles after the rainstorm to replace the drowned ones. So many devotional candles and flowers, soggy stuffed animals, wax-splattered cards and keepsakes, fluttering photographs. So much love burning back that darkness. Staunch Oakland love, stubborn and grubby and feminine. Incalculable grief and sorrow, rippling like heat, chittering like a million starlings.

I glance down. Where once I chucked the hourglass after returning to my car at Fifth and Mission, there's now a load of glass shrapnel and glitter strewn all over the passenger-side rug. 'Eh! Linear time is bullshit, anyway.' The Harpy starts cracking up, and so do I. Totes inappropes, but I can't ever manage to feel guilty for expressing mirth this close to the veil. *And we can't tell you why she's here, right now. But they know that this is church. This is a temple sojourn. This is a sacred space, and you are bearing witness.*

Now, on autopilot, I'm walking around to the passenger side of my car to retrieve the broken hourglass. It's still mostly in one piece, shattered near the top of one hemisphere. I carefully pick it up by its base, scooping a bunch of the glitter sand back into it. 'Less than five minutes,' I say to myself. 'Fuck,' I say to everything else. I wander back across the street. *Deep breath, Mer. Fire in the hole.*

I approach the fence and look, really look at what isn't there anymore, at what will never be there again. Peering straight down that pitch-black throat, my entire body starts shuddering. Through chattering teeth, I whisper some stuff I can't remember for the life of me; as soon as the words hit the air, they're gone. Not even echoes remain. One small, convulsive flick of my wrist, and all of the shimmering sand goes flying, blowing across the paper flowers woven through the chain link, dancing, pixelated, prismatic, with raindrops lit by the beams of streetlamps. I delicately set the empty broken hourglass down on the damp concrete, by a shrine under a corrugated piece of metal siding, next to a bunch of still-flickering candles illuminating the faces of young beautiful kindreds who will never slurp ramen again, or feel sunlight on their faces, or heal from ███████████

and it's all too big to see. It's too deep. It's too infinite, so I turn and walk back to my car, returning to the living, to my loved ones, to my home again, tears and rain still falling, humming a little fugue in G minor. Now I'm standing in the courtyard of the warehome down by the estuary where I've sublet a studio, touching my own face, my own body to remind myself what time it is, namely Now, still feeling the sticky grit of the broken hourglass's sand all over my fingertips. I grab my hat and bag, bounding up the rickety treehouse stairs to my own place. Therapy Day is winding down with one final ritual in the form of resurrecting fire in the pot-bellied stove in the corner of the room:

Wiggle toes, stretch limbs, crack knuckles, roll shoulders, wriggle hips, strip naked, squat 'n' chortle, build the pyramid of kindling. Take up your black matchbook with its gold-gilded statement of now rather dubiously poetic intent, 'MAY THE BRIDGES I BURN LIGHT THE WAY', and strike. Clap and briskly rub hands together, and watch the last glinting grains of sand tumble from your palms into the burgeoning orange glow. Tears still streaming. Love over will. Love above all. Manifest this, and all things, with joyful clarity and purpose. Dance with love. Do with love. Cash Askew, Em B, Jonathan Bernbaum, Barrett Clark, David Cline, Micah Danemayer, Billy Dixon, Chelsea Dolan, Alex Ghassan, Nick Gomez-Hall, Michela Gregory, Sara Hoda, Travis Hough, Johnny Igaz, Ara Jo, Donna Kellogg, Amanda Kershaw, Edmond Lapine, Griffin Madden, Joseph Matlock, Jason McCarty, Draven McGill, Jennifer Mendiola, Jennifer Morris, Feral Pines, Vanessa Plotkin, Wolfgang Renner, Hanna Ruax, Benjamin Runnels, Nicole Siegrist, Michele Sylvan, Jennifer Kiyomi Tanouye, Alex Vega, Peter Wadsworth, Nick Walrath, Brandon Chase Wittenauer. Be with love. Stay with love. We have chosen love. Here and now. So far, so good. Singing bravely, sweetly, into the flames:

Fuck shame.

Fingertips

merritt k

1.

A ritual to be performed every two weeks: take the train up to Broadway, walk up the street ten minutes to Helen Nails. Helen spins up a rotary tool, burrs the polish and hardened acrylic off your fingernails, clips and reshapes them if they've gotten too long. She dips a paintbrush into liquid and powder, painting on and shaping the resultant paste, which hardens into a translucent coating. Back to the rotary tool, smoothing things out.

She drags out the UV lightbox, paints a colour on one hand. Carefully insert your hand into the box, activating the light that cures the polish. Repeat the process. Rub in the sugar scrub she deposits on the back of your hands, rinse them off. Leave approximately one hour after you entered with nails sharp enough to puncture skin. Take a picture, post it online.

2.

I was a teenage nail-biter. A compulsive one—not so bad as some people I've known, whose cuticles frequently bled from their attentions, but a regular ripper and chewer. Given my childhood proclivity for my own fingers in my mouth, it's a miracle I never got into cigarettes. Maybe I didn't need them. I had an outlet for all my nervous energy in keeping my fingernails ragged.

When I finally started addressing the social anxiety that had defined most of my adolescence, my therapist suggested I try being more aware of my behaviours and body when I was nervous—a pretty standard suggestion to practise 'mindfulness'. I knew nail-biting was a nervous habit, I noticed myself doing it, and I stopped.

I don't mean to belittle anyone else's struggles with this kind of habit, but the truth is that I'm not completely sure how I cut it out. I might have slid back into it if I hadn't started painting my nails, which I hadn't been able to do since childhood—owing to the constant state of disrepair they'd been in for most of my teen years. Things got a little better around then. My hands stopped being vessels for anxious coping and became parts of me I was proud to show off.

I didn't have many parts like that at the time. If I'm honest, I still don't.

3.

My experience in growing up under patriarchy oscillated between hyperawareness of my body among my peers and a desperate attempt to forget about it during weekends spent locked in my room with books and movies. Two extremes, no comfortable middle ground. No sense of simple enjoyment in movement, capacity, or even just being. Constant scrutinisation of the self and anticipation of the other occupied all the space that the pleasures of embodiment might otherwise offer.

It wasn't until decades later that I heard of the term 'body dysmorphic disorder'. BDD describes a difficult relationship to the body—little things become obsessions and the mirror becomes something to either desperately avoid or spend hours gazing into. For someone with BDD, the smallest feature of the face or body can become the focus of intense loathing—the shape or size of a nose, a minor blemish, or a drooping eyelid.

The way the literature talks about BDD makes it seem like it's independent of social and cultural values. Maybe that's because psychologists would be out of a job if they couldn't point to universal psychological phenomena. But in the case of BDD, it strikes me as especially wrong. What's crazy about being appearance-obsessed in a society that overwhelmingly fixates on image and that explicitly assigns value to women based on their attractiveness?

Of course, the way psychology talks about disorders is now less focused on simply breaking norms and more on the concept of 'distress', and BDD definitely causes its share. There's the simple issue of time lost to fretting, social issues caused by appearance-related concerns, and even self-harm or suicide attempts. What looks to the outside world like a frivolous concern with appearance can feel to the sufferer like a life-and-death issue.

The value of having one little thing that is pristine, pure, and perfect amidst all this cannot be overstated. While wearing nail extensions hasn't cured my BDD, it's given me something to hold onto when things are bad. Maybe my hands just aren't a

focus of my mental illness, but regardless—I can look at them
and see one part I can deal with, recognise as mine, and even
feel positively towards.

Committing to nail extensions means having one part of me,
however small, be utterly perfect at all times. Barring breaks,
scratches, and the extremely rare—thank God—event of the
tear, my fingernails remain spotless. I can leave the house a
mess and still receive compliments on this one thing. More
importantly, I can feel put together even when I'm falling apart,
even when the world seems to be falling apart around me.

4.

Beyond a commitment to perfection, nail extensions also
reflect an ongoing investment in the body. Associated as they
are with excess and frivolity, they are a signal to oneself that
the body that bears them is worth spending time and money on.

In a very simple sense, seeing the nails as a rewritable canvas
is an invitation to take ownership over one's own body. Running
parallel to the notion of maintaining the body in accordance
with beauty standards is the thread that hey, this thing belongs
to/is you and you can do whatever you want with it. You can
get over-the-top nail art, you can tattoo all over it, you can shave
your head.

It's easy to be critical of the individualised, capitalist cult of
'self-care' as indulgence achieved primarily through purchase.
But such an analysis always risks sliding into blaming women
for being dupes stupid enough to buy into consumerist messaging about worth and value. Plenty of women already feel
guilty enough for treating their body as something worth caring
for—their struggle is less about recognising the limits of self-care

as a concept and more about learning to see the body as a real object deserving of loving attention. The trouble only arrives when this recognition is divorced from the context of patriarchy, or when it's treated as the ultimate goal of feminism.

Ritual doesn't exist outside of capital. Capitalism subsumes subjective time into clock time, it creates wage labour, it upholds exchange value rather than utility. Any attempt to create rituals for personal enrichment or appreciation inevitably gets sucked back into the system—'treating yourself' means going to the mall, the spa, the bakery. Don't worry, you'll pay yourself back in guilt later for these indulgences. Patriarchal capitalism demands a kind of two-faced logic of women: it sets up the conditions for 'indulgence' itself by presupposing 'good' behaviour, then dangles the possibilities to act 'badly' in front of us everywhere. You deserve it, but also how dare you.

5.

So much of beauty is a ritual, and it's easy to make it seem like more than it is by employing magical language. 'Glitter armour' and 'war paint' feel to me at best cheesy and at worst gross. Yes, makeup can be fun, but that feels more aspirational than realistic. Here and now, beauty is like a lot of other systems that suck but everyone has to relate to in some way—you're never outside of it, not really. I don't like getting lectures on this, either from men or from girls who just took their first women's studies class and are excited to dunk on femininity, but on some level it's true: beauty sucks and is scary and evil.

Beauty carries terrible costs. Most obvious is the personal cost to women who are implored to spend time and money in devotion to it. Related is the psychic and emotional cost of attempting to live up to beauty and always finding oneself falling short. But the costs go beyond consumers—consider the environmental and human costs of cosmetic production, costs that producers are happy to write off as externalities for others to worry about.

There have been two major feminist responses to the tyranny of beauty. One is to disavow the concept entirely, to refuse to participate in the injunction to present oneself as a normative (white) feminine figure. The other is to redefine the audience for beauty practices as the practitioners themselves—beauty for the wearer, rather than for men. The former approach is more associated with radical feminist traditions, the latter with liberal or 'choice' feminism. Both are admirable in their efforts to grapple with the burden of beauty, but each falls flat in their focus on individuals. The radical response places an inordinate amount of weight on the individual's capacity to embody anti-patriarchal values, while the liberal one can end up defining whatever a woman chooses in the context of patriarchy as good.

But what if we took the liberal feminist approach—that individual women's choices are all good—and twisted it a little? What if we decided that the individual's choices around expression and embodiment didn't actually matter that much, politically? What if we decided to forego the unending conversations around whether or not some bodily practice is feminist or not and resolved that all of these choices are essentially meaningless—that what matters is mass action rather than personal proclamations. The personal is political, sure, but they aren't identical. Maybe the personal is even just personal sometimes.

6.

The number one question I get about my nails is 'How do you use a computer/get dressed/go to the bathroom with those?' The answer I typically give is 'Very carefully.' It might seem flippant, but it's the truth. Long, sharp nail extensions that can rip tights, scratch skin, and smash off on all manner of everyday objects require care.

What are hands for? Pretty much everything: opening, moving, typing, cleaning, and fucking, to name a few. When I started wearing extensions I had to think about these activities more than I ever had—until I became more aware of my surroundings, I paid the price in broken tips. Something as simple as reaching for an object became an act that required more care than I'd previously mustered. And cleaning one's body or touching a lover's now meant considerable care to avoid injury.

It would be easy to paint all of this as an illustration of the ways in which the dictates of beauty confine and preoccupy women. In the same way as a high heel, the long manicured nail demands a certain kind of consideration, a practised movement, a restraint on the part of its wearer. I don't deny any of that, but I do wonder whether those experiences might actually have some value—whether it could be useful to be more conscious of how one's body operates and how one moves through the world, from a philosophical or even ethical perspective. Maybe it's the flagellant in me, but I think there's value in experiences that necessitate a deeper awareness of our bodies and surroundings.

7.

As far as I know, I'm one of Helen's very few clients who opts for long, tapered extensions. When I leave her shop, they're sharp enough to easily scratch skin—maybe even draw blood. Most women who opt for extensions seem to go for a natural-nails-but-better look, rather than an elaborate, over-the-top silhouette. That's more the territory of Instagram accounts, just like exaggerated contouring and novelty makeup application techniques.

Like contouring, the dramatic, aggressive nail extension can trace its history back to drag—a performative exaggeration of femininity. That these practices have now found their way to mainstream internet beauty culture is interesting in that it represents a cyclical pattern. Moreover, when men express distaste for 'caterpillar brows' or 'scary nails', it seriously troubles the simplistic notion that this kind of beauty culture exists for their benefit.

It's easy to state that we don't do things for men, but simply making that statement isn't enough to change a patriarchal culture. We still lust after beauty not just for its inherent value but its worth in exchange—the better treatment we know beautiful people receive and the fame, fortune, and social media validation that comes with a toned body or a pretty face. But beneath all of this, there's an undercurrent of something different.

Maybe sharing absurd beauty practices and the obsession with increasingly-dramatic looks is just one manifestation of a crowded environment in which YouTubers and Instagram users will do anything to differentiate themselves. But it also feels like a shift away from beauty tips expressly shared with the goal of enticing men towards something stranger—a coven of weird women playing and sharing with one another.

8.

The ritual space of the bedroom or the nail salon has been built upon by the virtual space of Instagram. While it isn't a magic circle in which the normal rules of the male gaze don't apply at all, there's something strange about it and similar online worlds. These platforms are places where women share images of beauty for the consumption of other women. I can't imagine that many men—except maybe a small percentage with hand fetishes—follow these accounts.

Here the difference between nail art and other beauty practices becomes clearer. Unlike fitness inspiration or makeup posts, which ostensibly might be followed by men for their voyeuristic potential, nail art Instagram feels like a space created by and for women.

This is the weirding of beauty, the decoupling of body maintenance practices from their patriarchal underpinnings to create a form that exists for itself, rather than for the pleasure—explicit or implicit—of men. How else to explain nail art that includes piled on gems, liquid seascapes, or even portraits of the wearer's favourite cartoons? Whereas no amount of disavowing the purpose of makeup can change the fact that beauty standards are a manifestation of patriarchy, it's hard to frame a hand adorned with lovingly-detailed images of the anime boys you want to see fuck as something that's pleasurable for a heterosexual male audience.

My own nails rarely ascend to such heights. Occasionally I'll have Helen add an accent stripe or apply a heat-sensitive colour-changing polish. Otherwise, they're a solid colour, albeit on a long, pointed shape. But even when I complete my little ritual by posting a photo taken just outside the salon on Twitter, the responses are less erotic than they are aesthetically appreciative—and they're mainly from women. I don't get unsolicited dick pics or requests for sex from strangers like I do when I post photos of my body. Actually, my hands are the only part of my body I regularly post pictures of at all.

9.

I stopped posting selfies for a few reasons, chief among them that the practice felt like an unhealthy quest for constant affirmation. It's not that I think there's anything wrong with selfies in general, it's just that posting them fed into my BDD—it became one more reason to obsess over my appearance and compare it to others. How many likes did I get this time? How many expressions of desire? And how many did that other girl get earlier today? It was too much.

Pictures of my hands just after a manicure feel safe. They elicit admiration rather than affection. And even if there is an erotic undertone buried underneath all that, it feels charged with power. Controlling my visibility is a source of strength. Resisting the demand to be seen, to make oneself visible has been a challenge, but a rewarding one. To be clear, I don't believe there's anything inherently moral about being more or less recognisable on the internet or anywhere else. This is just how I've navigated those waters.

Being unrecognisable except for my hands has become a part of my personal mythology. Sharpened talons and a grinning skull on the back of my left hand have become the only part of my body most people who follow me online have ever seen, and I'm okay with that. I'm more than okay with it—I draw power from it.

In a reversal of the disembodiment and dismemberment that culture constantly inflicts on women, I've located my self in my hands. And maybe that's appropriate. After all, my hands—rather than my mouth—are the vehicles through which I communicate online.

10.

While my nails might look threatening, I don't have any illusions about them actually being dangerous. At best, they project the signal that I am not to be fucked with—but even that's a stretch. They aren't protective in a literal sense. Instead, they help ward against the insidious effects of living in a patriarchal culture with a brain that tends towards obsessive thinking around the body. I'm not likely to fight anyone off with them, and if I ever tried, I might just end up hurting myself. But they do help me combat the idea that every part of me is flawed and doesn't measure up. They remind me that this body is worth maintaining and investing in. And they've given me a ritual to participate in, a space and rhythm weirded by women for our own ends.

Red Glitter

Sophie Saint Thomas

I chose the Frankencock.

She plucked it out for me from the black leather chest that contained her many dicks. Inside the chest was an extensive variety of dildos of various shapes and colours. There were white dicks, black dicks, purple dicks, medium-sized dicks, large dicks, dicks with veins, smooth dicks, a titanium dick, dicks with testicles, and dicks without testicles. When closed, the black leather chest doubled as a luxurious couch. The entire Manhattan apartment was decorated minimally with dark wood and black leather furniture. It was pristinely cleaned. She was a Virgo, after all. I felt like I was in *Fifty Shades of Grey* except everything was queer, poly, respectful, and took place in New York City. Nothing reminds you how outdated patriarchal penises are like a line of dildos sitting in a row on a black leather sofa ready to penetrate you. Double this when they're placed there by a beautiful person who fought tooth and nail for her achievements and resulting upscale apartment containing said chest of cocks.

The Frankencock looked like, well, the cock of Frankenstein's monster. It was massive, probably ten inches long with a four-inch circumference. The dildo was green and inhumanly veiny, and its testicles had bolts on it. It was a beautiful monster, like Frankenstein's. We got along swimmingly. When I came, I gave gratitude for where my life lead me. My giving of thanks was a form of magic. Practicing gratitude can be the most powerful spell you can cast. Using your orgasm for magic just means harnessing and intentionally directing sexual energy and the power of orgasm towards a goal—one that can be totally non-sexual in nature, such as getting a book deal. But sometimes it's nice to simply say 'thank you' when you come. Gratitude is a powerful form of spellcasting. Getting fucked on black leather with the cock of Frankenstein by someone I trust is, as the kids say, living my best life.

I've always been queer, and I've always been a witch. However, I didn't always use my powers or sexuality in a manner that served me best. I let myself be small. I accepted love and sex that was selfish and viewed me as less than. But I no longer live my life that way.

I don't know how to dismantle the patriarchy. Traditional attempts, such as reporting sexual harassment in the workplace, for instance, have gotten me fired. Asking male partners to please stop screaming at me for expressing myself has gotten me called names and screamed at even louder. And sadly, at time of writing, to my dismay and that of the many other witches who have tried, hexing Donald Trump has not succeeded in removing him from the White House. However, through my rituals that manifest intention into reality, I can work to dismantle my personal dependence on the patriarchy. As a result, I feel more powerful than I ever have in my life. It's a power steeped in independence forged through accepting and being true to myself.

I make my living by writing about sex and relationships. There's no way around the fact that my relationships impact my work and my lovers become muses. When I changed the way I engaged with problematic male figures through the aid of my rituals, such as sex magic, my writing became stronger, in more than one sense of the word. I became a better writer as I became more comfortable in my skin. Even after over a decade of writing about sex, sometimes I still struggle with shame. I worry what others will think of me, or that I will be seen as a two-dimensional sex object rather than an artist with a fascination about human sexuality and a desire to help others shed their shame for their normal, healthy desires. Such shame, fear of change, and fear that my open sexuality makes me unlovable lead me to stay in relationships after their time had passed. Shedding my own shame through rituals helps me write with more bravery. Perhaps by being brave myself, through my writing, I'll encourage someone to leave an abusive relationship or a partner who tries to bring them down, by writing about all the other ways to fuck and love that don't suck away your power like a vampire. A witch is just a person who is aware of and knows how to wield their power. And a vampire is no match for a witch.

I'm a Scorpio, which is the sign of sex, death, and rebirth. The tarot card that corresponds with Scorpio is the Death card, which in a reading rarely means literal death. Rather, the card often represents the death of a situation or habit that is no longer serving you; in other words, it means change. When I was little, I went through some big and scary changes. I grew up in the Caribbean, and more than once my family was forced to move because a hurricane destroyed our home. An outcome of the constant upheaval is that as an adult, change has been unwelcome in my life and I crave stability wherever I can find it. An unintended result of this is that in my twenties, I stayed in situations, especially romantic partnerships, far past their due date. Drawing the Death card meant dealing with change that I wasn't ready to handle, so I didn't. Instead I focused on the other symbols of the Death card: the image of the skeleton of death on its ghoulish horse is also often wielding a rose. I've always known that after destruction, life carries on—another outcome of growing up amongst hurricanes. Flowers grow from graves; out of death comes life. And now red roses are my favourite flower—hold the baby's breath. (I adore both flowers, but not mixed together.) I use red rose petals in two of my consistent rituals other than sex magic: tidying up my apartment and candle magic.

A former male partner of mine, T, who lived with me for about a year in my apartment, knew that red roses are my favourite flower. T often bought me bouquets of them (sans baby's breath) on special occasions. We were first friends, then lovers, and then partners. I cherish the memories best of T as a friend. He loved me and I loved him, but as a partner, he did not treat me with the level of respect that I deserved.

There was a string of incidences where T lost his temper and spoke to me in a sadistic manner meant to make me feel small. And then one night in the springtime, six months before I met the Frankencock, his demons once again emerged from the dirt surrounding his heart. This time, I didn't even react. I didn't cry or go after him as I often used to when he walked into the other room following the outburst. There was nothing left to discuss. After T's temper cooled he fell asleep; I stayed awake. I sat on the floor of my bathroom.

Sitting in contemplation on my bathroom floor has become a ritual of mine in the four years that I've lived in my Brooklyn home. Before I moved in, a woman lived there for several decades. When she died in the apartment, it freed up, and I moved in. The city instituted locks on how much you can raise the rent on such special haunted apartments, so my ghost guardian blessed me with a rent that's under market. Anyone who lives in New York City can confirm that such an experience is a miracle. So while sharing rent with a partner is easier, I can afford the entire apartment to myself as a writer in my twenties. Whenever I need to address dark feelings, I retreat to the bathroom. Sometimes I wonder if she died in there and this is why I'm drawn to sitting on its tiled floor during dire times.

In this night of bathroom solace, I knew that this relationship and my habit of putting up with shitty men had ended, no matter how many bouquets of red roses they bought me or how many times they professed their love. None of it mattered if it wasn't built on a foundation of mutual respect. The Death card no longer scared me. Still, ending a long-term cohabiting relationship is a major decision, so I slept on it. In the morning, I felt the same cool-headed understanding. I told T he had to move out. I gave him a month to do so, which—while kind and reasonable—turned into a disaster. I spent many nights that final month sleeping at my best friend Casey's apartment because I couldn't be in my own home with him. I felt angry and resentful that my home no longer felt as if it belonged to me, and I wanted it back. As the month came to a close and the situation became increasingly unmanageable, it was Casey who stood up for me and helped me reclaim my space as T finally moved out.

The night before T's departure, I slept in a hotel because he was still in the apartment packing up his things. When I woke up, alone, I realised something. I never had to date a man who treated me like shit ever again. I never had to date a *man* ever again. And though that last part was probably bullshit—despite my love for pussy and strap-ons, I can't pray away my queer mutual appreciation for penises any more than you can pray away the gay—I knew something had to change. I had to become strong and independent enough that I would demand respect, that I would never stay in a relationship just for emotional and financial security or because I was scared to be alone.

T texted that he was gone, so I came home. I was exhausted. It had been so long since I slept soundly in my own bed. The excitement of the next chapter of life awaited me, as did relief, but more than anything, on my way home, I felt anxious. I didn't know what to expect when I got back to my apartment. Would he still be there, angry? Would he be there with a bouquet of flowers in hand, a dozen red roses sans baby's breath, begging to have me back? Or would he simply be gone? It was the latter, complete with a note, and that inflicted the most pain. He left me with a reminder of his goodness and why I fell in love with him. It was a letter of apology, written with sincerity, on the same pad of paper I use to write out letters of intention when I cast spells and take notes for work.

My rituals aren't perfect. Despite my Virgo moon that screams at me if my underwear and bra don't match, my rituals are messy,

disorganised, and often spontaneous—like me. I was alone in
my apartment. It was dirty with a shambles not wholly my own,
but rather from the whirl of a prolonged and painful separation.
Drawers sat ajar, suddenly empty. Blankets I never gave much
thought to were suddenly obviously missing. The mess hurt to
look at. It was time to tidy up and reclaim my space. But before
I could move into the headspace needed to diligently clean up
the ruins of a relationship, I would need to make more of a mess.
I needed light and a ritual to prepare me for the difficult work
of cleaning up the remains. That meant candle magic. And
candle magic means glitter.

~

I didn't know how to carve my own candles when I moved
into my home at the end of the summer of 2013. So I had the
witches at Enchantments, the occult store in the East Village,
make a blue home blessing candle for me for my new ghostly
apartment. I came to Brooklyn after leaving another man, J,
whom I lived with in the Lower East Side of Manhattan.

Several traumatising events occurred in the months leading up
to my decision to leave J and move to Brooklyn alone. Any last-
ing rose-coloured lens of youth was shattered that summer. I was
sexually assaulted by a very violent person. My parents divorced
in a brutal manner. My mom got sick. I coped unhealthily with
alcohol until it brought me to such a bad place that I almost
killed myself in a blacked-out state. When I think of a tarot card
to represent this time in my life, it's not the rosy Death card, but
The Tower, which is far more frightening. The Tower represents sudden upheaval, disaster, often as a result of something
beyond your control. That was how I felt, terrified and out of

control after my assault and the tearing in my own family. So I began to make my own decisions. I knew it was time to give up booze. I enjoy cannabis and psychedelics, so I'm not sober by AA standards, but I've found what works for me. And despite my feelings for J, who is the first love of my life (yes, you get more than one), even if I didn't totally understand it, I recognised that I needed to take steps towards independence and freedom. So I sobered up and left. I did not leave J in a dignified nor mature manner, and I'm not proud of that. I snuck out in the middle of the night while he was out of the country. It was a vicious move. But what I do know is that the 2013 separation was required of me. I wouldn't work and write with the drive that I do unless I had to support myself, and I didn't have to support myself when I lived with J. And in retrospect, after going through a cohabitating breakup four years later with someone who took their goddamn time to move out, perhaps just getting up and leaving is a lot kinder than I thought.

I never got to burn my home blessing candle the Enchantment witches carved for me. I somehow lost it in my move from Manhattan to Brooklyn. Perhaps the candle disappeared because I needed to take control of turning the apartment into my own, and I did. I've been through hell in these walls, curled up sobbing, frozen in PTSD flashbacks. I've also experienced joy and happiness of my own creation that only comes from stepping into the independence of adulthood. I worked relentlessly at my writing. I smiled and laughed and came with various lovers. I curled up and snoozed with my cats. I danced alone at 2 a.m. to Bauhaus. It took four years and more than one bad relationship, but what was originally a barren row of rooms with a sleeping bag flung on the floor is now a fully furnished apartment (well,

I don't have a dining table, but whatever, couches are made for
take-out). The apartment became mine, and I became myself
in the apartment. It was a messy process of growing up that
included optimistically opening my heart and home to a partner with the end result of heartbreak. But that was part of the
process. It's not over yet; I still live here.

⤙

Now I know how to carve my own magic candles and always
have at least one burning in my home. After my split with T, the
one that created a deep gash in my trusting nature but taught
me how to stand up for myself, I carved two candles: one for
a house blessing and one for love uncrossing. Candle magic
is one of my favourite forms of spellcasting. Everything I've
learned, I learned from my other best friend, Annabel—an
astrologer who lives in the apartment next to me—and the book
The Enchanted Candle by Lady Rhea. With candle magic, you
enchant a candle with your intentions, and as it burns, your
intentions manifest. When the candle goes out, the spell is
complete. While any candle can do, the best are seven-day pull-
out candles that you can slide out of their glass jar. This way,
you can feed your candle offerings appropriate for the spell by
placing them in the bottom of the glass, such as rose petals and
honey for love. Various candle colours are for different desires.
For instance, green is used for money magic, red is for love, and
purple works wonderfully for creative endeavours. White candles can be used for any spell and work well for clearing. Blue,
the colour of the ocean, represents peace and serenity, which
is why it's the colour of choice for home blessing spells. Black
candles are good for karma balancing, or if you really want to

call someone on their shit. Some witches will strongly advise you against using a black candle, but I love using them. I've always been drawn to the bloodier-looking goddesses, such as Hecate, the Greek goddess of magic, crossroads, ghosts, and necromancy. While I must be careful to practise cultural appreciation rather than appropriation, I also work closely with Kali, the deeply misunderstood Hindu mother goddess of creation and destruction, who is fabulous at demon-slaying. And who can forget dear Satan? I don't think we need to be so afraid of black magic. The term black magic itself very often refers to certain hoodoo and voodoo practices, and it is frankly racist to label the terms white magic as good and black magic as bad. Humans are oh-so-messy and grey. My practice is glittery and needs all the colours of the rainbow to thrive.

Before I begin a candle spell, I meditate to calm my mind. You want to put emotion into your candle, but a brain scattered from too much time on Tinder and Twitter is not conducive to magic casting. After my meditation, I'll sage the area and all my supplies, including the candle. You never know what pesky energy could be lingering inside the candle, and you want it to be pure for your purposes and the deity you devote it to. I often work with Venus for love and Kali for protection, but I'll also use Rihanna for money magic and Freddie Mercury when I want to feel fab.

For my love uncrossing candle, I used a white pull-out. Usually, I tend to do a combination of following the spells in Lady Rhea's book and my own improvising. Lady Rhea founded the aforementioned shop Enchantments in 1982, which is why it's so well known for its candle spells. I meditated. I saged. I wrote a detailed letter of intention, ordering the removal of an unwanted obstacle in my love life, which in my case was a reliance on partners who treated me like shit. I fed my candle sugar and rose petals. I carved a sigil (a symbol believed to contain magical powers) into it as well as my name and the Scorpio symbol. I slathered it with uncrossing oil, purchased from an occult store in the Bronx. I then put down newspaper and rolled the white candle in red glitter until it resembled a dildo that could've been owned by David Bowie. Then I lit the fucker on fire and watched it burn. Along with my new, happy blue house blessing candle, my love uncrossing spell burned as I made the apartment my own dragon den. Even if you don't believe in deities or that the intentions crafted into a candle can be communicated to the universe through fire, candle magic is a powerful ritual. It forces you to sit down and meditate upon the changes in your life you wish to see, and then write them out. Magic requires hard work and follow through. I didn't expect just the candle itself to clear my love life of vampires and make me strong enough to live happily single, but by taking the time to make such intentions clear, I became aware of them. Awareness leads to action. You don't have to believe to benefit from rituals—for instance, simply carving a candle for the sake of making something pretty can be meditative—but having lived as both a witch and a sceptic, I've learned that life is more fun when you believe in magic.

~

T left on a Wednesday. The next five days I took off work and cleaned my apartment. I devoted an entire day to each room. Like J, T used to pay for a professional cleaner to come twice a month to tidy up the place. Now that would be on me.

I stepped into the long-misjudged role of 'women's work', one I was excused of for too long having lived with men who paid for cleaners. I'm not going to lie, I miss that part. I suck at cleaning. No matter how hard I try, I never seem to be able to get all the dirt from the corners. I've accepted my home as one that will usually contain some cat hair and dust, but perhaps one day I'll earn enough myself to hire a professional.

I scrubbed T away, skin flakes, semen stains, and shit molecules. I cleaned the entire apartment until it sparkled. I also scrubbed away the pain before him, from previous breakups and sexual assault. That, too, had to go; perhaps such pain had lead to poor partner selection. All the while, I knew the apartment would become filthy again. It looked like it was ready to get fucked up and I liked that. It reminded me of how I look stepping into the bedroom of a lover with my hair styled and makeup perfect. If things go well, when I fall asleep or hail a cab home, I'll have mascara smeared across my face. My lipstick will be gone, washed away by spit or rubbed off on orifices. My once-luxurious curls will be a gnarled knot of hairspray, formed by the hands of another.

When my apartment was as spick and span as my untidy self was capable of making it, it was time for a different type of cleaning. On my bookshelf sat an owl pellet. The bookshelf was from an Ikea trip with T. He put it together, not perfectly, but close enough. An owl pellet is not owl shit, as is commonly assumed. Rather it's a hard ball of owl vomit containing objects such as teeth, feathers, and claws of the beasts the owl devours but cannot fully digest. Owl pellets are used to absorb negative energy. They're like an air filtration machine but less expensive and for witches. Even though I had used bleach (I am not always the best witch when it comes to opting for natural cleaning supplies in an effort to save the Earth), I still could feel the pain. I ran the owl pellet along every wall, and I hissed. *Hsss! Be gone. Get out.* I hissed and I howled. I shoved a towel into my mouth, sat in the bathtub, and I screamed. I screamed into the towel with the force that I could never show T in return for all the times he screamed at me. I screamed and I hissed until I no longer wanted to make ugly noises. I screamed until I wanted to feel good again, and then I saged. Not only is sage believed to have cleansing properties, but unlike an owl pellet, it emits an odour of calm and comfort. After enough saging and screaming, it was time to clean myself.

I filled the bathtub, in rare pristine form, with warm water. When I had gone candle shopping at Enchantments, I also picked up a bag of uncrossing bath salts, which I filled the tub with. Along with my candle spells already burning, I lined the rim of my bathtub with tiny red tea candles. Red is the colour of love. I stepped one foot, and then the other, over the row of flickering candles to gently lower my naked body, smeared in matching red glitter and various magical oils, into the tub. I stood in the dimly lit tub and stared at my feet as they created small ripples. The water was scalding. Once it became bearable but still deliciously hot, I slowly lowered myself down to a squatting position, allowing the bathtub to take over my weight. Glitter and magic oils hovered around me. Finally, I stretched out into full relaxation and let the warm, magical salt water cover me up to my neck. Then I grabbed my magic wand.

It's not a magic wand like Harry Potter's, not even like the Hitachi. My wand is a waterproof sex toy that stimulates the clitoris using air puffs. There's a cute little suction cup on the end of a pink water gun. I swear they haven't paid me to say this, but I'm going to tell you because it seems cruel not to: the name of the toy is the Satisfyer.

Once upon a time, when I was in ninth grade, I squirted. Or I thought I did. My girlfriends and I had bashfully walked into the lone adult toy store in my town and each bought vibrators. I bought an aqua-coloured g-spot toy that in retrospect was surely not made with body safe materials. I didn't even know about g-spots; I just liked the snaking curve of the ocean-coloured toy in comparison to the rows of flesh-coloured sticks. At home, worried the sounds would wake my parents upstairs, it made me come. As I did, I noticed fluid pooling under me. I must have only been fourteen years old. I had heard about squirting, but I worried perhaps I just peed. A lot of people think squirting is peeing, but it's actually fluid from the Skene's gland, which passes through your urethra but is different than pee. If the patriarchy didn't control medical research, we'd have more information on the subject. I first fucked someone other than myself at sixteen, and at twenty-nine, in nearly a decade and a half of partnered and solo sexual activity, I had never squirted again. I knew all about it from my work as a sex writer, but I had decided that I wasn't one of those women. On this night of cleansing and magic, I was about to find out I was wrong.

I placed the suction cup, like those that line the eight tentacles of an octopus, over my clit. As I soaked in the salt water, watching the red glitter slide off my body and mingle into the water, I turned on the vibrator and enjoyed the deep sucking sensation that began in my pussy and spread throughout my entire body. For the first time in months, I felt my body fully relax as I let go into the pleasure. I imagined my future self, dressed in sequins and leather, at a book premiere, completely self-sufficient. I imagined myself feeling completely loved and content in a manner that was neither selfish nor clingy. I imagined the salt and glitter carrying away my self-doubt. I came. As I did, I felt a burst of fluid emanate from what felt like my urethra, but it wasn't pee. I took a deep breath and relaxed further, and a wave of even more of my come filled the tub, rippling down against my legs and becoming one with the glittery salty magic bathwater. Holy shit. I had just squirted for the first time in at least fifteen years. With that orgasm, I felt the release of not only the breakup, but all the pain and sexual shame I had been carrying with me. I've been able to squirt regularly ever since.

～

I've become more empathetic but less forgiving following that night of sex magic. I've ended new relationships at the first sign that the person isn't able to give me what I need — often to their shock — in situations I would have stayed in at another age and another time. I worry about becoming cold. I worry about having such high standards that I'll never find a partner. However, so far that's not been the case. I'm single but loved. I have lovers and partners who respect me, such as the owner of the Frankencock and others who may turn into long-term partners when I'm ready for another relationship.

There's a key ingredient in my life that I owe all of my strength to: friends. The best thing that has ever happened to me is finding my two best friends, with whom I can share my soul, my fears, my insecurities, and my love. My independence is both a result of and dependent upon my coven. I believe that of all the rituals, my friendship with them is what has dismantled my dependence on the patriarchy the most. They are a constant source of love in my life. When I'm feeling sad or insecure, I speak with them, rather than grab the phone to text a dude like I used to. They support and encourage my queerness. They remind me that who I am is wonderful. They hold no opinions back when I develop a crush on a shithead. It's much easier to choose lovers who respect you when you have such wonderful friends that you're never alone.

My rituals are ongoing, not a quick fix. Just like the world will take time to dismantle the patriarchy, my own unpeeling has been gradual. I'm still growing and healing and crying and smiling. You see, I used to date people who made an effort to make me feel small and unworthy, and at least temporarily, they succeeded. While men are often drawn to that which glows, with time, some want to crush it so no one else can enjoy the warmth. Being told that you are less than and treated in a manner disrespectful to your magic, can be hard to recover from. It takes time, and I honour that. Often making a rapid change rather than gradual ones results in snapping back to old habits. I know I must *continue* taking glitter baths, making love to myself, and reminding myself that a full life is not dependent on having a romantic partner. Such relationships are lovely, but it's difficult to find proper companions when you're unsure of yourself, so I work through my rituals to become aware of my self-worth and date those who reflect it while honestly aiding in my growth and calling me on my shit. I continue to burn candles to ward off vampires and attract abundance. I squirt often, most often alone, sometimes with lovers. And I continue to keep my apartment, my home and sanctuary, (fairly) clean, although I've accepted that my floor will always be scattered with cat hair and red glitter.

Touching Pennies, Painting Nails

Sim Bajwa

I don't really know what to call the rituals the women in my family practise and the power behind them. They wouldn't call it magic and would only sometimes call it superstition. They wouldn't attribute it to religion either; Sikhs are instructed not to believe in rituals. It doesn't help to classify it when all the information I have is from word of mouth, stories, and advice passed from woman to woman. Their rituals are simply a kind of faith. A faith in being able to keep your family safe, in being able to ward away anything that would bring them harm. A kind of *just in case* magic that changes and shifts between generations and families.

My childhood in Britain was different from my mother's childhood in India, and the way these kinds of rituals were performed for her when she was younger wasn't the way they could be performed for us. We didn't have the same kind of belief in this power and were only reluctantly willing to go along with it. To make sure that we would carry out her instructions, she needed to simplify. To share her power, she needed to tweak and adapt her rituals, to make them accessible to us. It didn't really matter to her if we believed in this power. The important part was that she did, and does.

When I was younger and had been getting sick a lot, my mother gave me a red ribbon to tie around my wrist. I never asked what it was for or why it was supposed to work. Another time, she had my brothers and I dip our fingers in a shallow metal dish full of olive oil, and then touch pennies she kept in a small bag. I remember when I was maybe sixteen, my younger brother had been getting in a lot of fights (he used to have a temper and no real grasp of consequences). My mum gave him yet another bag of pennies and told him to drop one in a running body of water every morning on the way to school. I'm not sure who told her this would help calm his temper or what the significance of the pennies was. I know that in India, throwing pennies in holy water is considered good luck, but my mum told him that any river or canal would do. In adapting all these rituals to fit our lives, she was sharing with us her power in a way she thought we could understand.

There were so many instances of this—half-remembered rituals that my mum performed and had us participate in, on the edges of my memory—and I regret not paying more attention. I can recall some details of her rituals, maybe a little bit about why they were supposed to work, but I can't replicate them. I never expected these gaps in my memory to bother me in the way that they do. My mother couldn't control how the world shaped us, couldn't control who made us feel bad at school or in the workplace, couldn't control if we achieved what we wanted, and at a certain point, the control she had over our behaviour disappeared too. But she could make the world a little smaller for us with these rituals. She could exert her power and feel comfort at having given her children some armour. If I've missed out on harnessing that power for myself, then I only have myself to blame.

I ran from my culture and the rituals and beliefs that my mother and aunts brought to it for so many years that coming back now feels alienating in a way I did not expect. I guess I thought that it would all still be there, happening around me in the same way as before, back when I had no desire to participate but was enveloped in it all anyway. And in a way, it is. My mum still walks through the house with incense every day, still only washes clothes on certain days, still does the odd ritual to ward away the evil eye—*buri nazar*. It'll be a ritual that her mother had told her about, or something one of her aunts mentioned. But I'm still outside this part of my culture, looking in. It feels strange to be writing about it all too—as if I'm picking apart something that just *is*. It makes me feel tentative; I don't believe, but my mother does. It's new ground for me to recognise these rituals for what they are: a way to capture hope and power.

My mother has stopped trying to explain things to me, though, and when I show an interest now, a desire to learn, she looks at me as if I'm still that petulant sixteen-year-old, rolling her eyes, so desperate to leave. I don't know how to explain why it feels urgent to know now. Her rituals have existed around me through my life, but this won't always be the case. The position we ended up in—one where my mother gives power and I reject it—is one I want to shift, and I know the responsibility for this is on me.

I come from an intensely patriarchal family. Though my own family unit—my parents, me, my two brothers—may not seem to be, I have a cousin who was only allowed to eat her meal after her father and brother. I have another cousin who wasn't allowed to wear anything except traditional clothing at home and was threatened with a slap when she pointed at some model in a perfume ad and said he was hot. There are other cousins—distant from me, some whom I've never met—who are told they don't need an education because they won't need it in their marital home. I've always considered myself one of the lucky ones, as much as it burns to call agency 'luck'. I got an education, I have a job, and whenever I challenged any instance where I felt I was treated differently because of my gender, I got scoldings and lectures, never a slap in return. But now I'm twenty-five, marriageable, and part of a family and community that refuses to see a woman as someone who has value on her own, outside of her relationship with a man.

It feels incredibly difficult—impossible and pointless at times—to resist and fight against their enduring belief that an Indian girl respects her family, keeps her father's honour, gets married, keeps her husband's honour, teaches her sons that they are to be honoured, and teaches her daughters that they are to honour. The peripheries might be different—you might have a job or not, you might live with your in-laws or not, you might drink alcohol or not, you might have a life outside of your husband and children or not—but the core remains the same. You are modest and self-sacrificing, servile and accommodating. You come second. You don't get to be selfish; you don't get to consider your own comfort first. There's no room for women who aren't cisgender and heterosexual. There's no room for women who want sexual agency. The men will do what they want and they're not going to listen to arguments or contradictions. They think of their anger as a right and their wives' anger as an indulgence. It's a trap, and maybe my mother and my aunts and cousins know this, because with these lessons, they also hand down seeds of female anger that seem to grow and bloom and twist to fill the space underneath our tongues.

Growing up, I was desperate to leave. I felt like if I didn't, the walls around me would get smaller and smaller until I lost myself. There would be no room for me to do what I wanted and my decisions would be made for me. This is the way I saw my mother when I was younger—every time she didn't do something she wanted to, every time she bit her tongue, every time she was underappreciated. I wanted to move out, I wanted my independence; I didn't want the language, the obligation, the thousands of tiny ways that I was treated differently for being a girl. I associated everything to do with my culture with limitations and being told no. I felt stifled and fearful that I would never have my own life and would march on behind my older cousins, all living the lives we were told we should aspire to. I thought I was stronger for being loud and vocal about what I didn't want to do, about what I didn't agree with. I thought the women who didn't were weaker and too scared and should just *speak up*. I didn't get that they were angry too, and that my rage was only an addition, not the exception. It's embarrassing to think about how reductive and self-centred this view was.

I feel like my family—up and down and spanning generations—is built on silent feminine anger, born from decades of ingrained male entitlement. It's an anger that manifests in bitten tongues, flared nostrils, a door slamming a bit too hard, everything just passive aggressive enough to be explained away. It can't be too overt because that would push things too far. It's the kind of silent anger that sits in your belly and festers. And it's *isolating*. It makes sense that my mother turned to ritual for relief from this anger. She operates within a network of women with similar beliefs and rituals, giving tips and tricks, making comparisons and giving advice. It's a space where gossip is exchanged and grievances are aired. Support is given and anger is validated. They bring their daughters into these spaces, lending them some power too. But I felt like an outsider in these spaces because my beliefs didn't align with my mother's; I didn't care about her communal power or about letting her into my spaces of resistance. I used to feel like if I let myself be interested, if I listened and gave my attention, then I would be giving in and I would lose my independence—and that was the last thing I wanted to do.

As soon as I could, I ran off to the closest city for university and then I ran off to Scotland—almost as far as I could possibly get while still being on the same island. Leaving was its own form of resistance, as I got the space I craved so much to work out who I was without strictures or limitations, but it didn't allow any room to come back home or to see anyone outside of myself. In all of this, I never stopped to think about the women in my family and what they felt or to give them the credit that they were due. I would roll my eyes when my mother told me that some things aren't so simple. That shouting doesn't always mean strength and that if a woman is silent, it doesn't mean she isn't angry. When she told me I speak as if I 'have a pair of scissors for a tongue' (while snipping with her fingers), I took it as a compliment, though she didn't mean it as something positive.

I learned to be more empathetic and understanding as I got older. At least, I learned that I needed to be more empathetic and understanding. When I was younger, I didn't have the patience to consider what it must be like to be in a marriage within a family that will allow men more mistakes than women and where women are supposed to tolerate their husbands' flaws while twisting themselves into an 'ideal' wife, daughter-in-law, mother. When this attitude has seeped into so many corners of your life, when the knee-jerk reaction to resistance is to feel guilt at neglecting your obligations and duties, how easy can it be to speak up against it? I *could* speak up when I was a teen-ager because my mother gave me the space to do so. She was the voice in my defence and she was the one who wanted me to go to university, to have a career. She would slip me money when I needed it, and she was the one who convinced my dad that I should move out for university. There are all these little moments that I remember now, where she would push for my father to treat my brothers and I equally. It was never a loud, angry demand but a quiet, steady conversation. It was subtle enough that I didn't really understand at the time how much she was on my side. I was so busy tying her up in all the forces that I felt held me back that I didn't see the way she resisted *for* me.

I never claimed any of my mother's rituals as mine, but along the way, in amongst my efforts to break away, I made some of my own. They're different from my mother's, but they have the same core. They shrink my world in times of crisis, where I control what I can with self-care rituals that make me feel a little more powerful, a little more able to deal with the world. I can't speak for why my mum's rituals centre around pennies and luck, around avoiding certain things on certain days, on drinking from copper cups at certain times. In the same way, she can't really speak for why my rituals revolve around my nails, my makeup, and my eyebrows.

My rituals involve me and no one else. This could be in reaction to a world that gives women less value, reaffirmed through the sacrifices I see the women in my family make every day. I resolved early on that I wasn't going to be the one serving a man, that I would never be the default for any kind of household or emotional labour, and that I wasn't going to give up even one thing that I wanted to do for anyone else. As a result, I ended up finding rituals that I thought didn't have space for anyone else. I paint my nails every other day—the ritual of removing, buffing, base coat, colour, top coat as familiar and calming as stretching. For no real practical reason, my nails are always painted, a splash of colour that'll clash or compliment what I'm wearing. Either is fine. There's a sense of emotion in it too—some days, a red or a blue or a green just doesn't feel right. Sometimes I get a colour in my head and I'll hunt it down. Maybe I need a plum or a mustard or some shade of grey with a hint of purple. Other days, I need glitter.

It's a small assertion of my space. My nails, the way they catch the eye, the space my polishes take up, my supply of remover and cotton pads. My day was bad, I'm broke, my co-workers in my all-male-except-me office were condescending and sexist, but for fifteen to twenty minutes, I know exactly what I'm doing and what the result is going to be. And I know tomorrow, my nails are going to be bright and glossy, and I will have made them that way.

Makeup has a similar rhythm and purpose as a ritual. Primer, foundation, concealer, powder, liner, lipstick. (Contour is hard and I can't be bothered.) It's another piece of control, a way to tell the world, 'Yes, I'm ready to deal with you.' I like how I look with a dark dark lip, big winged liner, and my hair wild and curly. I also like how I look with a bright red lip, carefully lined, with my hair straight and pinned back. It's like painting on a shield—one that I choose and tailor for the day.

The final part is getting my eyebrows threaded every two weeks. I've always had thick, unruly brows. The familiar routine of knowing when to close my eyes, knowing what auntie means by 'stretch', puts me on solid ground every time. My mum took me to an auntie's salon when I was sixteen to get them threaded for the very first time. This was one of the many women who I'm not related to, but who are aunties simply because they're older than me and they're Desi. I paid little attention to the women who worked in the salon, the women whose names my mother knew, and the things they talked about around me. I let their words pass by me as I considered the fact that I can choose what my eyebrows look like, choose how they frame my face, how thick they are and what shape they are. In essence, I ignored the spaces and ways in which my mother and her peers asserted their agency, because I was too focused on finding my own.

These are women who moved to a foreign country and built new lives, some who set up their own businesses, finding ways to be financially independent. They exist in the patriarchal framework that I always wanted to escape, but they have created spaces where they call the shots. In my family, my mother holds a huge amount of power, though it's not always obvious. She runs a business, she handles the finances; she might check everything with my dad first, but she's the fulcrum by which my family functions. She grasped this agency gradually over years and uses it to make decisions for her family, rarely focusing it all around herself. It was often easy for me to be oblivious to that because I wanted all the power over my life, and I wanted it right now.

The time, attention, and money that go towards my nails, makeup, and eyebrows are for me, and me alone. I don't care if the smell of my polish is annoying or if I'm needed to do something in the kitchen, but I can't because my nails are still wet. I don't care that the money I spend on my eyebrows could be better spent elsewhere (although anywhere that charges you more than £5 is a rip off, and you should find a Desi auntie's salon). I don't care if these rituals are inconvenient for those who want me to fill a predestined role, and I don't care if that makes me selfish. Because, hey man, what I want matters. I matter enough to put myself first; I matter enough to take up space with colour and clunky bags of lipstick and polish. I also know that performing these rituals keeps my resolve in place. They give me strength and they are also the foundation for my resistance, because if I can say, 'No, I'm painting my nails', then it's only a tiny step forward to say, 'No, make your own food', or 'No, I'll go out if I want to.'

There have always been stark differences in my mother's rituals and my own. My mum's are communal and intended to protect, to incorporate family and loved ones. Mine are usually solitary and unapologetically about what I want. In some ways, this reflects how different we are as women. She's much more willing to compromise and let things go and is naturally affectionate. I am terrible at letting things go or offering kind sentiments in general, I hate compromising because it feels like admitting I'm wrong, and I tend to forget hugs are a thing. She's sociable; I like being alone. She's more respectful than I am, friendlier, better with kids. In some ways, she's a lot braver too. This is a woman who, in her early twenties, moved to a different country where she only knew two other people, learned a new language, pretty much just rolled her sleeves up and got on with it. And then there's me at twenty-five, unable to travel around a new city without wide eyes and shallow breaths and looking at Google Maps every five minutes. She also takes very little shit from people—including me. The reason no one can ever offend me is probably because no one can truly roast me like my mum. We have very different outlooks on life. She is terrified I'll never get married or have children by twenty-eight (thirty at the latest). I'm terrified that I will—that the Natural Order of Things will take over and I'll give in to familial pressure—and that I'll be stuck in a suburb with a husband and children. Our common point is the anger that we clutch in our fists over continual patriarchal attempts to take our agency, and the power that we created for ourselves in response—and it doesn't matter if that power is tangible to anyone else. Having belief in these rituals is like strapping on armour, piece by piece, before wading back into the world.

Recently, there's been an unexpected shift in how distant our rituals are, and it feels as if tendrils of our resistance are reaching out and twining together. Circumstances changed and I had to move back home. It's been weird to tell my restless feet to stop twitching because realistically, I could be here for the long haul. I've also been forced to confront my own inability to see beyond what has always been and what the future could be. I'm spending more time with my mother than I have in seven years and realising how much our anger and our resistance overlap.

Our rituals are maybe not so distinct and separate, and maybe my own rituals aren't as solitary as I thought. My mum bites her tongue a lot less, and looking back, her anger has gotten less silent over the years. There are now moments when she decides she's going to say no. She'll tell my dad to make his own dinner and tell her mother-in-law to wait if she wants something, and she doesn't let anyone use her like an endless well of labour and emotional support. I find myself wondering if she has her own quiet rituals that I don't know about because they're all for her.

A couple of months ago, I went to an auntie's salon with my mum—something I hadn't done since I was eighteen. I got my eyebrows threaded and, for the first time, listened to conversations between women who work in the salon with their customers. They talked about their husbands and in-laws, how one woman will be a business owner and mother and wife and cook and cleaner, and still her husband will consider himself to be superior. A pocket of space that I would usually associate with my mum's rituals had opened up in a ritual that I considered mine. I had a moment of wonder, where something in my resistance paused and said 'Oh.' These women could be allies, not obstacles or another force to overcome, and I had missed this for a long time. My rituals could have included this all along, if I had only let them.

I think about what other secret spaces I missed because I wasn't looking, so focused on wanting to leave and carve out my own. Maybe a flaw in my resistance of the path that was set out for me, and my resistance against the belief that a woman's priority is never herself, is that I refused to be tied down in any way. I'm always so afraid of my wings being clipped that I won't let them rest. I'm trying now, trying very hard, to find some kind of balance. I don't want to be swept along into making sacrifices that are somehow inherently mine to make for being a woman, and I don't want to get too comfortable putting the men in my life before me. But it can't be a bad thing to try to open up my own rituals, to find where mine have common ground with my mother's. If I incorporate her into my rituals, let her in to understand why they're important to me, or let myself participate in hers, it doesn't have to mean that I've lost. It can mean sharing power and lending support; it can be both armour and a hand to hold. I feel like we're edging towards each other, however slowly, and I wonder where we'll end up. If I adapt my rituals to this new version of my life, where I live amongst everything I used to run from, then I'll only be doing what my mum did when she told my brother, it's okay, any river or canal will do.

Ritual in Darkness

Kim Boekbinder

The floor was cold and the room was dark, nearly pitch black. I sat holding my knees, rocking, barely breathing. I was in shock, I knew that much, and I knew I didn't want to be there anymore — not there and not anywhere. I rocked myself again.

'Are you okay?' I heard a voice say.

No one else was in the house. I realised the voice must be my own. I heard myself ask again.

'Are you okay?'

I answered. 'No.'

The night before I had watched in horror as a very large minority voted for an authoritarian white supremacist rapist to lead the 'free' world.

No. I was not okay. I might never be okay again.

~

Gather:
Sea salt
First aid kit

⁓

Before the 2016 United States presidential election, I had been having nightmares; hiding from Nazis was the common theme. Nazis at the door, SS officers coming to find us, me and others hiding in closets and behind walls and under tables and beds and floors. My brain had plenty of fodder for these nightmares as both my grandparents had survived World War II, my grandmother in occupied territory and my grandfather in a concentration camp.

People had been making Hitler comparisons for months, of course, and I had read the account of how Trump kept a copy of *Mein Kampf* on his bedside table—for the speeches. But it wasn't until I spoke to my grandparents that the fear really hit me. 'What's happening now in the US reminds us of what happened in Europe before the war.'

After we hung up I sat still for a long time, staring at the brick wall in my East Village apartment, thinking of how their past was now my present.

My dreams intensified after the election: I would wake in my beautiful bed from some of the worst nightmares of my life to find that my waking life was worse. Facing the world as it was shaping up in 2017 made me wish I could hide in my bad dreams.

I had a tour already booked, flying from city to city to play concerts. In November 2016, airports were terrifying places, full of older, wealthier white men. I thought it must be an order of magnitude worse for people of colour, for women wearing hijabs, for anyone already at risk of violence in the best of times.

⌁

Gather:
Rosemary oil
Multi-tool with a good blade

⌁

On a plane I watched the flight attendant in the aisle taking drink orders. As she neared me she shook her head sadly while staring at an older white man in a seat a few rows ahead of me. She was a beautiful black woman in her late thirties.

'Is everything okay?' I asked as she got to my row.

She leaned close and said, 'A man up there just grabbed everything out of my hands, didn't want to look at me or touch me, didn't say thank you.'

'Do you think it's because of the election?' I asked. She nodded, and then thought for a moment.

'I've been working here eighteen years and it's always been this way, but it is worse since the election.'

'I'm sorry.' I gave her a 'Pussy Grabs Back' sticker and told her about my song of the same name, and she laughed out loud, startling the people around us. For the rest of the flight, she laughed and gave me a high five every time she passed me.

⌁

Gather:
Vetiver
Kevlar gloves

~

'We'll make our corner of the internment camp pretty,' my friend C and I would joke before the election.

Three days after the election, on a respite from my tour, I went to her apartment for a gathering of close friends, many with visas from countries we all knew were 'undesirable', many of us visibly queer, or trans, or publicly anti-fascist and anti-Trump. We gathered in solidarity, drank in shock, reaffirmed our commitment to our friends.

In the early morning hours I watched an orgy bloom on the floor. There's no aphrodisiac quite like impending doom.

When I sang my song 'Sex Magic' at my next concert, I thought about this scene.

Come put your magic inside me
Your diamond tipped, your salty sweet
Your hardest hard, your softest soft
Come get me high, I'll get you off

~

Gather:
Blue Cohosh
Plan B, morning-after pills

~

In the days that followed the election, I read about the sharp rise in hate crimes against people of colour. Against women.

I read and researched. I bought books on fascism, authoritarianism, civil rights, resistance, and revolution. Mostly what I learned was that what we are experiencing now is not new, or novel, or special. Technology and culture change the details, but the core rot is the same.

I started putting together a go-bag—a pack of essentials that can be grabbed in an emergency. I researched first aid courses and made plans for what we would need in various situations: fire, flood, hurricane, active-shooter, power outage, martial law, total social collapse.

I made zines and distributed them randomly, anonymously. They were full of information: how to stay sane in an authoritarian regime; infosec/opsec; basic safety and first aid tips; and some angry words for those who had brought this nightmare upon us.

I held gatherings—maybe they would have been called 'teach-ins' at another time.

I felt history crashing in on me; it felt oppressive, it felt fake, it felt like we were trapped in an alternate dimension.

None of this could be true. I wanted to be anywhere but here.

But as bad as the shock was, I knew that the worst time would be when the shock faded and it was all normal.

I had panic attacks for months.

꙳

Gather:
Lavender
Water purification tablets

꙳

As 2017 progressed my shock remained, but behind it there was anger too. I was so angry that this could happen, that we had let this happen. Angry at the selfishness of the people who could vote for this. Fuck them.

And I felt more hopeless than I'd ever felt before. I've been dark. Dark, dark. I've been on the verge of no longer existing on this planet, but this was different—this was worse. The world has often been a troubling place full of bad things, terrible things, but progress was happening, or so it seemed. And while my personal demons may have held me down at times in my life, I knew that the world was turning on as always, that even on bad days there was hope out there, if not for me, then for someone. But now it truly felt like there was no hope. For anyone. The world was being taken over by greedy autocrats and insane, hateful racists. Not only in America. North Korea's Kim Jong Un seemed intent on vying for the title of 'World's Most Immature Despot', but Trump was giving him a run for his money. The Middle East was in crisis, spilling refugees by the millions into a Europe that was breaking apart on its own.

We thought neoliberalism, for all its faults, was enticing enough to keep its stranglehold on the global economy, but even it had failed.

And I felt a failure in my own creative expression and in the creative expression of others. It felt like all the art, the books, the music, the films that had been made about equality, love, fairness, fierceness, inclusivity, and community had all failed. We had all failed. Our art had failed. If the people in wealthy, prosperous countries, full of art and access to things most humans haven't even been able to dream about, if these people could choose genocide over equality, then what, exactly, was the point of any of it?

I didn't know what to do.

I kept singing.

'The Well' is a spell for justice. I wrote it years ago about war crimes the US commits to this day. When I sing it, I sit on the floor of the stage or in the audience. Sometimes I hold hands with an audience member. Often, people are openly weeping. Often, I am too.

Will I feel it, do you know
Will I fall, fall, fall
Will I feel it, do you know
Is there a bottom to this well?

～

Gather:
Burdock root
Wind-up radio

～

I read more. Books by activists, black women, who've been fighting this for years and years, and years and years. People who know that the struggle didn't just begin and won't suddenly end. I read books by women: Hannah Arendt, Angela Davis, Octavia Butler.

Knowing that the struggle is not new, that it has been going on for a long time, is comforting. Reading their words was helpful, because the struggle is bigger than me, bigger than now.

The world we're working towards isn't going to happen in my lifetime, but that doesn't mean it isn't worth fighting for with everything we've got, because every inch along the road towards a fair world is worth everything that I have and everything that I am.

The plague of sociopaths in power, of narcissists mortgaging our futures for their own gain, is an old problem. Fascists and authoritarians rise and fall. They always fall. Their world is not reasonable, rational, or sustainable. They will lose, as they always do. It's up to us to mitigate the damage.

In January I wrote this chorus:

We're the body
You're the disease
We can get better
We can be free

⁓

Gather:
Agrimony
Compression bandage

⁓

My Opa was a member of the Dutch resistance, a teenager at the time. He and a Catholic priest would forge documents to get Jewish people out of the country, onto ships headed for America, or Canada, or anywhere—ships that were often turned away. To make his documents authentic, my Opa had to steal a stamp from the SS office, an offence for which he would have been shot on the spot. He had to go back twice, two stamps for each document. He made thousands of these documents.

His family used to hide other Jewish people in the walls, until finally it was his family's turn to be swept up and taken to a camp. Somehow, they didn't believe it would happen to them, but of course it did.

In the camp my Opa watched his family starve to death. He watched people beaten, tortured, shot, burned alive. He was at Bergen-Belsen, a camp so notorious for its horrors that the Allied soldiers who liberated the camp were scarred for life.

When the British found him, he was lying in a mass grave, where he'd fallen; he weighed 78 pounds, he was six feet tall, he was seventeen, and he was an orphan.

These were the stories I grew up with. They were a distant history, a terrible relic of a terrible past. Look how far the world had come.

My grandparents always told me not to trust people. They told me not to dye my hair or stand out in a crowd. They told me I could love whomever I wanted, men or women or both, but that I should be private about it. They told me not to go against the grain. My grandparents loved me, wanted to protect me from the world they knew, the world I thought was ancient, past, never gonna happen again. Surely not.

Their concern was cute.

Until it wasn't.

~

Gather:
Candles
Flashlight/windshield breaker/seatbelt cutter

~

A week after the election, I started lighting candles with F in her small, beautiful apartment. She was in shock too. And we were both angry. We talked about hexes and curses, harm and hate, the dark things we wanted to do. What if we had the power to kill at a distance? Would we?

The anger was real, but the hate couldn't find a foothold in us. More than anger, I had care for others, and I wanted to light candles for them, for the people who would be most hurt by this terrible, impending administration.

At night we gathered our supplies. I recorded a special piece of music for the occasion, and it played in the background while we chanted:

Unity, Protection, Clarity, Understanding.
Unity, Protection, Clarity, Understanding.
Unity, Protection, Clarity, Understanding.

F worked the herbs and the salt in a circle on the silver platter; she anointed and lit the candles. We held our hands over the flames, and I felt myself leave my body, spreading out over the country and the world, protecting, protecting, protecting.

~

Gather:
Passport
Cash
Rugged backpack

~

It's been a year now since that dark day. The administration has tried to do many terrible things and we have resisted fiercely; they are fought at every step. But still they manage to do great harm: passing laws, attempting to build the stupidest wall in a global history of stupid walls, deporting people, arresting people, and making white supremacist ideals publicly tolerable.

Nazis have killed people in America this past year, slitting throats, gunning people down, running them over in cars. Nazis waving swastika flags and torches scream for 'safe space' to spew their 'free speech' full of hate and genocide.

I take this all very seriously. But I also know they have already lost. Because they always lose. Nazis are, quite famously, losers. The Nazis, the Confederates, the white nationalists, the KKK: losers.

Many more people may be hurt by this administration and its minority of hate-filled losers—people may die. I may die. But the Nazis will lose; of this I am sure.

I toured across America this year, playing concerts in Midwestern cities and desert towns, in rock clubs and in living rooms and in DIY spaces, and I have found in every place that there are thriving communities of creative, queer, intelligent, caring, wonderful people who will fight for their freedom and the freedom of others, because they know more than anyone how much is at stake.

I don't know how much damage the fascists will do. I don't know if we're going to be okay anytime soon. But I know that we can be okay. I know that it is possible. And I know that there are millions of us working every day for this very possibility.

I've done my rituals, my gathering. My pack is ready. I know where everything is, how everything works. I hope I never need it.

I gather the essentials; I light candles to centre myself, as a kind of meditation. I perform daily rituals of caring; I am mindfully kinder to strangers because this year has been stressful to us all. I prepare my first aid kit to help others if they need, and to help myself if I need. I prepare myself for a long resistance to tyranny. I prepare myself to fight for what I know to be right. Some of the rituals are boring, mundane things, like calling my representatives, because I know resistance is rarely glamorous and work takes many forms.

Resistance is in my blood. It's my birthright. My grandfather stood and fought and lost his family. And survived. Being a member of the resistance is one of his proudest achievements.

The Nazis, the alt-right, far-right, right, and centre, those so concerned with their 'free speech' have woken their own doom.

The great irony is that while Trump woke them — made their views seem tolerable, possible — they woke me; they woke many of us.

In their silence, I was dormant.

I've always been active in social justice activism. I've gone to hundreds of protests, donated money to causes, organised, and worked towards a better world. But I didn't push as hard as I should have. I would protest, but avoid arrest. I would stand my ground, but be afraid for my physical safety. I would voice my opinions, but surely I would never hit anyone. I would never advocate violence.

And now?

Punch Nazis. Punch them literally and figuratively. Make them afraid. Drive them back into the miserable hell they so clearly want to live in. Destroy even the possibility that their ideologies might be tolerated.

Let me be clear; I don't *want* to punch anyone. My hands have better uses: making music, making love. But my hands won't be free to do these things if the Nazis get their way. I'm ready to do what I need to so that the people I love can live free.

When the Nazis and their sympathisers weren't so concerned about their free speech, I was merely an annoyance to them, a person whose lifestyle 'choices' made them uncomfortable, a person they chose to see as a threat.

But now that they are loud, I have become dangerous.

Gather what you need.

Care for those around you.

Light a candle.

Punch a Nazi.

Gayuma

Sara David

As an orphan of diaspora raised by New York City schools, I grew up knowing none of my family history. I could have felt like a freak because of my fat, brown body, my clueless bespectacled braceface, or my clumsy English words, but mostly, I felt like a freak because I was always alone and peculiarly close to death. It is easy to feel like there is a vast, uncrossable expanse between yourself and anything resembling a home—easier still when your histories are purposefully or fatefully obfuscated by death, war, or shame.

To excavate stories that are supposed to remain hidden is to unbury your connections and find your roots. But then your work has just begun: you must water them if you are to bloom.

⁓

There are countless supernatural qualities of girlhood: being forced to hone and rely on our intuition; moving in synchronicity with the moon; the violence and gore of our transforming bodies. Every woman knows what it means to be a mortal monster, to be Medusa crucified for the vessel she was born into.

The occult world is by definition hidden, veiled—a liminal space with which every woman is familiar. All women are witches. In liminality we've been forced to see beyond—and in this we carry memory and past. As a queer Filipino immigrant living in a nation of vibrancy, potency, and poison, my rituals excavate the lives we've been forced to keep secret or leave behind.

But the occult world is orphic. Like Orpheus's voyage to try to bring his wife back from the underworld, learning the rules and languages of the spirit realm is a journey through darkness. We, the children of diaspora, the daughters of refugees, have traversed darker.

Estranged from my mother and mother tongue, I must find ways to feed my ancestors. The spirit world is a private universe and a natural home for women: Here, our suffering serves a purpose. It is calling me to my destiny.

～

My grandmother Aurora Basa was born on March 18, 1934, in Cavite City, Philippines. She was a healer and a witch.

Aurora's parents Joaquin and Marciana, a doctor and pharmacist, were prominent healers in Cavite who had converted their home into a clinic to help Filipino and American freedom fighters during the Japanese occupation of World War II. The healers gave generously to the rebels even when they had little to give. The family subsisted almost entirely on eggs laid by a single chicken on the property and used coconut water instead of inaccessible saline solution to fill recuperating soldiers' IVs.

Eventually, Aurora and her sisters received medical training, carrying on the family tradition of healing. While still a medical student, Aurora met a naval officer named Juanito at a dance held by the Cavite City naval base. The two were soon married and started having children just one year later, ultimately raising three daughters and two sons. While his wife was a healer, Juanito became a commodore under the Marcos Regime. Ferdinand Marcos, the United States-supported dictator, ruled the Philippines from 1965 to 1986, holding the entire country under martial law for many years and stealing as much as ten billion dollars from the economy as personal wealth.

A poor fate awaited all of them: Aurora, her husband, and the Regime itself. Our family would be splintered from inside out, in parallel with forces of diaspora and political change.

～

Magic in the Philippines existed before written history and varies considerably across our different ethnic groups — we are an archipelago of more than two thousand islands, after all — and is today mostly a merging of pre-colonial spirituality with Catholic religious elements.

Although our household religious practices have become a form of folk Catholicism, we have not forgotten the importance of spirits and our innumerable ancestors. Even before the arrival of the Spanish and Christianity, our islands were a syncretic battleground of Hinduism, Buddhism, Islam, and native, deeply rooted animist societies ruled by priestesses.

Pre-colonial Filipinos worshipped 'diwatas' (derived from Sanskrit 'devata', meaning deity or divine, with origins from

Hinduism and Buddhism), both male and female deities made by God to watch over his creation. Diwatas were worshipped and venerated as superior in beauty, knowledge, and strength; people would leave them offerings like rice, alcohol, fruits, or fish, hoping their prayers would be answered.

Aside from their own earthly social structures, pre-Hispanic Filipinos believed in an invisible spiritual realm coexisting with our own. This world was inhabited by spirits, including family members, elemental deities, and lesser gods who were honoured with rituals and feast days. These beings were believed to preside over all areas of life, including birth, sickness, marriage, harvesting, and death. Some of these spirits were considered friendly; others, tyrannical enemies.

Some portion of what we know about the archaic Filipino spiritual life was recorded in Spanish writings as early as the 1500s, but the Spanish also saw to the vicious destruction of indigenous spiritual practices — especially after Filipinos revolted en masse in the 1890s, seeking communal and agrarian reform in the colonial system.

~

My mother Vivien — the fourth of Aurora and Juanito's five children — was born breach, butt-first, which led residents of the barrio to believe she was born with the power to heal.

This idea manifested in different ways. When she was as young as a toddler, the elderly would sometimes ask her to touch or bless them with her healing hands. Sometimes she was even summoned by people in the village who'd swallowed fish bones while eating (she'd spit on her hands and rub it on their throats). Vivien is also said to have been the Commodore's favourite child;

he lavished his youngest daughter with affection and gifts no one else in the family received.

For much of her childhood, my mother lived a blessed, idyllic life of privilege as the daughter of a prominent naval leader. The powerful Commodore was heavily intertwined with and personally crucial to the work of the brutal Ferdinand Marcos and his corrupt government. Juanito's ties to the Marcos regime kept his family comfortable and safe inside a gated community, where Vivien eventually met my father Carlos. They were newly teenagers and he was a bad boy from America who smoked cigarettes.

Despite Marcos's 'reign of terror' — or perhaps because of its urgency — Vivien fell into a whirlwind romance with my father that ignited the intensity of her rebellion. Though Vivien had a bit of a rebellious streak ever since she was a child (swiping some of her parents' money or sneaking away in the night to see her friends), her defiant nature evolved after falling in love; she blossomed into a rebel fighter. The two were swept into the youth-heavy People Power Revolution to help devastate Marcos's fascist regime. Following the 1983 assassination of Ninoy Aquino, a radicalised senator and long-time opponent of Marcos, the young lovers dispersed literature and made yellow ribbons for students to don in solidarity with the anti-authoritarian movements against Marcos.

I'm unsure if my mother ever did any direct work to personally interrogate her father's complicity in Marcos' deadly work. She was only a teenager at the peak of his influence, and at the time every vocal radical getting attention was assassinated or imprisoned. Talking about the Commodore today, his involvement in the reign of terror is brushed off, and everyone from my close to extended family to random locals emphasise that he was a good man. 'He was a real gentleman', I've been told at least thrice.

At sixteen years old, my mom got knocked up. She and my father wed and she gave birth to my brother. Not four months after delivery, Vivien was back in the streets for the day of uprising against Marcos in the capital city of Manila. She and my father stopped by the palenque to stock up on food and drove to the city to hand it out to radicals at sit-ins, organisers who had been rallying for days, and the ever-present, booming homeless population.

The revolution succeeded, and then I came.

~

I was six years old when I left the Philippines for America; we fled in the night and I brought nothing save my inherited loneliness. On the Pacific islands and the island of New York, I was both familiar and displaced.

At twelve years old, I suffered the monstrous effects of my changing body. In the summer, I got my first period at the annual pool party and sat morosely on the edge of the pool. When asked why I wouldn't jump in, I said nothing and bled silently.

That fall, I was raped by my teacher, a man who was supposed to be my mentor. He collected me from class and had his way with me in his office. The first time it happened, I thought I'd die from the pain but instead, I lingered somewhere between blindness and unconsciousness. In my blurry haze, I thought I saw a hooded figure—someone who might save me.

But there was no one. The man called me a 'good girl', told me not to tell anyone, and my near-death became his weekly routine.

When I told a counsellor what the man had done, she let me know I could never tell anyone else. The man was too important, she said, 'someone doing good'. 'How could you even say something like that?' she asked.

I felt further away from humanity than the thousands of miles between me and my family. I said nothing and bled silently. I hadn't yet known that I'd descended from women who healed with magic after being shattered by men and war.

⌁

After the fall of the Marcos regime, the Philippines was at war with itself, and my family, too, crumbled from within. The Commodore left Aurora for his mistress. My mother left her family for a new life in the United States. And eventually, each of Aurora's daughters followed her there.

After all of her precious daughters moved to America, Aurora was increasingly falling under some sort of dark spell. Some say that the Commodore was seduced away by his mistress with gayuma—love magic—and that Aurora honed her ancestral protective magic to keep herself and children safe. Some believe Aurora grew bitter at the separation and tried to use gayuma to win the Commodore back. Regardless of whether the Commodore's wife or mistress performed gayuma, the selfish and narrow-minded application of love magic cost these women more than they knew.

The Commodore vanished from a boat and was assumed dead, and soon after that, his mistress also vanished in a strange whirlwind of fear, conspiracy, and blood money. Aurora never knew another love after the Commodore. She was hit with karma two-fold: bad luck and bad health.

She was eventually struck with uterine cancer, poisoned where she bore her husband's children. It's said that she cried out for him on her deathbed, that the last word she said was his name.

As Aurora's only granddaughter, she treated me preciously growing up, carrying me close to her chest and insisting I sleep next to her. I remember how she'd show me her gold jewellery pieces—displayed delicately on fabric on the kitchen table—sharing the stories behind each gift. 'This was for our first anniversary,' she'd say, letting the gold chain dangle from one hand and holding the pendant with the other. She'd often grow wistful afterward and tell me, 'Never give a man your whole heart, iha.'

After her death, there was a karmic ripple.

All three of Aurora's daughters ended their marriages and careened in different directions, my mother in the most dramatic way by switching professions and abandoning her children, again, to move thousands of miles across the country for a man.

Where my grandmother built walls, my mother tore them down and erased all proof. After the Commodore broke her heart and abandoned their family, Aurora remained faithful to him. As if believing the pendulum had swung too far, Vivien put her whole heart into romantic endeavours, happily leaving her family behind.

I resented her throughout all of it, but now see it was necessary to untangle the havoc wreaked by love magic that began before either of us were on this earth. Love magic sets a trap we mortals can't help but fall into: the idea that romantic love is the only one worth summoning. Aurora was moved by pain and Vivien by pleasure, but love magic is about something greater than both.

The purpose of love magic is not to win love, but to remove karmic obstacles in the way of love. (Whether that love is the romantic one we set our sights on, who's to say?) Love magic is a gift of strength, a power so great it can topple regimes but so orphic only you can understand. Love magic is justice.

⤙

I visualise the distance between me and my family as more than just an empty space: I see it as oceans and land—and laid over it like an opaque mirror, a world inhabited by the spirits that guide me.

This is how I feed my ancestors: Once a week, I lay out a bed of banana leaves. On it, I place incense in a coconut shell, an offering of fruit (mangoes, calamansi, santol, rambutan), any herbs and vegetables I've grown or collected, a bowl with money (preferably coins), and pictures of my grandmother and other ancestors who are important to me. I light the incense and, after a few hours or days, eat the offerings. I burn the banana leaves before replacing them with fresh ones.

When it strikes me, I speak to my altar by singing songs or reading passages I know were cherished by my loved ones.

⤙

To unbury history is to keep our ancestral traditions alive, and to connect with our ancestors is revolution. The tools available to Filipina witches today look only a little different than those available in the past.

As Spain transformed our archipelago into the only large Christian nation in Asia, working-class Filipinos still could not afford the offerings of Western medicine. The indigenous spiritual healer class did not completely dissolve but dispersed into a kind of magical diaspora that echoes the Philippines' cultural fate. Our shamans became Christian medicine men and women, mostly exorcists and herbalists running apothecary services, sometimes in the guise of formal clinics. To some degree it appears the older pagan spells were simply swapped out for Catholic prayers, with other trappings of the practices preserved.

Today there are dozens of words for 'magician' or 'witch' in the Philippines, but the word I hear most often is simply 'bruha'. Filipino witchcraft today is arguably less feminine (and no longer dominated by women practitioners). Because of the Spanish destruction of most pre-colonial Filipino culture, the diwata fell from being goddesses to evolve into the equivalent of mythical enchantresses or nymphs—beautiful and alluring creatures who live in the forest, trees, or water. The pre-colonial traditions concerning diwata have carried on today in the form of folk Christianity, succinctly illustrated in how every barrio has its own patron saint.

Even with pagan elements stripped away, our lives are imbued with the rituals of honouring or pleasing the spirits and our ancestors. The magic of the islands dispersed and my matriarchs lost touch with the spirit realm, but their power didn't disappear—it became smaller and quieter, a constellation of events that seem disconnected unless you know what to search for.

⌣

Before I knew I was enshrouded by the ghosts of my ancestors, I felt death hovering over me. Before I'd learned about my mother witches, I knew there was power in my words. 'Be a good girl and don't tell anyone.' 'How could you even say something like that?'

I never knew the details of my grandmother's fight against the Japanese occupation. I never knew my mother's role in the People Power Revolution against Marcos's US-backed dictatorship. I only knew what I had to learn on my own: how to survive.

My adolescence was a blur of black, white, and red extremes. The life of a school girl: waking, eating, extracurriculars, bleeding, homework, crying, sleeping, waking, not eating, being devoured by men, bleeding, not sleeping, being devoured by myself, waking, eating, bleeding, being devoured by darkness.

As soon as I was able, I ran away and never looked back. In college, the man—the teacher, the mentor, the tormentor—sent letters to my campus mailbox almost weekly. I collected them for a year without opening or reading them. That summer, I brought them with me to a backyard bonfire and lingered after everyone had gone home. Opening them, all the letters said the same things: he loved me and never wanted to hurt me. He's so, so sorry for being such a sick man. I watched every letter burn and spoke his name once, clearly and with purpose.

He died within a year.

I didn't wonder whether I killed the man with my words; he was already old and karmically doomed. The love spell was cast when I killed him in my mind, killed the weight I had carried and the obstacles he put between me and a life with love.

The love between my parents wasn't ignited by the revolution—the revolution was an act of love that birthed me. The greatest love magic we can perform is to seek justice for the oppressed. Uncovering our indigenous histories and ritually appeasing our ancestors arms us with an ancient, unnameable power.

The tools the women in my family have used to mitigate disaster and effect change are powerful. In addition to Western medicine, my grandmother practiced white and black magic. People were healed by her; the people she cursed died. My mother was also born a witch, recognised by her community. When my mother and I immigrated to America, the role of ritual and inherited power in our lives also transformed. The magic of our family evolves alongside us and is as old as our nameless ancestors.

It is the same story with the diwata, our island goddesses. Just as the colonial magic is sanitised and partly devoured by the foreign plague of civil, social, and religious patriarchy, the magic and ritual of my diaspora changes, too, blended with our most basic rituals: the rituals of staying alive.

~

Years ago, I journeyed back to the Philippines to learn my cultural and familial history. I interviewed locals and relatives to learn my past, but instead, I learned my present and future. Documenting the lives of my ancestors, I met the members of my spiritual court, the forces that guide my intuition.

It's a strange thing, to feel like you made a choice of your own volition only to find that fate had chosen it for you long ago. In uncovering my family's silenced histories, I found an eerie, humbling connection—a deep reassurance that I am significantly small but exactly where I'm meant to be.

It's said that when the Spanish arrived to the Philippines in the sixteenth century, the inhabitants were heavily adorned with gold. The Spanish made sure to take all that gold from the locals, even going so far as grave robbing or forcing people to surrender their gold under the threat of torture or crucifixion.

To honour the revolutionary spirit of my ancestors, I place my gold in a bowl of water and leave it in the sun for a few hours. Then, I wash my hands in the bowl, making sure to push the water downwards. When I leave my home—the one thousands of miles from the islands of my ancestors, the one I've built alone out of darkness, the one kept warm by love—I always wear an excess of gold.

Pushing Beauty Up Through the Cracks

Katelan Foisy

It's a late night at the apartment. Rain knocks at the window, coffee brews, and I'm separating a collection of herbs and dirt, placing them into piles. Behind me, a paper moon attached to a starry night sky and dark maroon drapes. I'm sitting by the vintage Victorian loveseat and antique elephant plant stand painted to look like the one in my grandparents' home growing up. The large 1920s radio acts as an altar table. On it is a mix of antique candleholders ranging from the 1920s to World War II, mirrors, Victorian tintypes, stray tarot cards, cake toppers, and a collection of oils and dirt from sacred places. Relics from hotels that no longer exist are framed on the walls and sit atop a collection of vintage suitcases on a painted wardrobe cabinet. My house is a collection of golds, jewelled reds, dark blues, and greens. People who come here compare it to a museum or a vintage theatre set. Spread across the floor, the herbs lay on pieces of wax paper. One will be crushed and burned as incense; the rest will remain in the mortar to be mixed with soil, whispered to, and sprinkled into fresh paint. These are the first few steps in creating portals, the doorways into time frames we may or may not see.

Art has long been a tool of resistance. Beauty stimulates inspiration. Inspiration arouses curiosity. Curiosity unveils questions, which lead to revolution. Art becomes survival during times of war and oppression. The first thing a dictator destroys is beauty, because beauty and creation are hope. In my own art, I create doorways, visual spells that weave in between time, memory, ancestry, and spirit. They shift paradigms, becoming energetic sigils themselves. Each piece of art has a specific ritual procedure. For some, it's the ritual of photographing and merging past and present; for others, it's about placing pieces of history within the layers. With the veil thinning, political, environmental, and socioeconomic upheaval at hand, I have been focusing on history and land memory within my art, mostly between the time periods of World War I and World War II. As I study these periods, I notice patterns occurring: the new tax bill that mimics those from 1929, women's right to vote and the votes themselves being questioned, people of colour being targeted by authorities and pushed out of a country that boasts freedom. These are some of the many issues that have repeated themselves over the years and resonate today as we face war and recession, as well as ongoing racism, sexism, and classism. The issues have never resolved, only evolved. As an artist I believe art and magic can be used to bring these issues to light, even if only subconsciously.

I work mostly with mythology, portraits, and fairy tales to create a subconscious spell, introducing the viewer to an energetic message. I mix dirt from historical places and add it to paint to create a portal between land and memory. The portal manifests when the person makes initial contact with the artwork, allowing for the information within to be dispersed and the viewer to take that information and use it in the way they deem necessary. This communication unveils itself over time; the connection between the artist, land, and spirit allows a magical doorway to open that in turn invites the viewer to enter the magic unfolding through a beautiful piece of art. The initial reaction can be to take it in, but the subconscious magical work digs deeper, creating the portal through which change can occur. It becomes a problem-solving spell, providing the power to create a solution to the matter at hand. Creating magical art pieces allows me to process what is happening around me as well as allowing for an energetic solution. Being part Romani and Cree, I'm attracted to folklore and historical art and stories; they help me to see how issues mirror each other over time.

   While I usually focus on folklore told by elders, I'm attracted to particular artists because their chosen mediums—often day-to-day items—and depictions of what they experienced reflect my own practice in many ways. Artists who find beauty in times of despair are inspiring to me—artists like Ceija Stojka, a Romani Holocaust survivor, writer, and artist, who used writing to detail her account of growing up in concentration camps, including Bergen-Belsen, Ravensbrueck, and Auschwitz. She later took up painting, using toothpicks, cardboard, glass jars, postcards, her fingers, and salt dough, painting scenes from the Holocaust that spoke to how Romani culture may have been stripped from her people physically but nevertheless remained in their hearts. Or Helga Hosková-Weissová, who was transferred between Terezín, Auschwitz, Freiberg, and Mauthausen; she began keeping a journal after witnessing a butterfly land on a flower as she entered a camp. On her father's advice to draw what she saw, she drew day-to-day life—lice and bedbugs, a cart with bread, waiting in line for food. Or Charlotte Salomon, who created paintings portraying scenes from her life during the time Nazis prepared to take over France. Her collection of 769 paintings—entitled *Life? or Theatre?*—used only three colours of paint to illustrate her thought process on whether she should take her own life or instead undertake something wildly eccentric. These are just a few examples of how art can weave beauty and personal experience into statements of resistance.

Resistance in art is the documentation of the time around us and the stories we not only develop but also retell as time moves forward. Beauty is never to be dismissed. It may appear frivolous while simultaneously conveying something darker. Beauty can be gritty and unkempt. Beauty wears masks; it plays with artifice. It can seep into the ground and come up through the cracks. Beauty is dangerous.

These are the things that filter through my head as I pound wild rose, thorns, deerstongue, sacred dirt, and bits of deer hooves from an old rattle into dust. As the pestle hits mortar, I whisper sacred stories into the mixture and gently blow on it three times to 'wake' the ingredients. Tonight, the stories come from a shapeshifting woman. Once human, she was raped and left for dead, but she was revived by the original Deer Woman spirit who lures promiscuous and abusive men away from the tribe and into the forest to their demise. There is not one Deer Woman but many. To women, she is a protectress, bringing the matriarchy back to the tribe and watching over childbirth. Over the next month, she and I will become close. Every night, I will mix incense and burn it while I paint. Every night, this mixture will be stirred into paint and layered on paper in between prayers. I listen to the news as I work — stories of Planned Parenthood defunding, women being sexually harassed and abused — and while this upsets me, I know it's important to allow this energy into the space. I ask her to answer the pleas of the women consciously and subconsciously calling to her, and then I go blank. I allow her to take shape while I take a backseat. I become a neutral vessel for her to come through. Her breath becomes my breath. We are opening a doorway from past to present and calling on our ancestors. The guides of our ancestors become our guides. This is how I document time and spirit within a painting. A lot of the time I won't remember the process or the specifics. All I know is that in order to allow her in, I have to let ego out.

There was a time in both my ritual and my art that I would become emotionally overwhelmed by it. It was messy and obsessive. It often backfired or I would become entangled within it, reliving the trauma myself instead of creating the change needed. I had to learn to let go of emotion, to take a step back and maintain a more analytic stance to allow the real magic to happen. The realisation that my art and magic do not require angst or trauma to be powerful was one of the greatest gifts I could give myself. My work became transcendental in nature, lifting me outside of myself and allowing for spirit to come through. Emotion is often ego-based; it connects back to the 'me' energy that I generally want to keep out of my process. Instead I become a problem solver. I assess what type of energy is needed and work from there. This process takes time and patience and practice, and it's hard to explain until you've tried it yourself. But once I let go of ego, I was able to turn off my emotional connection and allow the necessary energy to come through.

William S. Burroughs once said, 'Black magic operates most effectively in preconscious, marginal areas. Casual curses are the most effective.' While he's talking about curses, I find this to be true with most magical workings. Often before I start a painting or visit a place I need to photograph, I will do what I call a skin-shedding session. I visualise layers of emotion shedding away until there is a new skin void of ego. I take a few deep breaths, allow my mind to go blank, and then begin the work, focusing only on the historical aspects or spirits needed for that particular working.

Slowly, the images come: I see her hair and face, but the way she wants to be depicted is not as a deer-hoofed woman with a beautiful face. She wants to be a warning for all those who see her. I start by drawing her skull, my movements rocking me back and forth as I outline her hair and body. Scientifically, female deer can grow antlers if they have enough testosterone in them. This Deer Woman harnesses the power men would use to wound women and uses it to grow her own. Her antlers are a warning. She's nearly as tall as me, her hair is like mine, she wears similar dress, we move in unison as I mark the paper with detail; it is raw and messy, and I haven't even applied the paint. I know this piece must be done in sections; it's too big—in scale, in concept, in power—to complete quickly or all at once. Guided by her hand, I draw her. I take the herb and animal mixture from the mortar and sprinkle it into the paint. The

brush mixes it in. I mix browns and whites to make bone. My
wrist flicks with each movement—some long and fast, others
tight and detailed. I work nearly non-stop, hours passing with no
concept of time or my own memory. I know when this happens,
the magic is in the mania; the ritual of process can't be broken.
I'm thinking of women while I paint, those who keep fighting
no matter what comes their way. I'm thinking of Standing Rock.
I'm thinking of Standing Rock and the women there protecting
what is sacred. This is her thought, her energy pouring through
me. The Water Protectors protect the Earth Mother and Deer
Woman protects the matriarchal energy of the tribe, something
that has been lost through years of colonialism. This painting
doesn't figuratively depict anything in the world around me,
but symbolically, it's all there.

The process of painting is a journey through doorways,
through time, across lands. My paintings contain secrets, residing in the symbolism and paint. The mixture of herbs and dirt
within the symbols provides openings for a portal to emerge;
these portals can reveal unsightly truths no one likes to acknowledge. On either side of Deer Woman are tiger lilies. In medicinal
terms, tiger lilies help with menstrual cramps; they can cure
inflammation of the vagina, neuralgic pain, and nausea brought
on by pregnancy. They can be added to soup or made into tea
to help treat depression and stabilise moods. They can also be
used for UTIs and heart conditions. The darker connotation
of the tiger lily goes back to 1904 and a children's book, *Peter
Pan*, and the character Tiger Lily. Although the book wasn't
controversial at the time it was published, it's more than problematic in the way it depicts Native Americans. This children's
tale did not receive the same criticism that later children's books

such as *Mary Poppins* and *Little House on the Prairie* did, but all contained racist stereotypes of Native Americans. The tiger lily reminds us, even as a subconscious spell, that we must be aware of how we depict and perceive things.

In addition to the tiger lilies, I painted beetles that became totems of adaptation and of earth's creation. Without these, change cannot fully take place. Deep within the layers of paint, I sprinkled brick dust from my grandmother's home, a place of love and stability for me throughout my life. The centipedes I painted crawling up beside Deer Woman became guardians. There is a myth that tells of a giant 'leech' with a serrated sucker mouth that shapeshifted to defeat an evil shapeshifter in the form of a dragon-like creature, thereby saving humankind. The 'leech' eventually became known as the centipede. And then I painted Moth, who brings transformation and messages from the spirit realm. Weaving these images together brought on a sacred spell of protection, myth, history, time, and a portal back to the matriarch. Her final destination was Que4, a community radio station and art space where she could be seen publicly and her message heard. I believe you can create magic with images, the same way I believe that you can work to heal wounds and create personal progress with film and photographs. While Deer Woman was my painted portal, in between painting sessions I made gateways, layering photographs and playing with time.

Art will open doors you never knew existed. Jo Teeuwisse, from Amsterdam, purchased 300 negatives depicting World War II images from a flea market and superimposed them over modern-day streets. Her work creates a narrative that connects the two times. She interviews people who have experienced the war first-hand and researches the images and backstories to create a unique and accurate history of the era, giving the viewer a doorway into past and present. This is what I call time travel. Time travel allows the viewer to experience multiple time frames at once, allowing historical moments to merge and removing the disconnect of the black and white photo, pulling it into present day. In one of her photos, the doorway of Haftl Krankenbau Schonungsblock Block 19 is featured. The past image is in black and white and shows prisoners of the camp in black-and-white-striped uniforms being released by what looks like Russian liberators. This image is superimposed onto a present-day image of the same door and steps in colour, allowing the viewer to look at the significance of the place from a new time and angle.

My own experimentations into time travel developed from my interest in the land and its history. I started to create 'The Memory Keeper' series as a book of spells for the 2016 *Psycho-analysis, Art & The Occult Conference* in London. I had been living in New York for twenty years, and my time there was coming to an end. Sometimes you move to a place knowing there's an expiration date. When I moved to NYC, I saw how it changes constantly. I was fine with change, even inspired by it; change is one of the only constants we have in our lives, and it allows us to grow and learn as people. But by 2008, New York had started to change even more rapidly. Areas of the city that had previously remained relatively untouched began to take a new shape. Friends who lived in certain neighbourhoods, especially Brooklyn, started seeing their families and neighbours pushed out to make way for a new, richer crowd. I was angry seeing this happen and wracked my brain for solutions. Being someone focused on history, I was dismayed to see so many businesses and buildings closing — especially those that had withstood changing times. Places such as Coney Island High, CBGB's, and the Chelsea Hotel started to close down, having been bought out by larger companies or knocked down and replaced entirely due to rising rent costs. NYC was losing the places that made it special. By the time 2016 rolled around, restaurants like Lanza's and bakeries like De Roberti's, places that had stayed in business throughout the Great Depression, were now closing their doors. I was never fully connected to the idea of living in NYC, but I knew during my time there I would work with the land, connecting the people who lived there to the history of it and collecting pieces of it for later use. Once that time was up, I'd have to find the next place and move on.

Chicago was calling, but I wasn't sure how I'd get there. I'd been there on business trips and each time the city felt like home. I was drawn to the architecture and was curious about what the land had to tell me. I'd been interested mostly in the Native American roots of America, as well as the time period between the First and Second World Wars, the Great Depression, Prohibition, and the history of the mob; I was also fascinated by technology (the rise of radio and vinyl records), politics, music (the preservation of jazz during a time when it was seen as the Devil's music), and the arts (the shift from Victorian, art nouveau to art deco, as well as fashion and the rise of silent film) during these periods. Chicago, like NYC, played a big part in those histories.

Before I left NYC, in that nebulous space of leaving and arriving, within the pages of a Victorian photo album, I created 'The Memory Keeper' spell. I took photos of myself and my travels to places that played a role in those histories. Within

each photograph, I made what I call a 'time stamp'. Good time
stamps can be made using a sign that has remained throughout
the years, or a dock in the early morning with no one else around.
I survey the land and breathe in deep. I look around to see who
is there and where the best shot may be. I look for images that
could be timeless. I also often use vintage or antique cameras.
As times change and technology develops, it's important to
continue to work with the technology of the past. Working
with analogue allows us not only to have a backup, but also to
understand the time that went into working with this technology.
I enjoy relearning how to use the equipment and tapping into
the process of using it. As the digital age makes things easier,
working this way allows me to appreciate the time and effort
put into the arts before our time. Often I'll document a place
with both the past and present merged, layering photographs
or film with both past and present footage. The book weaves
a spell through time and place: it explores Coney Island and
NYC; remembers the selling of Manhattan and Brooklyn; looks
at the beginnings of the mob and its effect on politics, entertainment, radio, art, and technology. It summons the Los Angeles
of silent films, the Chicago of jazz nights and mob bosses, the
Las Vegas of mob politics and gambling, the Atlantic City of
seedy politics and more gambling—cities where there was a
connection to the history and land memory I was drawn to and
interested in working with.

Parts of the spell book are created as fiction, a story in which
I create a tear in time. I created a character for the book, a silent
film star writing to her lover while they travelled and met up
in hotels along the way. Part of the spell process is preserving
the memory of what is no longer there. I purchased vintage

stationery and postcards from the hotels, some no longer existing, tapping into the ever-changing energy of the cities and America itself. I photographed and filmed the places I went and made them look like 8mm films and stills. I had long been interested in silent films, and placing myself within that context connected me to the history of the land that I was trying to relate to. The films went along with the book and became visual spells themselves: spells to tap into historical aspects and create portals into the future, spells to open communication with both the spirits and the land. The films became cut-ups — text or images cut up and rearranged to create a new body of work. They were spells rooted in the land, showing the physical journey from one place to another. I took film stills, printed them, and placed them in envelopes with letters written on the scans of the old hotel stationery. Writing the letters made them magical incantations, petition papers, allowing the spell to form through ink on paper. By tapping into the past and merging it with the present, I create a tear in time, allowing the magic to create a portal into the future, which paves the way for me to not only get to where I need to go on the land, but also to create a sigil helping to create shifts in the energy of that land.

I found that as I worked with these images and words, my connection to the land unfurled a deeper understanding of the timeline in which cycles are repeated. When you place yourself into another time visually, it shifts the way you think. It made me more aware of the energy surrounding me, so I could then tap into the spirit of the land and allow it to channel through me. Channelling that energy through me paves my path forward. I can easily move through time and create a network of spellwork to allow for the magic to take form in whichever way is needed. For the book, it took me about a year to fully see the magic happen. After moving to a new city and getting the apartment I had written about without knowing it existed, now I'm starting to see the work come full circle. This can happen quickly or it can take months or years, depending on how big the issue is. The journey was one of understanding the timeline of art, political ties, technology, and entertainment, and then looking into the repetitions we make over time. Each of the cities I explored had a piece of this information, and by traveling to all of them, I was collecting a fuller picture—not only for my own personal journey, but to expand my work into a spell that would help others.

Looking at the history of the land, I was able to connect the repetitions in time. A good example of how this works is Coney Island. Coney Island was originally called Narrioch, mean-ing 'land without shadows'. As Dutch settlements grew and Native Americans were swindled and pushed out of the land that would eventually become Brooklyn, the name changed to Conyne Eylandt, which is seen on seventeenth-century Dutch maps and is purported to mean 'Rabbit Island', coming from the Dutch word 'conyn', meaning rabbit. The name was anglicised to Coney Island when the British took over in the mid-seven-teenth century. Rabbit as a totem is related to fear. In order to champion fear, it's important to tap into the source. Any fear of moving away from what is known can be overcome by making friends with rabbit. For me, the rabbit totem was about moving away from what I had known and grown comfortable with in NYC and starting over in a new city. With these few bits of history, I notice the repetition of time—from white set-tlers pushing Native Americans from their own lands to the gentrification we see in our cities today. This was part of the reason I was leaving NYC, but I also knew that remaining in the US meant it was inescapable. The world around us relives the memory embedded deep into the soil. Privileged groups decide they want what marginalised groups have and they take it. This is the way that the United States of America was founded. It is fundamental in understanding our history and pivotal in working with the land to change it.

Within the book, I could see many of the same repetitions I saw in Coney Island playing out in other cities. As I created the pages, collecting information from the land itself, I knew I was onto something but still didn't know exactly why it was so important. I began to realise that I could connect the stories from my own journey to the Deer Woman, who I originally started to paint in NYC. My connection to her deepened as I collected information from the land. From there I could get to the root of the issue and push beauty up through the cracks. I could create a body of work that contained codes within it to dismantle the current situation, both personally and politically, piece by piece—the work becoming a magical sigil in itself, not only a shift in my own personal transformation and journey, but also a code to work at a national and global level. While this book and this painting were originally created to facilitate my own personal journey, I now knew they had a larger purpose. I wasn't working through a personal trauma; I was working with trauma that the land itself held within it. This is land memory. I was witnessing it in real time and pulling at the root. I was creating beauty to combat something much deeper.

How does a piece of art become a sigil of resistance? If we can make a book of images and words or an art piece into a spell to change our own personal lives, imagine what we can do for others. By creating portals, working with myth, creating art that contains symbology and pieces of the land and imbuing those messages into the paint, photographs, and magical workings I create, I'm shifting the paradigm from not only preserving and documenting these cycles, but also challenging and changing them with my own magic. In her Vice article titled 'We Must Risk Delight After a Summer Full of Monsters', published August 2014, artist and journalist Molly Crabapple states, 'Beauty is survival, not distraction. Beauty is a way of fighting. Beauty is a reason to fight.' She is right. The first thing a dictator does is destroy beauty. Beauty is power. Art should be looked to as a guide in a time of uncertainty and possible war. The goal of resistance art is to preserve the memories and cultures that any dominating regime is trying to erase. Resistance art does not have to be overtly political in nature; it can be shrouded in veils and masked in beautiful symbols. It needs only to take root just below the surface for it to grow. And then that beauty can flourish, the way a plant can break through concrete.

Ritualising My Humanity

J. A. Micheline

Every day I remake my body into the shape of a person. Being born a monster means I do this daily before the mirror. The remaking is done so often that it is easy. The remaking is done so often that it is hard.

The voice is first and, arguably, the most important. My human one is somewhere in my upper oropharynx, as opposed to my monster voice, closer to the front of my mouth and breathing along the surface of my tongue. Neither is particularly kind. Neither is particularly unkind. But it is the sound, the feel of the vowels, the volume and timbre that allow humans to recognise each other. In times of trouble, I swallow my loud, natural-born-monster voice and remake myself. I use a trick I learned from my father. My human voice quiets in direct pro-portion to my rage. Emotions — all of which are monstrous — are to be discarded daily if they are not useful. Fury can be used but channelled; despair cannot.

Key among the remaking is also language. So long as I eliminate stranded prepositions and common conflations of subjective and objective case, I am free to speak my monster mind. A good friend once told me that my voice was 'deceptively sweet'. I have sometimes wondered about the significance of this statement, what the deception was, but it's just as Jaboukie Young-White once said: 'Anything is possible when you sound white on the phone.' Sweetness and whiteness become almost equivalent, particularly within the context of femininity. My power grows with my ability to deceive.

I was born black and so I was born a monster. My blackness is so abhorrent, so evidently dangerous to whiteness that it has been linguistically aligned with evil—'black magic', 'the dark arts'. A direct line is drawn from D. W. Griffith's 1915 film *The Birth of a Nation*, described by James Baldwin as both 'one of the great classics of American cinema' and 'an elaborate justification for mass murder', and the murder of unarmed black people at the hands of law enforcement as you read this page. The film, widely considered the foundation of modern American cinema, portrays black sexuality as a threat to whiteness—specifically as a threat to white women, who ostensibly belong to white men. Freed slaves, characterised as unworthy of their freedom, attempt to change miscegenation laws for the sole purpose of marrying white women. A black man stalks a white woman until she jumps off a cliff to her death. The clear and present danger of blackness—as physically painted onto white men in blackface—was such that some have attributed the resurgence of the Ku Klux Klan to its widespread and critically acclaimed release. It was a part of the Klan's recruitment materials for decades. And it is, of course, still screened regularly in film schools today.

My skin marks me as dangerous. The onus has been placed upon me to demonstrate the contrary, to prove my humanity. And so I look on with some mix of confusion and resentment seeing women—very rarely black—claiming monstrosity, declaring their dreadfulness, and wishing that men would see them as harpies, sirens, demons, and other such world destroyers. My experience of monstrosity is definitively lethal. It is waking up to a hashtag that could very easily be you or your loved ones. It is the use of white grace as justification for murder. Though it is characteristic of many nonblack women, it is white women in particular who seem to want to leverage this grace for something more intimidating. But from a black perspective—what could be more intimidating than that?

This is not to say I don't understand this desire. Women are, on the whole, encouraged to behave in a 'lady-like' fashion and are subsequently punished when we deviate from this course. It's a matter of control. The standards of femininity—delicacy, demureness, and deference—are meant to rob us of our agency. By these rules, we are too fragile to face the world unsupervised, too breakable for our own good, justifying male dominance. This performance convinces both us and our jailors that this—the authoritative man and the submissive woman—is the natural order of things. Even when we become aware of these artificial performances, we become caught between nature and nurture, between femininity that we genuinely enjoy and femininity that has been insisted upon us. To embody a harpy, a siren, a heart-eating demon is to buck these unreasonable demands on our personhood; to become monstrous is to become an entity that a man would not dare seek to control—to become something beyond either nature or nurture. After centuries of making us afraid, isn't it time they feared us?

Still, it is also worth noting that these (hollow) patriarchal protections are not extended to black women in the same way in which they are extended to white women. White women have protested loudly—and justly—about their infantilisation, about their depiction as damsels in distress. Meanwhile, black women—and many other women of colour—have never been afforded the privilege of childhood or the role of a damsel. Take it back to *The Birth of a Nation*; the fear of black sexuality and the depiction of black people of any gender as hypersexualised has persisted to this day. This, too, has been a justification for violence against us, sexual or otherwise. Our children are never allowed to just be children; our twelve-year-old victims of violence are suddenly adults. Our women will never be rescued from the tower; they have never been worth saving.

I'll say it again: I understand where this all comes from. Non-black (cis) women—you're tired. I see that. You're tired of being treated delicately, tired of being told what to do, tired of these attempts to make you comply. So you elect to become dangerous. You bare your teeth and sharpen your claws. You hammer nails into your baseball bat. You're the villain now.

Or, at least, for the moment.

To become dangerous is a different paradigm to being born dangerous. I can file my teeth down to their bloody gums, clip my nails until they're raw, hold my hands up and beg you not to shoot—but monstrosity has been insisted upon me externally. My black body, the bodies of black enbies, the bodies of black (especially trans) women, the bodies of black people have been deemed monstrous. We were born dangerous and are killed, disenfranchised, and disrespected with absolute impunity as a result. We have neither the luxury nor the privilege to become dangerous; we are too busy having to constantly prove to a white world that we are not. Your becoming is only meant to last insofar it allows you personhood; it can be shed and escaped at will. My birth is inescapable. It has been decided for me. It has happened *to* me. I can remake myself multiple times across a single day, but that externally-insisted danger will always be enough to take that personhood from me. And it is, at times, infuriating to see you symbolically pursue that which guarantees my lack of agency purely for the sake of your own. I'm filled with quiet resentment as you perform rituals of danger.

My rituals exist to reinforce my humanity, to evidence that I am not dangerous, to demand that a violent world see me as a person. I attempt, constantly, to perform dignity despite being afforded none. And, what's more, I attempt this knowing that it will not work. So the question must be asked: for whom are these performances—both yours *and* mine—and what is their significance when we know they lack efficacy?

If my rituals are a demand to be seen, are evidence of my personhood, that suggests they are less for me and more for the white male world. Indeed, it could be argued that my particular enactment of humanity upholds rather than subverts the structures that oppress me. Instead of acting naturally, I am performing exactly as whiteness and maleness wish me to, as though this will somehow mitigate or undo that which binds me. Respectability politics—a term coined by black academic Evelyn Brooks Higginbotham—has never granted any marginalised person their freedom, but one could certainly interpret my rituals as compliance, as a misplacement of priorities. Perhaps

I should join you white women in your witchy revolution. Perhaps I should leave the concern for parallel constructions, for sotto voce behind. Perhaps I should find myself a candle, a pentacle, and an altar. After all, your performances serve not to comply but to undermine and warn. *Dead men can't catcall*, you remind them. Even if your performances are *for* them, as mine are, at least they serve to undermine the idea of delicacy. At least you're not proving them right. But despite being a woman, despite understanding the temptation of performing danger to prove them wrong, being black makes it very hard to follow as you make your way down this dangerous road. I know the very real bodies we will pass along the way; they don't look all that different from mine.

This is not to say that there are no black witches, no black enbies or women embracing their own externally-imposed monstrosity. Blackness contains multitudes and there are a great many of us who have weighed these truths and found agency in danger and defiant otherness. What's more, blackness contains its own witchy traditions—specifically, religions—that embrace the ritual and the supernatural. Voodoo, hoodoo, voudou, vudú. Some of these traditions, Haitian voudou for example, are particularly known for their acceptance of the more marginalised amongst us—queer, trans, and nonbinary practitioners. Multiple voudou spirits experience same-gender attraction. Others are described as being deux-manière, doubly-gendered. The religion is very much considered a place of solace for queer Haitians. It is said that the only place that lesbians feel safe identifying as such is within peristils, voudou temples, and the level of acceptance is such that most queer and trans advocacy outreach programmes tend to be based in peristils themselves.

But, as is often the way of a violently anti-queer and trans world, voudou's association with the marginalised has resulted in the demonisation of the religion itself. Even so, voudou and peristils are places where queer, trans, and nonbinary Haitians—and their diaspora—can find some belonging. True black magic.

Black and nonblack people alike are in desperate pursuit of places of power and self-reverence. But in the performance of these places—and especially in the borrowing of black and/or Indigenous traditions—one must consider the marked difference between the embracing of danger in spite of one's monstrous body and the pursuit of this danger to escape a frustratingly human form. I want to whisper:

You know not what you seek.

Honour the dead.

Turn back.

Maybe my ability to create fear is something I should treasure. For all of the huffing and puffing of white women in ripped denim vests and fingerless gloves, I can generate much more fear with much less effort. Even if my efforts at dignity fail me, danger remains in my arsenal. I can always forsake my human form and reveal a black-as-fuck monster. I can terrify in a way that others cannot. It remains in my back pocket, waiting for a day or even a moment when I am too short of temper for dignity. Those days, those 'fuck it, mask off' moments are few and far between, but they do come. And in that moment, I am briefly satisfied to have scorched my enemy, but then later I am just furious with myself for having become all they said, even justly. For having given *them* the satisfaction.

My rituals do not protect me—after all, nothing can—but they do, somehow, preserve me. Just as I imagine that your pursuit of danger preserves you. They give calmness of spirit, a path and light forward. They hold me together; I might fall apart without them. Still, I am worried about choice, about birth and becoming. I am happy to be as I am, but, as is the case with all women, I cannot be sure what happiness is truly mine and what belongs to others. My ability to make and remake myself is such that these remakings are essentially me, such that I am not sure how much has been remade. It feels natural to me not to raise my voice, to make reason a priority, to remain self-affirmed. It feels natural to present myself with as much dignity as possible. This feeling of naturalness may even be the goal of these remakings. I imagine that you want to feel dangerous as much as I want to feel human. I don't know what it means when your danger and my dignity become like breathing to us, when the masks are masks no more. Did we win or did we lose? Or is it enough to simply feel like we've won?

The feeling seems like it should be enough. And it is here, too, that I understand your becoming dangerous. Outside of the context of anti-blackness, it feels good to be a danger. It feels good to be in control—and control is what I wish to embody, more than anything. A quiet voice and a measured tone are, to me, emblematic of the control I possess, even if the control is false. The feeling of control is almost victory enough, given the fear with which I (and we women) are made to live our lives. But I think we must also interrogate what these assertions of control reflect in the multiple frameworks of power. It is not that I wish to take this feeling of control from my fellow women, but insteadI want to ask them to think of what they are doing, what it means, and why it means what it does. I want nonblack women, white especially, to understand the different impacts and meanings of danger.

And I also want to tell you a secret.

As I have said, I take quiet satisfaction in an ability to remain calm, an ability to let the justness of my rhetoric stand on its own. Still, as the good Lorde reminds us: the master's tools will never dismantle the master's house. No amount of calm or assuredness will prevent my suffering. But it is deeply sustaining to be able to arm myself with respectability while giving an overwhelmingly male and overwhelmingly white world exactly what it said it wanted and exactly what it deserves.

Even when I was young, I knew what this white world said of angry black women: too loud, too emotional, too volatile. And all for no reason. I also knew what they saw of themselves—softspokenness, rationality, and even-temperedness. Constantly, I—we—were told that we must become like them, despite the unreasonableness of this task. We were told, in the face of violence, disenfranchisement, and disrespect, to remain calm.

So, I did.

My rituals very much reflect my decision to become the ultimate danger: a white man, or rather, what the white man purports himself to be. What is so galling about these ludicrous attempts to reshape women, to reshape people of colour, to reshape Indigenous, trans, and queer people, is that the standards to which we are held can never be met by oppressors themselves. White men insist upon logic while dismissing emotion, only to irrationally lose their tempers when it is pointed out that anger, too, is an emotion. And in the midst of these demands for reason, they present weak, poorly formed arguments. They paint themselves as near portraits of perfection, while falling dramatically short of their own self-image.

In an attempt to survive, before I knew that I'd done it, I became what they asked of me. I became soft-spoken; I became committed to reason; on most days, I became even-tempered in the face of conflict. I became the white ideal. And I am so satisfied to be the monster that they have created. I am so satisfied to see how much they pale in comparison.

My quiet words only contrast their tendency to shout. My sharp rhetoric only highlights the softness of their foundation. My patience only provides them rope — rope with which they inevitably hang themselves. My rituals serve ultimately to expose their lack of dignity. My rituals serve to let them wither in adequacy. My rituals serve to remind them that nothing they own was deserved.

In truth, my rituals — the same ones I use to perform my undangerous and thoroughly human body — are weapons. In unabashedly affirming my own dignity, I am become dangerous.

Simulating Control

Nora Khan

I am on a swept virtual rampart before a stoic virtual fortress overlooking a roiling virtual sea, dappled in warm virtual afternoon light. I am in one of the earliest chapters of *Dark Souls II*, easily one of the most punitive games of all time, a title built for masochists. According to recent statistics, forty-two players die every second in the game, clocking over 150,000 mortalities per hour. The average player, regardless of their skill level, dies tens of thousands of times. A pillar in the centre of the game holds count of how many players have died and continue to die. This unreal glut of deaths is the running joke of the game; it is a fact, a given, an ever-lengthening asymptote to climb up and along. Each move and act in this world is defined by the high chance of being just moments away from perishing. This makes *Dark Souls II* a very lonely game.

In this small coastal town, I slow down in a wheat field and breathe, watch the sun setting on the bluffs, on the gorgeous

ruins, on the wheat. I gather focus before the next plunge
through the broken archway, down the path, on into impossible battle. I am in a blissful space between this brief, brilliant
life and yet another resurrection by a campfire. This town feels
like a space of resistance to that cycle, as it is both out of real
time and the game's time. The stones look swept clean, now
wildly lit red and gold by the setting sun. The game's harmless
NPCs—its mages, gatekeepers, soldiers, priestesses—are all
still present, but they register on the periphery of my awareness,
skirting around this calm with their bickering, digging, and
nervous guarding. I forget my likely-futile mission—to un-pet-
rify a statue, to find a cleric's sacred chime, some old-as-hell
feather, some futuristic shards with necromantic properties,
I am sure. I look over the water. The peace here brings me to
a standstill.

The oceanside fortress is deeply familiar. I am shot through
with nostalgia. I have been here before, somewhere in my mind.
I linger at its base, before its modest steps, now something like a
hundred deaths deep. Not only have I been here before, but I
have built almost precisely this fortress by the ocean before and
many hundreds of times. I have constructed it from foundation
to spire. The exact shape, colouring, and position of the mental
fortress changes each time, as it is a hyperreal composite of all
the fortresses by the ocean outside of vaguely medieval towns
in dozens of dungeon crawlers I have played through the late
1980s and 1990s to the present. But as in this game, the specifics
of the fortress are not quite as important as the feeling it produces as a controlled space, its reveal of itself within an order of
movement. The overlook of the fortress by the sea is consolation
after a struggle. It has only opened up before me after I have

moved up through its dungeon, so I can watch the sunlight cut across the stone sides, widening angles in high drama.

〜

My own mental game begins in a narrow stone corridor at the opening of a dungeon. I am tussling with a yowling mass, an abstract object that takes on various faces before receding back into amorphousness. The room is hellish, meaning blood-lit. I grip this tulpa, which manifests a trauma—a cluster of harmful words, a violence, a painful memory of harm—and then place it firmly on the floor to flail and direct its gruesome energies at me. I watch it and then walk backwards, slow as though through water, keeping the flailing being steady in my vision, distancing myself from it physically and emotionally with each step. I pause, and a metal dungeon door, substantial, several feet thick, studded around its grated windows, slides down from overhead. There is a delicious ch-chunk as it clicks past me, rolls down, and slams. To ensure its heaviness and its solidity, I press myself madly against the door, press and press to try to get back to the other side, until I slide down against the wall onto the ground, my legs weak from the effort. I can hear the psychic detritus, still activated, but its noise is fainter.

When I have exhausted myself against the door, I walk forward several feet, the map of the ground opening up before me. Behind me, another heavy door slides down and shakes the ground as it hits. I press against it to try to hear the noise of the object. Its outlines are dimmer now. It is secured in a closed space, neutralised. I walk forward, and the stone corridor begins to widen, the torches leading up a winding way. Another door rolls down behind me. Four steps, and then another. Four

steps. Registering each shuddering gate, I walk past torches to
the end of the hall, to the base of a wide stairway that curves
up into the black.

~

Why am I even here, in this dungeon? The simple answer is
that my brain has slotted me here to map my way out of the
grip of a demon that usually represents a traumatic event or
a flashback rooted in complex post-traumatic stress disorder
(CPTSD), emerging from a childhood and early life dismantled
by emotional and physical violence. In order to get through
the day, I need to be able to separate myself quickly from the
memory or event; it will debilitate me if I cannot protect myself,
effectively deflect, and reconstitute myself from the ground up.
When I am stuck on a traumatic episode from ten, twenty years
ago, I'm sixteen, six years old again. I am there. I am seeing and
feeling it all again. The flashback sets in me as total paralysis
and derailment. I lose focus. I can't speak. People have told me
it looks like the colour has drained from my face, that I look
like I'm a thousand miles away, which I might as well be in
that moment.

This mental mapping and struggle out of the dungeon is my
first and primary ritual. It is a simple and effective way to com-
partmentalise pain and give myself distance. I learned that tool
on my own to manage anxiety or desperation and break up
obsessive loops around negative, destructive feelings. Many
years later I would learn just the compartmentalisation tool
again in cognitive behavioural therapy and realise I had been
doing such imaginative self-preservation rituals for years.

I now see that I have relied on forms of such simulation-based healing in the absence of therapy and a supportive social network, which my chronic depression often weakens dramatically. Working through trauma demands space and time, financial security, and professionally-trained, profoundly empathic listeners. It requires education in emotional intelligence and a reliable safety net. Most people in America have limited or non-existent access to most of these things. So when overwhelmed or spiralling, I would (at ten, at fifteen, at twenty, at twenty-five) go and sit down cross-legged in a quiet room, then press play on a walkthrough. I had many set pieces, depending on need, some more soothing and cool than the dungeon, the spatial equivalent of a ten-hour psytrance meditation video on Youtube: a seaside forest with brisk streams running through it; a cavernous medieval court; or a trail through hills in Hawaii leading to a ledge on which I watched the ocean crash over a house, flood it, loosen its foundation, and drag all its contents out to sea. After more extreme violence, I needed more elaborate walkthroughs. I would slot the vile trauma into a form, place the form into the dungeon, then manage the form through creating space between.

I am not sure when the dungeon became my main go-to of these sets. I do know how it has developed over time. I call the dungeon retreat and the following ascension out of it the Undoing. The Undoing evolved into a complex and knotty set piece that could jumpstart my own creative process. And—now I see this—my need and commitment to be creative and generative was directly linked to the origin experience of trauma or erasure.

Allow me a quick mini-walkthrough of my CPTSD here. CPTSD wracks my mental undercarriage to such a degree that processing and resolving basic, offhand slights and offences becomes very difficult. A hypersexualised advertising image that seems to valorise assault, a slightly too-sharp tone of voice—these can all deconstruct my peace and focus for the whole day. These instances—what's one day?—may not seem like much, but days add up to weeks add up to years.

And then there are all the casual erasures by intimates, the dismissals by professional acquaintances, the accretive small violences common to the daily experience of women of colour. The fact of my origin actually says nothing substantive about me, other than what I want it to, but in writing it out, it is inevitably a marker that overdetermines 'who I am' to some reading, precluding the possibility of self-definition. Stating the fact is its own double bind, but it has to be made explicit for this essay to make sense to the people I write for. The page generates the same suffocating issues as in life. Identity, like trauma, is ultimately an endlessly mineable resource for publishers, for editors, who care most about cultivating a woke look. I speak to define myself but I am reified by my choice of words.

Living in a psychic underworld of a billion microaggressions endemic to living in a country and civilisation built on white supremacy: this is the baseline. Such fun! The baseline is the indecent, violent freedom others feel to erase the truth of my experience and feelings and perspective because (if we dig down to the foundation) they do not see me as real. That is it. At least a couple of times a day, I'm on the receiving end of a phrase or statement that emphatically denies my inner life, that denies my humanity, my creativity, my value, and my ownership of my ideas. Casually buried in an e-mail, in a message, in an off-hand remark, a denial of my possible singularity in favour of such incredibly boring assumptions and tropes and stories about who I am, what people generally like me must be like.

And there is nothing worse than a boring story.

Such fun! I wrote above, and this is of course some more deflection, as you'll just die without laughing at it all. I'd just die. Such fun, I wrote, but could it, in fact, be a kind of perverse fun? Could it all be a matter of fighting cleverly enough, nimbly enough, out of the dungeon, knowing full well that each time that you'll die and start at the beginning again? Why do people play *Dark Souls II*, if not for the possibility of a more elegant, longer run-through with fewer deaths and less psychic harm?

~

The stairway begins to narrow, and a small rectangle of light appears. The noises have faded. I follow this stone staircase, spiralling up, and pass through the light. The stairs lead outside and hug the long curve of the castle. The camera's eye scales out of my perspective to a god's-eye view, circling the fortress. I am outside of myself, and I see my small body holding the wall for balance, trying not to look over the edge to the sun dappling the cold glittering water below. I watch my little body inching up and around the curved wall.

When I reach the terrace, the camera slots back to my eyes. I look down as I walk, notice how the rough stone ends precisely at the vertex of a burnt orange triangle, which reveals itself as one of ten in a gorgeous tiled compass. I walk to the centre of the compass and look out to the sea. The terrace circles around the fortress tower and is a cross between Robert Irwin's Central Garden at the Getty and the overlook at Hearst Castle—the former built for people to reflect on their relation to light and sound, their being-ness, and the latter for a media baron to look over his domain (America), his parties full of expensive and charming people, and the hills of the California Central Coast.

~

I started playing games at six. Through each successive console, from SNES to Gameboy, the Sega Genesis to PC games like *Doom* and *Diablo*, the dungeon crawler was my favourite genre. Though I was too young for the dungeon crawler's Golden Age (yes, there is a golden age), its effect can be traced in every role-playing game and war fantasy in the next twenty-odd years of increasingly elaborate titles. In the early dungeon crawler's simplest form, the protagonist just had to escape and successfully erase the obstacles thrown into his path. The plot was not really the point, but instead, the immense pleasure of the labyrinth's complexity, the pleasure of surrendering to the demands of strategy.

Having played since I was so little, it seems natural that my still-forming sponge brain absorbed the logic, structures, and mechanics of game worlds. They changed my thinking in an irreversible way, as so much technology shapes us irrevocably. The *automap*—a small partial map on the bottom right of the game screen that opens up through world exploration—has become the subconscious or background framework I see through, opening the possibility of new landscapes for endless psychodrama to unfold upon, changing the meaning of the psychodrama. My personal conflict means so much less within a ruined city, up against the epic of transatlantic trade routes, or underwater in a submarine.

My daily lived psychic reality intersects well with the overall beautiful logics and patterns of war games. Spending thousands of hours running through three-dimensional models reveals the 'real world', as it is also a system, a maze, a grid of objects to contend with, analyse, and define on an emerging internal map. I can find a way to gain agency in its bounded space and then try to transfer those lessons out into the world.

The foremost beauty of games to me is how they can model ambiguity as a role. The roles within a game don't need to be so precisely defined; in fact, the mechanics are built to make modularity a feature. I can be a man, a tank, a tree; I can be tall, short, strongly built, weak; I can take whatever form fits my inner life. Games' most fantastical and outright surrealist characters morph and die and resurrect in dozens of forms. A game character's physical presentation usually isn't aligned with their actual (internal, spiritual, emotional) powers. The humble chambermaid can be the most radical and all-seeing player, a visionary. The daughter needing to be saved can cause incredible chaos, controlling from her seemingly submissive position. The dog can be a prophet. The land can heal itself.

So on the terrace, I can be the main warrior, sure, but also be the blacksmith, the archivist, the scribe, the shipbuilder. I can be both a knight and a queen. I can be the enforcer tying the community together or the alien mage passing through with one vital piece of information. And there is my ideal possibility, to become the joker, a trickster, like Loki, who intervenes at will, who absorbs nothing harmful, who elides, who creates on their own terms, who doesn't have to play the game at all.

~

The terrace air is clean. There are men and women in hooded gowns, crimson, black, purple, like the ones I wore in lower

school during the Christmas parade, which wound through
Ghent in colonial Norfolk. We wore hooded gowns like these,
carrying candles to the Episcopal church to sing. They look
up at me and right through me. Their faces flicker between
being all smiles and open curiosity to being retiring, closed off.
They symbolise commitment, their lifetimes spent in pursuit
of strange feelings and ways of seeing. They shuffle around, in
one hand a book, a pen, or an empty sheet of paper. Though
they are old, they still say that they are learning, that they know
nothing at all. They have spent decades contemplating God, the
nature of reality, the arcane, in gnostic isolation, indifferent to
the world. In games, they manifest as infuriating oracles who
answer in ambivalent riddles. They aren't there to help or guide.
They are just there to demonstrate the sublimity of detachment
from being too in the world, to contemplate, catalogue, and
generate new languages, fictions.

~

This terrace is my space of retreat after the full Undoing is
complete. Not-yet born ideas incubate in tiger's eye, capping the
stone balustrade at intervals. The first ideas are cherished for
being untested, for being raw seeds. The terrace is completely
mine, where my role is as I define it. I inhabit the costume I want,
the flesh I want, the voice I want. I can be monstrous and endless, or I can be a speck of dust. I do not have to be anyone for
anyone. I do not have to speak in any particular way to please
any particular person.

In creating and navigating these controlled spaces of undoing—the dungeon, the stairwell leading to the terrace overlooking
the ocean—to cope with trauma, I found a way to write myself

out of uninteresting framings of my inner life. By the time I have gotten to the terrace, I have shed not only the original trauma, but how others in my real life have foisted roles on me, either in ignorance or intentionally. I imagine myself shedding all the remnants of a colonised mind and colonised thinking, all the images, tropes, and roles that do not serve me. What remains? What is now possible in this blank space?

On the terrace, I feel blank and calm. I feel at ease with doubt, with uncertainty, with half-formed thoughts. Offences and pain pass through me as easily as through a sieve. I reserve any certitude that I really know certain things, that my path is set out for me, that there is a proscribed set of possibilities for how my life will turn out. On the terrace I feel sure of the radical possibility inherent both in me and in the people around me, my students, my family, my friends.

There are many healing, generative effects that emerge from this undoing and following blankness, especially for writing. The blankness allows for doubt of language's sole grip on defining reality. The other figures on the terrace: their sentences mean one hundred things at once. In order to ever write about ideas that I did not yet have language for at the time of writing, I had to reject academic, canon-based ideas of which stories were even worth telling. And it will take a lifetime to sort through the imperialist aesthetics and values that shape which languages our cultural gatekeepers can even hear, register, understand.

In one of my favourite sermons, T. D. Jakes describes one's life as a massive bow and arrow. The amount of struggle we endure pulls back the bowstring, deeper and deeper, causing one's life, the arrow, to fly further, on fire, in the direction of one's talent and dreams. I also see the amount of work I've described in the Undoing, the labour it takes for a marginalised mind and body to climb out of the pits, scale the walls up to the terrace into a state of integrity, into a state of clarity, to be able to make anything at all, as directly proportional to the number of risks they might and do take in making.

Ultimately, the terrace is where I feel most strongly that it *matters* to struggle to make art in my way, with my own voice. To erase ventriloquism in myself. To ever examine why I am speaking, with claims to what, to what end, in service of what power. The terrace is the space to imagine alternative futures for others suffering around me. Making anew is really making for a more bearable lived reality in my body. Making what I feel called to make is how I can honour the silences the brilliant women before me endured, and the many dreams they had to give up.

The terrace is the free place I must make sure is always waiting for my return after months and months of distraction, of being hobbled at the knees by depression. After years of constantly being in my own way, of not letting the doors below just slam down so I can *move*. Of not looking at the automap to see that the edge is an unseen door, a way into the divine, the big, big love.

Somewhere in my psyche, I'm sure, the drive to continue being an artist, to build things of worth, stems from trying to change the meaning of the past. I write about children, to imagine other ways things could have been for me. I write the stories I needed to read when I was younger. I try, as difficult as it is, to write as here about creatively coping with trauma to give someone else like me a glimpse of other paths out of the banality of violence that don't involve self-harm, self-immolation. In this mapping

I find alternative endings. In those endings, a kind of correction and absolution.

~

The fortress expands. Its terrace stretches out to the horizon. A statue of a goddess appears. Titanic, one hundred feet high, Durga or Athena or Az'rael, depending on my moment's psychological and emotional need. Whichever form, she is my highest angel, and her civilisation-ending statue rotates slowly, twists out of the compass as she ascends into the star-studded night, ribbons of plasma spiralling around her. She is my ikon, my model for the depth of understanding, compassion, rigour, honesty, and power that I must draw on in the face of audacious erasures. You cannot erase Durga! She is eternal.

Around her, the gowned figures float as celestial beings, their faces more clear, their names visible in the sky behind them. Watching her rotate in my mind, my body separates and transmutes into rings of light that expand like smoke circles over the sea. I want to only ever come here to think about unseen things. I want to walk out of the dungeon again and again, no matter how many deaths are imprinted on the pillar in that coastal town.

I Am, Myself, a Body of Water

Leigh Alexander

The sea is my place. My dad always says that when my mom's family crossed the Atlantic to come to America, they reached the shore and they stayed there. The joke being, of course, that they were no great explorers, that they preferred ease.

But the northeastern coastline is uneasy. Its green-bellied swells are thick with dark curls of seaweed. We have jetties of slippery black stone and precarious dunes where loose sand whispers over insectoid seed pods. Tiny bubbles sing up from glittering sand to show where the mussels have buried themselves, and gulls stalk these speckled avenues like wardens. Up where the sand is blinding white and too hot to touch, the blanched claws and shells of crabs are everywhere. Among them the great, dark, primordial shell of a horseshoe crab lies belly-up like a beetle, its thin clock hand tail pointing back towards the mournful water from whence it came.

The Atlantean seashore isn't a place of ease, but rather of delight alternating with danger. The infinite roar and sigh of the waves, boat sails flecked colourfully along the horizon (*the stuff that dreams are made of/it's the sails against the sky* sings Carly Simon—favourite of my grandmother). Just as you surrender to the soft rocking and sighing of open space, your foot touches something slick and eldritch, and you start. Four, five, a dozen waves will carry you gleefully on your belly in your purple and orange swimsuit, but the next will yank and drag you along the sea floor, leaving you shaken, coughing, somewhere far down the dizzying shoreline frantically searching for the family blanket.

So it probably wasn't that it was easy. Regardless, my maternal family did not leave it, and neither would I. When I was small I hid in the sea, pretending I couldn't hear that it was time to come home. All kinds of yelling could be drowned in earfuls of water. By the time I could be forced ashore, roughly rubbed with a sandy towel, my jaw rattled and my lips were blue.

~

'I'm a mermaid,' the girls would say when we played in the water, twining legs together and splaying feet. The seawater would unspool the dark tangles of my coarse and difficult hair, making a slick rope I could toss back over my shoulder like Ariel in Disney's *The Little Mermaid*, which to kids at the time was a Very Important Film. In the water I didn't think much about the differences I felt between me and the others. If I felt large, then the sea could make me weightless. If I felt coarse, it would make me light and smooth my hair with gilded salt. The lace pattern of sunlight on my body under the water made me feel I had transcended that body altogether. Some part of me thrived there, certainly more than I thrived anywhere else. I knew already that the sea held infinite mysteries, infinite possibilities.

I was in a special school, one with great talking oaks on the playground, howling ghosts in the library chimney, aliens in the great tiled toilets. You might be thinking: Oh, a special school, how magical for kids. But 'special school' really means I spent a lot of time with my ear pressed to the door of my parents' room, trying to prise words out of the whispers that were talking about me. It means praying as hard as I could in the car at pickup time, *please let us drive away*, before the teacher yet again waved my mother over to talk about me. It means my body and spirit yanking one another out of shape, scrabbling frantically at the border of adolescence, at last tripping over it, dragged along the floor of it.

Were the other kids in the special school like that? Little bits of broken glass that needed to be polished by the persistent rhythms of the natural order? I can't remember; I was only about eight, and because it was a special school, there were only two third graders in a big, mixed group: myself and G. On the first day, we were sat together and assigned to be a *you two* during the welcome exercise, a crafts project involving curly paper crowns. Our crowns were more elaborate than the work of the little kids. Right away we thought we knew better than everyone else, being older, being special. We became difficult.

I honestly don't remember whose idea it was that we should become witches. We murmured incantations, blew ripples across the great troughs of leathery mud we stirred in the parking lot. Then science class. Then we wrote spell books, spotted with the blood of markers. It would be getting cold, the New England leaves crimson against a white sky, school bell jangling like a banshee. That feeling was magic. Probably if you'd asked us then—me, with my curly mop and a frame that curved like a thumb, and her all pale jangly elbows and knees—if we were witches, we would have denied it. We were teleportation agents, telekinetics, astral craftsmen, psychic detectives, and magi, maybe. It depended on the use case. It depended on what we were reading at the time and what the current escape plan was. Wherever we planned to star-travel to hide from being in trouble.

Why were we always in trouble? Listen, smart girls can't do anything right. The world tries to destroy us. One who speaks too assertively is rude, a know-it-all. One who is quiet is weak. One who reserves herself is offending her potential. One who is ambitious is unbecoming, one who works hard is indelicate; we teach girls to shrink themselves, and so—well, listen, okay, admittedly I threw tantrums. I would do things like tell the teacher I had appendicitis. I told her about how ignoring my appendix pain would lead to a rupture, peritonitis and sepsis, but she was unmoved.

And I told other stories. There was a ghost in the girls' bathroom; we're sorry we scared the first graders, but there really was one. The veneer of iridescence on the classroom floor was ectoplasm, not glue, and if it was glue, we were not the ones who squeezed it out as an experiment. And the reason we broke through the fence at recess and disappeared from the playground into the roadside woods was because druids were hypnotising us.

I guess I must have been bored. They say that intelligent children act out because they are bored, which I've always liked—the possibility that my childhood was sad because I was simply *too intelligent*, and not because there were any problems at home. It would be nice to be able to decide that the world around me was misshapen, instead of only me, in trouble again, in trouble all the time, punished, grounded, a perpetual state of lack. Supposedly then it wasn't that I was 'challenging', but that I was 'not being challenged'.

Back then I had some of my greatest meltdowns when forced to do math. No matter how my appendix allegedly threatened to rupture, no one yielded. I'd end up banished to a black bench in the hallway, drawing runes in the tears that spotted the lacquer. Very dramatic.

'I'm a lot more strict than your teacher.' One day, the headmistress of the class adjacent mine sat beside me on the black bench and spoke to me gently. She was a great, tall old woman, the boss of our entire floor, and I had admired from afar the tight ship she ran, the disciplined older kids who read Shakespeare.

She said: 'You wouldn't like to be in my class, would you.'

'Yes,' I wept, surprising even myself. 'I would.'

'No, you wouldn't,' she said. 'I wouldn't tolerate this kind of crying. You wouldn't make it in my class.'

I put my head on her knee and cried miserably: *I want to be in your class, I want to change to your class, can I please be in your class, Miss Evans hates me.*

But I stayed in the same class. That's about when I decided: G and I were going to blow this entire popsicle stand and return to the sea.

⤳

In those days, everyone knew that when you sang, invisible energy would come out. Just big huge swirls of it. If you don't believe me, just watch Disney's *The Little Mermaid*, which as

I said, we were all doing a lot of at the time. So here was our escape plan: I would sing out some invisible energy from the front yard of my house, and G was going to sing from the front yard of her house, and when the swirls collided in mid-air, the resulting energy splash would *rain* down on us, transforming us into mermaids where we stood.

It sounds a little dubious, I know, but it's not like I was an experienced practitioner of magic at the time. This is an incantation designed by an eight-year-old, based on having viewed Disney's *The Little Mermaid*. And I had other logistical concerns, like what colour tail we were each going to get, and how, once we were mermaids, we were supposed to make it over a hundred miles to the sea. I had only thought so far as the local duck pond. I could flop down the sidewalk to the duck pond, at least.

This was one of the funny stories of my childhood, while there were still some. My mom mostly talks about precocious things I did when I was little, times I was called upon and chosen. What stories would my dad tell about me? Not sure. I turned thirteen and at my Bat Mitzvah he spoke before the congregation—he was the only black guy in the synagogue—telling of how he learned he had a daughter, me, and how it made him glad. But I don't remember what his reason was, if he had said any, why he was glad to have me. In those days I was mostly just aware of being challenging—all those gut-dropping messages from school, the tear-stained letters I shoved under my parents' closed doors, and all the yelling. Every day yelled at, and sometimes yelling back. And in the sore, lonely silences in between, I was painfully aware that my grandmother was gone. She had died just a few months before.

She was the one who was glad to have me. Even now, two decades later, I can still imagine the sound of her voice, delighted, saying: *Hi, Sweetheart.* And she was the one who always took me to the beach, to the long, warm, brown days in which I wrote down some sigil of myself that time and challenge would not erase. She had spent every summer living by the sea, for as far back into her history as I know. Her friends still had houses there, with sandy ash-coloured porches and high-pressure showers we were always invited in to use. My mom and her siblings still talk about this seaside of legend, as if it were our true birthplace. As a small girl, every time I thought the waves might carry me away, I would look for the speck of her poised in her sun-chair to reassure myself. Every time I looked at her she'd be watching me, smiling. *Hi, Sweetheart.*

When we went to the beach, any hurt I was feeling would be washed away. Even the misshapen and unwelcome swells of my unruly, racialised adolescence could be filed down, just for those moments when I was being loved and rocked by the infinite waves. I had no colour and no weight. I was myself, a body of water, spoken to only by the moon.

Surprise: This is not the story of how my childhood friend G and I became full-on mermaids. That particular ritual, unfortunately, was one of the ones that did not work, along with the forever-blood-sisters one we would try later (that one went way wrong—she's a Trump supporter now!). But still something took root in me around then: The lifelong urge to come to the ocean to escape difficult things, to find an equalising force that cradles and thrashes me in turn, polishes me with sand and salt as if I were not broken glass, but really a pearl, a little mote of loveliness found among flesh and sinew, in a shell.

I never once have forgotten about the invisible terrors that might be lurking right nearby—the ghoulish touch of marine polyps, the imperceptible jellyfish stings, the barnacled boulders, the lungfuls of sudden waves. The uneasy truce I make with fear is part of it—every time I float in the sea, I remember that it kills people, all the time. It can kill me. Whenever I am rocking, colourless and polished and weightless among the waves, I consciously make my peace with the thought of a sudden undertow that might pull me into the void calmly and silently. It's just a thing that could happen, the presence of a threat more certain and indiscriminate than the labyrinthine self-criticisms and anxieties experienced by a body on land.

I get ready to die. Not because I want to—I have many telekinetic performances yet to conduct, many astral battles yet to win, many sea rites to complete—but as I float I just keep in mind: If no one were looking and if no one loved me, I could disappear all of a sudden. I make peace with the image of a speckle of me in the sea, vanishing soundlessly. Like I never came.

Here is how I bring myself to the ocean: I run through rural Cape Cod towards the sound of buzzards. Or I am the first to push out of the car in Maine, leaving my shoes behind. I clatter down slopes of stone towards the playful inlets of Dover's or Brighton's British shores; I take the long, drowsy-warm F train to Brighton Beach, New York, to walk straight for the marine horizon, weaving among umbrellas and radios and Heinekens. I have kicked along the warm Pacific in Bali and put my feet in the cold Pacific in Vancouver, both in different Octobers, which is when my birthday falls.

Usually, though, I arrive by the most direct route possible, as soon as possible. It doesn't necessarily matter the season, just the commitment to walk straight for the pea-green shadows without hesitation. I make sure I rarely shriek or wince. I must be seen to make a natural homecoming, even if no one is looking at me, and no one ever really is. Before anything else I make sure to get my head underwater. If you ever feel cold or unwelcome in the ocean, make sure to get your head underwater. I know you think you will be cold, but you won't. It only takes a moment, and once you've done it you will feel brave and completely reborn.

Next I like to float on my back, not a float with effort and pointed feet (I never want to be reminded of the swimming class at day camp), but a gentle sort of body suspension on the surface of the waves. I like to know that salt can just carry me, that it doesn't mind, that I will not be too challenging. Something that works for me is contorting myself into my most grotesque posture—yours can be whatever works for you. Is it how you guard yourself when someone swings at you? How you curl up to pretend you're not hungry when you are? The monstrous shapes you pinch and scowl into the mirror? Whatever it may be, the sea doesn't care. It will consciously make sure your face turns up to the sun so you can breathe.

Here is how I bring the ocean to me: I swim. I recommend you try this, even if you aren't good at swimming. If going way out to sea, towards the silent place the horizon line grows smudged and no one can see you anymore scares you, swim parallel to the shore. I always make a visual landmark—the little pile of your things, a hotel along the waterfront, the sparkling jetty, something like that—because the enormous blue curve of the sky will overwhelm your sense of anchorage to this planet before long. What I do isn't really swimming, if I'm being totally honest. I let myself be pulled. It's nice not to be obligated to perform.

I spend time in there. I like to imagine that there is no difference between the water within my body and the water without it. The sinews of my corpus, yanked all out of shape by years, maybe even generations of anger and displacement, are suddenly forgotten, lunar waves assembling me into order. I like to watch the horizon line grow indistinct, sea and sky and silence, the rare occasion of my slow breath. What I love most is when I leave the water walking crooked along the dizzy diagonal shore, tripping in foam, grasping helplessly for the old gravity. All pain then stops, all struggles minor detours between one visit to the sea and the next.

∼

I have now met the sea from all over the world. One February somewhere around Helsinki, I checked into a hotel for work and ran towards where Google Maps had thought I might find some ocean. I literally ran, in winter sport gear a few kilometres alongside featureless fields of snow for what felt like far too long—until, with a gasp, I realised the fields *were* the sea, that the silent ice I could see for miles had a frightening marine-coloured underbelly. *So you can be hard, too, old friend*, I thought.

Just a few months ago on the north coast of Spain, I walked barefoot along a dark silt shore in a rainstorm, listening to a church bell. If that sounds like a dream, I promise, it was real, and it was amazing. I guess not all of my magic spells fail.

Really, it was just that mermaid one from when I was little that didn't turn out. Which is probably for the best. Thinking about it, shouldn't a 'mermaid spell' be the sort of thing that turns a mermaid into a girl, and not the other way around? Besides, Hans Christian Andersen's *The Little Mermaid* is actually an awful story—she gives up her voice and her home for the world of ragged human knees and men's opinions, and it still wrings her out and kills her.

I wonder if my maternal family was always drawn to the sea because they have always been in pain, and learned the magic of the ocean for the curing of it. They may have been escaping difficult things, too, and it's maybe telling that I don't know, and not because I haven't asked. The insurmountable, roaring sea has to carry our stories for us, toss me confused and stinging among them, send me back in again and again to try to find myself in its unbounded waters.

But I imagine they found not that the shoreline was easiest, like Dad joked, but that it was best. I'm pretty sure my thighs come from that side of the family. My loud voice could be from any of them, too. The ocean can prevail over any of those things, turn me into a sun-dappled queen with my legs knit together like a tail, scintillating far away from the indignities of the landed world. My lips become blue, I'm polished and remade like sea glass, I somersault like a crude dolphin. I am laughing as I write this, like I haven't done since I was small.

Contributors

Cara Ellison is a Scottish author and videogame designer, though she started out making radio at BBC Radio 4 and fell into the land of videogames by accident. She's critiqued most aspects of games in word form anywhere you'd expect to find them, from *PC Gamer* to *The Guardian*. A comfortable solo world adventurer, she wrote a book called *Embed With Games* about travelling the world asking questions about why people make games and what they are for. Permanently uncomfortable in one type of writing or design, she makes TV shows, comics, videogames, and essays, and has difficulty sitting still, frankly.

Maranda Elizabeth is a writer, zinester, identical twin, high school dropout, recovering alcoholic, and white non-binary amethyst-femme. They write about recovery with BPD, complex-trauma, and fibromyalgia; writing, creativity, and friendship; politicizing recovery; queer mad poor crip lineages; and surviving social assistance and poverty. Maranda's work explores themes of loneliness and disposability; synchronicity and meaning-making; and memory and making a home. They have published a zine anthology, *Telegram: A Collection of 27 Issues* (2012) and the novels *Ragdoll House* (2013) and *We Are the Weirdos* (2017). They read Tarot for misfits and outcasts, and publish a column on LittleRedTarot.com, 'See the Cripple Dance'. Maranda grew up in Lindsay, Ontario, (Ojibway, Chippewa, and Anishinabek land), and currently resides in Toronto, Ontario (traditional territory of the Haudenosaunee and the Métis). Read their work at marandaelizabeth.com.

Laura Mandanas is a Boston-based Filipina American writer with a keen interest in loose leaf tea, nicknaming her girlfriend's biceps, and destroying the patriarchy. Her background is in industrial engineering. You can read more of her work at Autostraddle and lauramandanas.com.

Catherine Hernandez is a Toronto-based writer and theatre practitioner. Her book, *Scarborough* (Arsenal Pulp Press, 2017), was the winner of the Jim Wong-Chu Award, shortlisted for the Toronto Book Award and longlisted for Canada Reads 2018. It made the 'Best of 2017' lists for *The Globe and Mail*, *National Post*, *Quill and Quire*, and *CBC Books*. Learn more at catherinehernandezcreates.com

Avery Edison is a comedian and humourist who has written and performed extensively about her experiences as a transgender woman. Her writing has been published in *The Guardian*, at McSweeney's Internet Tendency, and The Toast. She lives on Twitter, where she spends all day making terrible puns and talking too much about her genitals.

Gabriela Herstik is a fashion alchemist, witch, and author based in Los Angeles. Gabriela examines what it means to be a modern day witch in her Nylon Column 'Ask a Witch' and loves to dissect the intersection between glamour and magick, especially through style. Her debut book *Craft: How to Be A Modern Witch* will be released with Ebury Press/ Random House in March 2018. You can visit her website at gabrielaherstik.com and follow her on Instagram and Twitter at @gabyherstik.

Marguerite Bennett is a GLAAD-nominated, *New York Times*-bestselling comic book writer based in Los Angeles. Her superheroic credits include DC Comics' *Batwoman* and *DC Bombshells*, as well as stints on *Batgirl* and *Lois Lane*, and Marvel's *A-Force*, *Years of Future Past*, and *Angela: Queen of Hel*. Elsewhere, her credits include *Josie and the Pussycats* and *Red Sonja*. Her creator-owned titles, *Animosity* and *Insexts*, can be found through Aftershock Comics. Her prose has appeared in *The Secret Loves of Geek Girls*. Her work is full of queer characters, heroines, villainesses, talking animals, bloody revenge sagas, female monsters, murder, and kissing.

Sam Maggs is an Associate Writer of video games at BioWare, an occasional comics writer for IDW, and the bestselling author of *Wonder Women* and *The Fangirl's Guide to the Galaxy*, both from Quirk Books. An authority on women in pop culture, Sam has spoken or written on the topic for *The New York Times*, Vulture, NPR, *Marie Claire*, *PC Gamer*, *The Guardian*, and more. She is named after *Bewitched*'s Samantha Stephens, but please don't ask her to do the nose thing. @SamMaggs / sammaggs.com

Deb Chachra, PhD, is a professor of engineering at a small college outside of Boston, Massachusetts. Her research interests include biological materials, infrastructure, and engineering education, with an emphasis on gender and the student experience. In addition to her scientific publications, she has published essays in the comic book *Bitch Planet*, the scientific journal *Nature*, and many other outlets. Her professional goals include revolutionalising engineering education and overthrowing the patriarchy.

Mey Valdivia Rude is a bisexual Latina trans woman living in Los Angeles. She's the Trans Editor at Autostraddle, a writer, comic consultant, and a trans activist. She's a bruja, a femme, and a bratty bottom who loves comic books, witches, dinosaurs, and crying. She has a cat named Sawyer and a very successful Twitter.

Larissa Pham is a writer and anti-violence advocate in New York. Her work engages with themes of the self, intimacy, and narrative, often within the context of visual culture. She is the author of *Fantasian*, a novella from Badlands Unlimited, and her work has also appeared in The Paris Review Daily, Guernica, The Nation, *Rolling Stone*, and elsewhere. You can find her work at larissapham.com.

Meredith Yayanos is, among other things, an artist and a monstrous feminist agitator. She lives, works, and fights in California, New York, and incalculable liminal in-betweens.

merritt k is a writer and podcaster living in Brooklyn. She hosts the podcasts *Woodland Secrets* and *dadfeelings*, writes about body accidents and digital weirdness, and can be found on Twitter at @merrittk.

Sophie Saint Thomas is a queer writer based in Brooklyn, where she lives with two marmalade cats, Mama Cat and Major Tom Cat. Sophie grew up in the US Virgin Islands. She is a regular contributor to Vice, Cosmopolitan, Mic, Noisey, Broadly, *Marie Claire*, High Times, Nylon, Playboy, GQ, Refinery29, Harper's Bazaar, and more. Brooklyn Magazine included her on their annual 2016 30 Under 30 Envy List. She loves to drink tea and study the occult and believes vanity is a delicious sin.

Sim Bajwa (@simuella) is an bookseller and writer based in the West Midlands. She graduated from Edinburgh Napier with an MA in Creative Writing in 2016, and her work has been published in *Helios Quarterly*, the Dangerous Women Project, 404 Ink's *Nasty Women*, and *Shoreline of Infinity*. She's currently working on her first fantasy novel and her favourite things are nail polish, cats, and tea.

Kim Boekbinder is a Noise Witch, casting neon spells over shadowed rooms around the planet Earth; she also tells stories on paper and on film. Kim loves you, she'll fight for you, but if you come for her friends, she'll fight you.

Sara David is a writer who was born in the Philippines and raised in New York. She's currently an editor at Broadly and lives in Brooklyn with two cats, Jubilee and Enzo.

Katelan Foisy is a multimedia artist and writer. She has displayed at The Worcester Art Museum, Ohio History Museum, MODA, WEAM, and Last Rights. She has graced the pages of the Grammy Award programs and the stage of Cynthia von Buhler's 'Speakeasy Dollhouse' plays. Katelan has been featured in *NY Times, Elle, Paper Magazine, GQ Italy*, and *Time Out NY*. She has written for Motherboard/Vice and Electric Literature and held events with Atlas Obscura, OVADA, and The Project Room. Her illustrations are featured in the forthcoming *Sibyls Oraculum* (Destiny Books Spring, 2018) with Tayannah McQuillar and *Chaos of the Third Mind* (Fulgar Ltd, UK, 2018) with Vanessa Sinclair. She was called a 'female Jack Kerouac' by Taylor Mead.

J. A. Micheline, or JAM, is a writer, critic, and editor newly based in Chicago. She writes cultural criticism, prose, comics, and the occasional angry tweet before bedtime. Her still-in-progress novel, *Super Charismatic Nucleus*, was shortlisted for Cambridge University's Lucy Cavendish Fiction Prize in 2016 and her critical work has been featured in *The Guardian*, Vice, The A.V. Club, and elsewhere.

Nora Khan is a writer in New York City, where she is Acting Editor at Rhizome. Her criticism and fiction, focusing on digital visual culture and philosophy of technology, has appeared in 4Columns, Flash Art, Art in America, *California Sunday*, Conjunctions, *The Village Voice*, and elsewhere. Her book with Steven Warwick, *Fear Indexing the X-Files*, was published by Primary Information. Her writing and research have been supported by a Thoma Foundation Arts Writing Award in

Digital Art, an Eyebeam Research Residency, and an Iowa Arts Fellowship. Learn more at noranahidkhan.com.

Leigh Alexander is a writer and narrative designer (*Reigns: Her Majesty, Where the Water Tastes Like Wine, Monitor*). Her journalism (*The Guardian*, How We Get to Next, Medium, Motherboard) tackles offbeat futurism, digital society, immaterial labour, technomancy, and how the internet, politics, and pop culture intersect. She is the author of *Breathing Machine*, a memoir of early internet society, and her occasional ASMR video series 'Lo-Fi Let's Play' explores ancient computer adventures. More projects can be found at leighalexander.net.

Acknowledgements

Thank you to every single person who backed the *Becoming Dangerous* Kickstarter and helped make this book a reality. You're all magical.

Thank you to Hope Nicholson, owner of Bedside Press, for everything, including selfies. Thank you to Phoenix Ivy Roots for conversations about the words we use. Thank you to Shannon Winterstein for the elements. Thank you to Simon Berman for his help. Thank you to Cara Ellison, Matt Johnson, and Chrissy Williams for early readings and encouragement. Thank you to Kieron Gillen for being such a huge fan of witches. Thank you to Jasmine Elliott for believing in my weird book ideas and helping to make them as good as they can be. Thank you to Jamie McKelvie for his unending support. And thank you to my cat, Bruce, because who writes an acknowledgements section and doesn't thank their cat?

Katie West
Editor, *Becoming Dangerous*

To Our Readers

Weiser Books, an imprint of Red Wheel/Weiser, publishes books across the entire spectrum of occult, esoteric, speculative, and New Age subjects. Our mission is to publish quality books that will make a difference in people's lives without advocating any one particular path or field of study. We value the integrity, originality, and depth of knowledge of our authors.

Our readers are our most important resource, and we appreciate your input, suggestions, and ideas about what you would like to see published.

Visit our website at *www.redwheelweiser.com* to learn about our upcoming books and free downloads, and be sure to go to *www.redwheelweiser.com/newsletter* to sign up for newsletters and exclusive offers.

You can also contact us at *info@rwwbooks.com* or at

Red Wheel/Weiser, LLC
65 Parker Street, Suite 7
Newburyport, MA 01950